LIFE IN A NOBLE HOUSEHOLD
1641-1700

WILLIAM, FIFTH EARL AND FIRST DUKE OF BEDFORD

LIFE IN
A NOBLE HOUSEHOLD
1641-1700

GLADYS SCOTT THOMSON

M.A., F.S.A., SOMERVILLE COLLEGE
OXFORD

JONATHAN CAPE
THIRTY BEDFORD SQUARE
LONDON

FIRST PUBLISHED 1937

JONATHAN CAPE LTD., 30 BEDFORD SQUARE, LONDON
AND 91 WELLINGTON STREET WEST, TORONTO

PRINTED IN GREAT BRITAIN BY J. AND J. GRAY, EDINBURGH
PAPER MADE BY JOHN DICKINSON AND CO. LTD.
BOUND BY A. W. BAIN AND CO. LTD.

CONTENTS

LIST OF ILLUSTRATIONS

The paintings, all of which are at Woburn Abbey, are reproduced by the generous permission of the Duke of Bedford.

PREFACE

This book calls for little or no prefatory explanation. It is based upon the household papers—account books, bills and letters—handled by the officials and servants of William Russell, fifth Earl and first Duke of Bedford, and reveals the great variety of information that this type of historical source contains.

My original intention was to include a study of the finance of the estates, from which the family income was derived. But it soon became evident that this called for separate treatment in another work and I have, therefore, so far as finance is concerned, confined myself here, in the main to asking how a family of noble birth in the seventeenth century spent its money.

The extracts, except for unidentifiable names, have been modernized in spelling and likewise in punctuation. The dating used in the text is according to the modern style, but double dating for the first three months of the year has been used for the extracts whenever it seemed necessary for the sake of clarity.

I have to express my grateful thanks to many friends who have ungrudgingly given me help and advice. In particular, I am indebted to Mr. W. G. Constable for reading and criticizing the chapter on the portrait gallery; to Mr. Graham Pollard for some valuable notes on the library; to Mr. J. L. Nevinson for his advice on the many intricate questions concerning a nobleman's wardrobe; to Monsieur André Simon for helping me to attain to a measure of understanding of the history of a wine cellar; and not least to Professor R. H. Tawney, who, with characteristic generosity, has allowed me to take up his time with discussions on seventeenth-century finance and land management.

I owe two debts which are beyond acknowledgment. One is to the late Sir Charles Firth, sometime Regius Professor of Modern History in the University of Oxford, whose pupil I am proud to have been. It is much to have the recollection of his wise and witty comments on the epoch with which his name must always be associated. It is even more to have the memory of the encouragement he gave me when this book was first planned. The other is to the Duke of Bedford. No words can express the thanks that are due to him for his most generous permission to use the family papers upon which this book is based. Much less is it possible to thank him adequately for the unfailing kindness shown to me while the book was being written.

GLADYS SCOTT THOMSON

September 1936

LIFE IN A NOBLE HOUSEHOLD
1641-1700

CHAPTER I

INTRODUCTORY:
THE RUSSELLS COME TO WOBURN

In August 1625, a family of refugees, father and mother, their ten children and some servants, arrived at Woburn Abbey in Bedfordshire. The father was Francis, Lord Russell of Thornhaugh. He had borrowed the house from the owner, his cousin, Edward, Earl of Bedford, to whom he was the heir apparent. The reason for asking for the use of the house and the hasty flight thither was that he and his family might escape from the plague, which was rife in the pleasant village of Chiswick, where they had been living.

The disease had been raging in London throughout the spring and the summer months. The last bad outbreak had been twenty-two years earlier, in 1603, the year of the death of Elizabeth and the accession of James I, and many had remarked it as ominous that the infection should have returned with increased virulence the year of the death of James and the accession to the throne of his son Charles. The funeral ceremonies for the old King had been shortened; Parliament, after sitting for three weeks in Westminster, had removed to Oxford; and although the state entrance of Charles and Henrietta Maria into the city on 16th June had kept some in their places, many of the richer citizens had waited for neither duties nor pleasures. They had betaken themselves and their families to what they hoped was the safety of the higher districts around London, especially Hounslow Heath and Highgate Hill, and farther afield to the outlying villages; and the plague had gone with them.

Long before this time, in many previous epidemics, Chiswick had been marked down as a very desirable place of refuge. One of its finest houses, the manor house, had been especially reserved in an Elizabethan lease granted by the lords of the manor, the Dean and Chapter of St. Paul's Cathedral, for the reception of the Master of Westminster School and his forty King's Scholars in times of sickness in London. As usual, in this year of 1625 others than the Master and his scholars had fled to Chiswick. The inevitable result had followed. Early in July cases of plague had been reported in the village. They had not remained isolated cases. Each week had shown an increase in the numbers of those infected, and as the numbers rose, so had the alarm and consternation of the inhabitants.

The nucleus of the village was the clustered group of houses of fishermen and boatmen. But at all times a number of wealthy residents made their homes round about. The situation was pleasant and most convenient in that it was within either rowing or riding distance of Westminster.

The house of Francis, Lord Russell, stood not far from the parish church, on the river bank, with steps in the garden leading down to the river, whence he could take boat to Westminster. There he had lived since his marriage to Katherine Brydges, the daughter and co-heiress of the late Lord Chandos, and there ten children had been born to them. Their eldest son, William, was now twelve years old.

Close to Lord Russell's house was the dwelling-place of his trusted friend, Sir Stephen Leasure, the noted Parliamentarian. Not far off, a house had recently been acquired by another nobleman who could scarcely be called an intimate friend of Lord Russell, although they were well acquainted with one another. The new-comer was Robert Carr, Earl of Somerset, sometime favourite of James I. The royal countenance had smiled upon the proceedings which had secured the divorce of Frances Howard, Countess of Essex, from her husband, and her subsequent marriage to Robert Carr. For two years the couple had led the Court. Then, 'dazzled thus with height of place,' Somerset and his lady had learned to know 'the narrow space 'twixt a prison and a smile.' Revelations had been made which pointed to the Countess having made certain of her divorce by the method of administering poison to Sir Thomas Overbury, and Carr, it was whispered, had been her willing accomplice. This had been too much for the King. Husband and wife had been committed to the Tower in the autumn of 1615. The Countess was expecting a child, and in the Tower, on the 9th of December of the same year, a little girl had been born and, being taken to the church of St. Martin in Ludgate for her christening, had been named Anne. In May 1616 the Countess had confessed her guilt before an appalled House of Lords, among whom was sitting Lord Russell. The conviction of the Countess was followed by that of Somerset, although he, unlike his wife, had not made and never did make any confession. For six years the two had lain in the Tower, until the clemency of King James had released them. But they had not been fully pardoned and their freedom of movement and choice of residence had each been severely restricted. Four years later, in the last year of the King's life, he had at length bestowed upon his one-time favourite and his wife a full pardon, whereupon they and the child Anne, now aged ten years, had come to live in the village of Chiswick in the near neighbourhood of Lord Russell. Had that nobleman, already well known for the strictness of his principles and for his inclination towards the Puritan party, had the gift of second sight, he would have regarded the little girl with an apprehensive eye. But the passionate courtship between his boy, William, and Somerset's child, Anne, still lay hidden in the future.

Life in Chiswick, the children still young and King

Charles only just seated on the throne, with the troubles of the nation, like Lord Russell's personal troubles, still far ahead, was pleasant enough. Lord Russell and his lady had a particular affection for the place and always said that they never wished to leave it. They had not reckoned upon the plague. In the last week of July 1625, the number of deaths in the village rose to an alarming extent. Some of the more wealthy inhabitants had already left; others were on the point of doing so. Sir Stephen and Lady Leasure, hardy folk, determined for the time being to stay and brave the dangers. Lord and Lady Russell, with their ten children, felt the risks were too great. They must quit their home for the time being.

The question arose whither they were to go. Lord Russell had a country mansion of his own to which it might have been supposed he could very well have removed his family. This house stood on his estate of Thornhaugh, in Northamptonshire. Thornhaugh had come into the family with the first Countess of Bedford, and had ultimately passed to Lord Russell's father, Sir William Russell, sometime Governor of Flushing and afterwards Lord Deputy of Ireland, for whom the Barony of Russell of Thornhaugh had been created. The house was a good one and pleasantly placed. The present Lord Russell had been brought up there. But for some reason which he never betrayed, he disliked Thornhaugh and, even under the urgent necessity of getting out of Chiswick, he preferred to borrow Woburn Abbey from his cousin rather than to take his family to the house in which he had spent his childhood.

There was a certain justification for the decision. The part of Bedfordshire in which Woburn Abbey stood had been esteemed as far back as early in the sixteenth century for the excellent quality of its air, an important consideration in the time of plague.

Apart from this, Lord Russell had a particular reason for

being interested in Woburn. His cousin Edward, Earl of Bedford, had been foolish enough to involve himself, as a young man, in the rebellion led by the Earl of Essex. He had escaped with a fine, but it was a heavy one. On top of this, his wife, Lucy, blue-stocking, friend of poets and favourite at Court, knew more about spending money than saving it. The only way, her husband had decided, to meet her debts and to help pay his own fine was to sell some of his estates. Woburn and the London property called Covent Garden, upon which Lord Salisbury had an eye, had been selected for the sacrifice and permission to alienate both had been sought. But the young Earl had made a mis-calculation. The proposed transaction had come to the ears of his cousin, now Francis, Lord Russell, and of the latter's father, who was then living. They had promptly petitioned the King that permission should not be given to alienate any part of the estates, to which they were the heirs apparent. King James had been pleased to grant their request and Edward, Earl of Bedford, had found himself unable to dispose of his manor of Woburn with the ancient abbey standing in its midst. Both the land and the building, such as it was, together with the London estate, had been saved for the family by Lord Russell, who had now asked leave to borrow the abbey house for the time being.

To Woburn accordingly Lord Russell and his family went. The flight was made, at the end, in haste. Much that was needed was left behind. Even when the family at last reached the abbey, matters were none too comfortable. The house had long been standing neglected and empty. It was in a poor state of repair and the furniture was scanty. The letters that went back to Chiswick from both the lord and the lady were full of commissions to the Leasures, asking them to go into the Russell house and look out necessities which had been left behind and send them down by a servant. Lady Russell had remembered to bring her pet bird with her, but its sustenance had been forgotten. 'I know not,' she wrote to her friend, 'what to do for my bird. If Mr. Warwick be safe, let me desire to have some seeds sent me from him by this messenger.' Lord Russell wanted some important papers that had been left locked up in his study and had perforce to send the keys and ask Sir Stephen to go to the house, open the boxes and get out the documents. Neither husband nor wife, however, had ever contemplated that their stay at Woburn would extend to more than a few weeks. They fully hoped, and repeated in their letters, that by the early autumn they would have news that the plague was stayed in Chiswick and that they might return to their own comfortable home there.

The hope was not fulfilled. It is true that towards the end of August the number of plague deaths recorded in London itself began to drop weekly, but the infection in Chiswick increased rather than decreased. 'I have received a letter,' wrote Lady Russell very sadly on the 18th of September, 'from Goodman Early, who sends me word that the sickness grows very grievous.' It was so in truth and Chiswick was emptying even faster than before. The Leasures themselves, who had held out almost to the last, finally yielded to the advice of their friends and left. As for the Russells, they found they had no choice but to stay on at Woburn.

Even so, they were far from being safe from infection. Cases of plague appeared in the town of Woburn in September and there were three deaths. In October the number rose with alarming suddenness to sixteen, of whom six were of one family, the schoolmaster at the free school and his five little children. The times were indeed, as Katherine Russell wrote, 'full of mortality and alterations.' Happily for the family in the abbey above the town, no case of plague was reported in the household and early in the following month, with the coming of the cold weather, it was seen that the worst, as far as Woburn was concerned, was over.

Then came brave news from Chiswick. There, too, as the autumn wore into winter, the infection began to subside. The exiles at Woburn Abbey began to consider at least the possibility of returning to their beloved home. 'Nothing,' wrote Lady Russell to Lady Leasure in a letter which accompanied two capons, a goose and four woodcocks by way of a present, 'shall so hasten my remove from this place with a good will as the enjoying of you, which is the cause that makes me so much love Chiswick. After Christmas, God willing, we shall come.'

After Christmas they went indeed, back to the beloved Chiswick, in time to attend the coronation of Charles, which had been fixed for the 2nd of February. It was a great day for little William Russell, just thirteen years old, for, as part of the celebrations of the occasion, he was made a Knight of the Bath.

That was in February 1626. In May of the following year, on the third day of the month, Edward, third Earl of Bedford, died. His wife, Lucy, who survived him only twenty-three days, had borne him children, but all had died in infancy. His cousin, Francis, Lord Russell of Thornhaugh, succeeded to the title and estates as fourth Earl of Bedford.

The estates were vast. There was a choice of houses on one or the other of them fit for the residence of an Earl. The announcement made within a very short space of time by the new owner was all the more surprising. Woburn Abbey, a somewhat dilapidated building standing on what was then one of the smaller properties, was to be his principal residence.

As far as the house was concerned, it had been in none too good repair when the monks had left, eighty-eight years before this time, in 1539, since, a year previous to the dissolution, a fire had wrought considerable damage, which had not been repaired when Henry's commissioners took their survey. For eight years after the dissolution the building, with its site and part of the manor, had remained in the hands of the former steward of the monastery, Sir Francis Bryan. Not until July 1547 had a grant been made by the boy King, Edward VI, of the abbey with certain lands to John, Lord Russell, Lord Privy Seal, soon to be Earl of Bedford. This was in accordance with the wish expressed by Henry VIII on his deathbed the previous January. The dying King had earnestly desired that certain of his ministers should have grants of land to the value of a hundred pounds a year, an attempt on the part of the father to secure their loyalty to his young son. Woburn, as granted to Lord Russell, had been reckoned to be worth £168 18s. 0½d. a year, so that an annual rent had been imposed of the balance of £68 18s. 0½d. The property thus bestowed was comparatively small in extent, for the outlying lands, which had constituted by far the greater part of the monastic wealth, had been retained by the Crown. Nor had the estate been of any advantage, as far as possession went, to the new owner, for it was not until after his own death that the reversion of the first lease granted to the monastic steward had fallen in.

This had not troubled the first Earl of Bedford, who had never thought of the Woburn grant as of any particular importance, which indeed to him it was not. He had other estates and two particularly fine houses. His wife had been heiress of Chenies, in Buckinghamshire, as well as of Thornhaugh, and at Chenies he and she had rebuilt the manor house and had taken it as their principal residence. On the great property of Tavistock in the west, which had been granted to him 'to support his dignity as President of the Council of the West,' the principal house was Bedford House in Exeter. This he had built on the site of the Dominican priory which had been part of the grant. He had little need, therefore, to think of Woburn, even supposing he had been able to get possession of the abbey.

The second Earl, succeeding his father in 1554 and gaining possession of the house, had evinced slightly, but only slightly, more interest in Woburn than his father had done. He had lent the abbey house or had leased it at intervals to various relatives. He had even sometimes stayed there himself, had indeed on one occasion been forced to do so when his Queen had signified her arrival during one of her progresses. Elizabeth had had perforce to be accommodated. But it was all mighty inconvenient, the owner had grumbled, since the house, in its tumble-down condition, was very ill fitted to receive royalty. He had had no thoughts of doing anything in the matter beyond what had been absolutely necessary, nor of making any serious attempts at reconstruction. After all, he had the fine manor house at Chenies.

After his death in 1585 things at Woburn had gone from bad to worse. Hitherto the estate itself had been fairly well kept up in spite of the dilapidated condition of the house. But under Edward, the third Earl of Bedford, the grandson and successor of the second Earl, the era of complete neglect all round had set in. It had certainly not been worth while, in the opinion of this young nobleman, to spend money on Woburn, even supposing he had had any to spend. If, by reason of the machinations of his uncle and cousin, the Russells of Thornhaugh, he had not been allowed to sell it, the place, estate and house alike, must just be left to go to pieces.

Into the dilapidated abbey of Woburn, with the dilapidated estate around it, stepped Francis, fourth Earl of Bedford. It may be that part of the attraction which Woburn had for him was that very condition of neglect. Here was a great work of reconstruction to be done, an attractive thought to a man of his vigorous and constructive mind. The gradual bringing back of the estate to a measure of prosperity must, no one knew better than the Earl, be a long business. But the house could be dealt with more easily. The Earl decided on rebuilding.

The time was propitious. It was a great building age and the Earl was already in touch with one of the foremost architects of the day. He had on hand a bigger scheme than the mere reconstruction of a dwelling-house, for he had determined on building over part of the Covent Garden estate. To this end he consulted Inigo Jones. The result was the creation of the Piazza, with the church later dedicated to St. Paul on its east side. It is probable that the architect had already advised on the rebuilding of the house at Woburn. The exact dates are uncertain, but the ancient abbey presently gave place to an admirable example of a seventeenth-century mansion.

It is fortunate that twenty years later the fourth Earl's son and successor employed the mathematician and surveyor Sir Jonas Moore to draw up a survey of his manor of Woburn which has survived and which includes a plan of the house. It is still more fortunate that the fourth Duke of Bedford, when he, in his turn, in the middle of the eighteenth century, decided to rebuild, should have desired his architect, Flitcroft, much against the latter's will, to leave the north side of the older building exactly as it stood and to build the newly constructed dwelling on to it. Enough, therefore, is left of the seventeenth-century house to make it possible, with the help of Sir Jonas Moore's plan and an old print, to vizualize the whole as created by Inigo Jones for the fourth Earl.

The house was erected on the exact site of the old abbey. But nothing of the latter was allowed to remain. The eminent architect had no interest in preserving an old structure. His aim was rather to replace it by the most perfect building in the style of the day that he could contrive.

With this object in view the new mansion, which was to borrow the name of abbey from its predecessor and but little else besides, save the old stones used for the foundations, was built round the typical square seventeenth-century courtyard and, with its gabled wings, high-pitched roofs, stone finials and grouped chimneys, had much in common with other contemporary buildings in the county and elsewhere. The principal entrance was in the west front. There was the great hall, out of which the eating parlour opened on one side and a small parlour on the other. A bedroom and another small parlour flanked each. On the floor above a series of five living-rooms had windows looking westward over the park. These were the state rooms. One of them, the great salon, had its walls decorated with stars and was referred to as the Star Chamber long after the reason for the name had disappeared with the change of decoration. The last room at the south end was the library, or study, and that at the north end the state bedroom. At the back, running the whole length of the wing, was the portrait gallery, with eight windows opening over the courtyard.

This west wing was reserved for state occasions. The family lived in the north wing. English architecture was still submissive to the Italian avoidance of the sun and the living-rooms as well as the family bedrooms in Woburn Abbey looked north, as did those of many another mansion of the day.

The living-rooms, parlours and withdrawing-rooms occupied the ground floor. In the midst of them, set between the two principal withdrawing-rooms, was one of the most popular contrivances of the age, a grotto. The walls of this room were completely covered by shells worked in an elaborate pattern and were then further diversified and ornamented by a fantastic arrangement of figures and stalagmitic forms. Over the two inner doors, each leading into a withdrawing-room, were placed, with no sense of

23

incongruity, the elaborate painted arms of the fourth Earl of Bedford impaled with those of his Countess. The grotto was intended, when the furniture, mainly gilded wooden chairs, should be added, as a pleasant sitting-out place for the family. A chilly one it must have been, except in the warmest weather, for it opened direct on the north side into a three-arched loggia leading to the garden, with neither windows nor door as protection.

It was the existence of this grotto which inclined the fourth Duke, when he was rebuilding a hundred and twenty years later, to insist upon the preservation of the north wing. All learned in seventeenth-century architecture would agree that he was right in so doing. The room is a remarkably good specimen of its kind, one in which the influence of Inigo Jones is particularly evident. For many a long year after the designer and the man for whom he had designed it had been in their graves, it continued to be a source of pride and pleasure, a unique specimen to display to visitors.

Upstairs, above the living-rooms and the grotto, a number of large, finely proportioned rooms served as sleeping-chambers for the family and, in common with the rooms below, never saw the sun. They had, however, at least a pleasant outlook, for the windows opened on to the best part of the formal seventeenth-century garden which was now constructed to run round three sides of the house.

Altogether there were some ninety rooms in the new house. Eleven sitting-rooms, with the great hall and the gallery, were allotted for the use of the family. The remainder were bedrooms and, chiefly in the east and the south wings, rooms for the use of the staff. They included the vast kitchen apartments, with a hall for the men-servants and another for the women, as well as bedchambers and office rooms of all kinds.

Of the ten children who had come to Woburn Abbey with their father and mother, the bodies of two little brothers

INTRODUCTORY

only too soon found their places among the pathetic row of little coffins in the vault at Chenies, where the chapel erected by the first Countess to contain her husband's tomb remained the burial-place of the family. The other eight children of the Earl and Countess, four boys and four girls, grew to manhood and womanhood in the new house.

When the building was finished the portraits of the seven eldest sons and daughters were ready to be hung upon its walls. They had been painted by the Hungarian portrait-painter, Priwitzer, in 1627, immediately after their father had come into the title. All the pictures—the little girls in prim black taffeta frocks, with pearl necklaces—are delightful, but easily the most conspicuous is that of the eldest son. William, Lord Russell, was then fourteen years of age and was destined to live for another seventy-three years, during which his devotion was to be given to his great estates, but more particularly to Woburn, where his boyhood had been spent. To sit to Priwitzer he had been dressed in the sweeping pink robes of the Bath, which he had acquired the right to wear two years previously at the coronation. The badge of the Order is around his neck and he holds the hat, with its long feather, in his right hand, while resting his gloved left hand on a sword.

A few years later the portraits of the boys and girls were joined by a great picture which Van Dyck had made of their father. He was forty-eight when the picture was painted in 1636. It is a noble portrait of an austere nobleman with a thoughtful, even a care-worn face. He is dressed with severe simplicity and plainness, entirely in black save for the broad, plain white collar extending from chin to shoulders. No jewellery or ornaments, not even a sword, are visible. On the other hand, he is not the close-cropped Roundhead of popular fancy any more than were Cromwell, Hampden and others. Since the beginning of the century hair had been growing longer and beards and

25

moustaches dwindling. The Earl, like most men of fashion of the day, of whatever political colour, wore his hair flowing to his shoulders and cut in a sort of fringe in front, with a clipped moustache and a small, pointed chin beard. He stands looking directly at the spectator, coldly ignoring the endeavours of the charming white and brown spaniel at his feet to attract his attention.

Care-worn, as the painter saw him, the Earl might well appear. He had been a busy man while he was yet Lord Russell. As Earl of Bedford his responsibilities, both public and private, were more than doubled. The fourteen years which were all that were allowed him of life after he came into the title and took up his abode at Woburn Abbey were years of increasing anxiety in public affairs and in the year of 1636, when he sat to Van Dyck, the weight of political responsibility was heavy upon him, for the struggle between the King and his Parliament was beginning to take a course of which no man could foresee, although many might fear, the end.

The journeys from Woburn to Westminster, with the subsequent anxious consultations, were tiring enough. For the fourth Earl they were only a fraction of his work, for he was simultaneously absorbed in a great project concerning his own lands. When he had inherited Thornhaugh from his father he had received some more property along with it. This was the manor of Thorney, with the former abbey buildings, which had been put with Thornhaugh to make a younger son's portion. Thorney, in the midst of what was correctly described as 'marishy' country, had been regarded by the original grantee, the first Earl of Bedford, with even less favour than Woburn, although admittedly the fen district was excellent when it came to a question of fishing or sending hawks after water-fowl. His grandson, Sir William Russell, however, had learned a good deal while he was Governor of Flushing. For one thing he had per-

FRANCIS, FOURTH EARL OF BEDFORD

ceived how skilful the Dutchmen were in draining their own 'marishy' country. As early as 1590, he had brought some Dutchmen across to see what could be done in the fens around Thorney. Now his son, the fourth Earl of Bedford, was continuing the work on a much greater scale. The project of the draining of the fens had taken shape.

This implied a heavy task, since for the Earl to have a project before him was to take an active part in it. Such work, when combined with his political interests, would have been enough and more than enough to occupy the time of most men. The Earl found it possible to interest himself also in such plans as the building on the Covent Garden estate and the reorganization of the great estates lying around Tavistock in the west and the smaller, but to him supremely important, estate at Woburn. Every detail concerning these had to come before him and copious notes scribbled in his curious angular hand around and over the papers of his bailiffs and agents testify to his determination to supervise everything. Before his life had come to an end it was evident that his careful and progressive management was bringing its reward in the shape of the great prosperity of the estates, with an increased income for their owner. It was, however, his heir rather than he himself who reaped the harvest which he had sowed.

While their father laboured at business, both public and private, the boys and girls had been rapidly growing up, as a family will do, and as each of the three elder little girls had attained the age of fourteen suitable marriages had been arranged for them. In the meantime, their eldest brother, William, when he had reached the age of nineteen years, had been sent abroad for a two years' tour of the Continent in charge of a tutor. He returned at the end of the year 1634, no longer a stripling, but a good-looking young man upon whom the eyes of many parents with daughters were promptly turned. For his own father and mother his marriage with one of those daughters became of paramount importance. To their consternation, they learned that their son had already made his own choice.

'We have here also another considerable heir,' wrote the Reverend George Garrard, a busybody, to Strafford,

'my Lord Russell, this winter come from beyond the seas, where he hath spent two years; a handsome, genteel man, and there is much looking on him. There are three young ladies ripe of marriage; it is thought he will settle upon one of them: my Lady Elizabeth Cecil, the Lady Anne Carr and the Lady Dorothy Sidney. Yet the voice goes that he bends somewhat towards the Lady Anne Carr, though it is said his father has given him the admonition to choose anywhere but there.'

Lady Elizabeth Cecil would, on every score, have been welcome to the young man's parents as their son's wife. Lady Dorothy Sidney, eighteen years old, the Sacharissa of future days, was enjoying the friendship of Edmund Waller at Penshurst and might or might not have turned from the poet to the good-looking young man who was also a good match. Her mother, the Countess of Leicester, would certainly have welcomed an alliance with the house of Russell. But Garrard had gauged the situation quite correctly. William, Lord Russell, heir to the Earl of Bedford, a nobleman whose austerity was a byword, had made it abundantly clear to his parents and to the eyes of the world that he would have Anne Carr and no other. They had been children of ten and twelve years old when the plague had come to Chiswick and the boy had gone with his father and mother in flight to Woburn Abbey. Now she was nearly twenty, he had turned twenty-one and the two of them were, as Mr. Garrard next reported to the Earl of Strafford, 'all in a flame with love.'

The path of their love ran far from smoothly. The Earl

of Bedford would not hear of the match. It was impossible to forget that Anne was the daughter of the infamous woman who had been successively Countess of Essex and Countess of Somerset and that that lady's mother, Katherine, Countess of Suffolk, had herself, in her generation, borne an evil reputation. Any father, even were he less of a Puritan than the Earl of Bedford, might well have hesitated before welcoming the child of the one and the grandchild of the other as his daughter-in-law. Nor could he have forgotten the day when he, in his place in the House of Lords, had heard the Countess of Somerset confess herself a murderess.

Young Lord Russell listened to his father's remonstrances and repeated that he would marry Anne or no one. The Earl of Bedford flatly refused his consent to the marriage.

A year and more than a year passed. At the end of the time neither father nor son had changed his mind. In the meantime, the world looked on and speculated whether constancy in love would not triumph in the end. Even Garrard was moved to put the rhetorical question that, after all, were not marriages made in heaven, and finally the King himself let it be known that he thought the Earl of Bedford should give way.

The Earl was by no means minded to do so. Nevertheless, his son's unswerving determination and the King's known wishes were having their effect upon him. In July of 1636 Charles and Henrietta Maria paid a visit of two nights to Woburn Abbey and it was freely reported that after they had left the marriage would take place. That report was a false one. Matters remained as they were and it was not until the following winter, two years after the young man had first made known his intentions, that the father began to show signs of yielding.

It became generally known that Bedford had told his son that he would permit the marriage if, and only if, Somerset could give his daughter a dowry of twelve thousand pounds. The Earl of Bedford may have thought and hoped that in saying this he had thereby erected an insuperable barrier, for it was also generally known that Somerset had been forced during and immediately after the trial to sell plate, furniture and pictures and to mortgage some of his lands. The lookers-on surmised that Somerset neither would nor could raise the sum required.

The world had a surprise. Somerset made a great gesture of renunciation in order to secure his daughter's happiness. Garrard, that indefatigable gossip, reported that he had said to the Lord Chamberlain, who was most kindly disposed towards the young couple, that one of the two, he or his daughter, must be undone, and that he would rather undo himself than make her unhappy. In February 1637, when it was clear that the pair were as much in love and determined to marry as ever they had been, Somerset approached the Earl of Bedford with certain proposals. Drawn up and signed in his own hand, they lie now at Woburn Abbey, with remarks by the Earl of Bedford scribbled across them.

Somerset offered as his daughter's dowry an immediate payment of one thousand pounds in sterling and another nine thousand pounds within six months. This last was to be secured in part by a mortgage on his house in Chiswick, with all its contents, which included such tapestries and plate as had been saved from the sale at the time of the trial. But this covered only a very small part of the amount due and another mortgage was proposed for the remainder. This was to be on certain lands in Scotland to which Somerset, and his daughter after him, had a reversion. Lastly, yet three thousand pounds more, to be paid on Somerset's death, were also to be secured on the same Scottish lands. In return, the Earl of Bedford agreed to allow his son and daughter-in-law two thousand pounds a year, with a proviso that this was not to be binding upon him unless and until he had received the money from the Earl of Somerset.

The first thousand pounds was duly paid and the security for the remainder appeared to Bedford, a shrewd business man, good enough. There was, too, the conviction that his son, who had been constant for so long to his love, was not likely to prove inconstant now. He agreed that the marriage should take place in July of that year, 1637, and on the 11th of the month William and Anne were married at St. Benet's Church, Paul's Wharf, London.

About the time of the marriage, possibly, as Sir Lionel Cust thinks, to celebrate the occasion, Anne's full-length portrait was painted by Van Dyck. It hangs now at Woburn, showing her in a rich white silk dress, cut square at the neck, with a pale blue bow at her breast. She seems to be stepping from off a Persian carpet on to a plain, boarded floor. A spaniel is looking up to her, as in the portrait of her father-in-law. This pale, delicate, beautiful picture has been reckoned one of the most charming of the artist's female portraits and in it, as in the other likeness he made of her, now at Petworth, can be read the secret of why the marriage falsified the fourth Earl's apprehensions and fulfilled the hope he later expressed in his last will, that the wedded life of his children should be blessed. The simplicity, modesty and charm of the lady are in marked contrast to the bold, hard, good looks shown in the two portraits, the one of her mother and the other of her grand-mother, which hang by hers at Woburn.

The happy married life of his son was a source of satis-faction to the Earl of Bedford during the next three years and the satisfaction was enhanced by the birth of two little boys, of whom the eldest was christened Francis and the second William. This was well, since from the financial point of view the marriage contract provided no satisfaction whatsoever. First came the failure of Somerset to pay the nine thousand pounds, or even part of it, on the date when it was due, and then the gradual realization on the part of his creditor that it was unlikely that it ever would be paid. It must in fairness be said that the default was not entirely due to Somerset, for he was prepared, since he could not raise the ready money, to allow the mortgage on the Scottish estates to take effect. Nevertheless, he did not grieve too greatly when his Scottish relatives, determined that the lands should not pass to an English Earl, nor ultimately to the wife of one, intervened. His emotional outburst, lamenting the misery of his daughter's childhood and expressing his fervent desire to make amends for it, was very soon a thing of the past. Anne ceased to be his greatly loved daughter and became instead, with her husband, an object of suspicion. Within a year of the marriage he was showing every sign of becoming estranged from her. No doubt the lawsuit into which he was plunged, over the matter of the non-payment of the dowry, was in part responsible for his change of mood. He certainly resented his daughter's prosperity and happiness. Anne, indeed, had a firm hold, not only upon the affections of her young husband, but upon those of his family, including her awe-inspiring father-in-law, who is said to have grown to love her dearly.

The Earl had need of consolation in his home life, for the political horizon was clouded and the air was thick with rumours of trouble to come.

In September 1640, the Earl of Bedford, as a known 'moderate' in political affairs, was named one of the sixteen noblemen who, after the close of the disastrous Second Bishops' War, were appointed to negotiate with the Scottish commissioners. The meetings were held first at Ripon. Then they were transferred to Westminster. Once the commissioners came to Woburn, perhaps on their way to Westminster. At all events, their arrival caused some commotion in the household, since there was no table in the abbey long enough to accommodate these guests at dinner. One, therefore, had to be borrowed from the house of Lord Brook, the Earl's son-in-law.

It was one of the last occasions on which the Earl was to entertain guests at the abbey, for his life had but a few months to run. They were anxious months during which he was occupied with the business in which the Earl of Strafford was the central, tragic figure, and each month the prospect looked darker than before.

On 3rd November 1640, the Parliament that future generations were to know as the Long Parliament assembled at Westminster. The Commons, in a state of agitation and alarm at what they believed to be a plan to overthrow the constitution of the country as they understood it, proceeded with their attack on the King's ministers. On 25th November, Strafford, who had taken his seat as usual in the House of Lords, was impeached and sent to the Tower. But could he be brought to the scaffold? Would the charge of treason hold good when the crime was adherence to the King against what Parliament believed to be the interest of the country? The Lords were doubtful. The moderate party among them were for the restraint of Strafford, but against the death penalty. Amid the turmoil and perplexity eyes were turned hopefully upon the Earl of Bedford. He, if any one, it was thought, might evolve a plan which should save the life of his fellow peer.

The contest dragged on through the winter months. But Bedford was not to see the game played out. In the first week of May 1641, the Bill of Attainder which the Commons had substituted for the impeachment was before the House of Lords. Bedford was not in his usual place. The previous week he had been staying at his town house, Bedford House in the Strand, a tired man. Very shortly he was a sick one. His eldest daughter, Katherine, Lady Brook, was in the house and it was she who, after her father had been evidently ill for a day or two, first noted with alarm the symptoms of smallpox. It proved to be one of the earliest cases of a particularly bad epidemic in London.

Immediately his illness was identified, the Earl expressed a wish that all his family should keep away from him and remain in another part of the house. He lay upstairs in his curtained and valanced bed in his tapestry-hung bedroom, with its red velvet furnishings, watched over by the doctors. The first physician called in was Dr. John Craig, who was physician to the King and who had also been physician to James I and had created some notoriety for himself by alleging that that monarch had died of poisoning. As the patient grew worse rather than better, the Countess summoned in consultation Sir John Cademan, physician to Queen Henrietta Maria. This worthy man at once decided that the case had been wrongly treated and said so, according to his own statement later put forth in pamphlet form, at considerable length. Sir John Craig not unnaturally resented the opinion thus crudely expressed by his newly arrived colleague. The two began to argue, and the sick man was heard to murmur from his bed that, on the whole, he thought he had better die in order to please the doctors.

The sarcasm was painfully true. Neither of the two medical men, whichever had been right in his diagnosis of the case, could save the Earl.

On Saturday, 8th May, he was seen to be desperately ill. He lay only half conscious, but still fighting for his life against the disease which was rapidly overwhelming him, while at Westminster another battle, also for a life, was being waged. That day the Lords, sitting in their chamber, passed the Bill of Attainder, which now only required the royal signature to send Strafford to the scaffold. In the course of the day two deputations from their House went to Whitehall to urge upon the King the necessity of giving his consent to the Bill. Charles asked for time, only to learn that it was too late. All that night between Saturday and Sunday the angry mob which had followed the Lords to Whitehall surged up and down before the palace. The noise could be heard even in the Strand. But no events in this world, not even the terrible sound of the fury of a people, had power to stir Bedford now. For him the earthly scene was closing. Upstairs the doctors watched the dying man; the family remained in anxiety in the room below. The end was not long delayed. Smallpox took its victims quickly. Towards ten o'clock on the Sunday morning, the 9th of May, Francis, Earl of Bedford, passed, in the words of Sir Thomas Cademan, 'to the Highest Court of Parliament.' That evening the King signed the Bill of Attainder.

For five days the Earl of Bedford lay in state at Bedford House. During those days the tragedy of Strafford's life and death was played out. The execution took place at Tower Hill on the Wednesday. Two hundred thousand persons, it was reckoned, were there to see Strafford die — 'Strafford, who was hurried hence, 'twixt treason and convenience.'

On Friday, the 14th, another crowd were in the Strand in front of Bedford House. By three o'clock in the afternoon three hundred or more coaches had assembled to follow the procession which set forth to Chenies. Thither the body of the Earl of Bedford, his Parliamentary robes spread upon the coffin, was borne in heraldic state, in accordance with the wish that he had constantly expressed, that he might be buried 'at Chenies where my great-grandfather lies.'

The Earl had made many wills in his time. It was an exercise of which he was fond. All the wills had been long and elaborate; the last one was particularly so. In it a new clause had been inserted by which a special bequest was made to his son and heir, William. He was to look, directed his father, in the study, where he would find a number of

35

manuscript volumes. These, said the Earl, had been written by his own hand 'more by prayers than with pains.' The son was now charged to take particular care of these and, in his turn, to bequeath them to his heirs.

This was faithfully done and the volumes remain in the study at Woburn Abbey to-day. In all, there are ten folio volumes. The fourth Earl of Bedford had found time, in his busy and laborious life, to cover their pages with his musings on religious doctrine and dogma.

CHAPTER II

A BUDGET OF 1641

WILLIAM RUSSELL, Earl of Bedford, the fifth of that name, came back to Bedford House in the Strand after the last ceremonies for his father had been performed at Chenies and he and his wife and the two little boys remained for a few weeks in London.

Bedford House in the Strand stood on the north side of that thoroughfare, next to Exeter House. Formerly the family had owned two houses in the Strand. One, which had been called Russell House, had been acquired by the first Earl early in his career. That had stood on the south side, between the Savoy chapel and Ivy Bridge Lane, with its gardens sloping down to the river. Many years later, almost at the end of his life, in 1552, the Earl had put up a less pretentious wooden mansion on his Covent Garden property on the north side of the street. He had, however, seldom, if ever, used this house as a residence, nor had his son, the second Earl, after him. Both had usually lived at Russell House on the river side whenever they wished to be in town and, as it chanced, both of them had died there. Then the property had gone to the second Earl's widow and had been sold, while the family had migrated across the Strand to the other house which stood on the Covent Garden site.

Bedford House had been completely reconstructed during the minority of the third Earl and had been made into a very fine mansion indeed. But for the owner it had served chiefly as the prison to which he had been strictly confined by order of the Crown after the Essex rebellion, being forbidden even to ride out, until at length he was allowed to go into the country. His successors, the fourth and now the fifth Earl, reaped the main advantage from what had been done.

The house was built round a courtyard. The main entrance was in the Strand. To the east of the building, between it and Exeter House, were the stables, which had their own separate entrance. Behind the house was a built-up terrace walk and beyond that again a formal seventeenth-century garden. On the other side of the garden wall was the Piazza, with its new buildings, the church of St. Paul and the handsome houses around, all of which, both church and houses, had been erected under the supervision of the fourth Earl. There, too, clustered under the wall itself, were the stalls of the fruit and vegetable sellers who had marked this district down as a desirable spot for the selling of their wares.

The windows of the principal room in the house, a long room running the entire length of the north wing, opened on to the terrace, whereby it was known as the Terrace Room. The walls were hung with tapestries. The furniture, couch, elbow chairs and high stools, was covered with figured satin or velvet, some red and some green, and all decorated with silver lace. Usually the room made a brave show of colour, but in this time of mourning everything was covered up with black stuffs.

Across the courtyard, in the south wing, a parallel long room, or gallery, faced the Strand. Here the hangings were of green cloth and gilt leather and the furniture of red velvet. There were several other living-rooms and also a waiting-room, furnished in green silk and silver, in which the Earl received visitors who came on business, except when they were taken to his dressing-room. The two little boys had their nursery and, over and above the bedrooms occupied by the family, there was ample accommodation, both business rooms and bedrooms, for the staff. This last was very necessary, for, although Woburn Abbey was the family residence, yet the London house was, for its part, the centre for the Earl's financial and business affairs.

On 17th May 1641, a week after his father's death, the young Earl took his seat in the House of Lords. He had, however, no intention of remaining in London any longer than could be avoided, even though business, both public and private, would, he knew, frequently bring him back. Throughout his life William, Earl of Bedford, was first and foremost the country gentleman. To him the supervision of his estates was of far greater interest than the changes and chances of the political arena, into which he entered reluctantly and which he was only too glad to abandon whenever possible. Of all his estates, Woburn, neither the most ancient, nor the wealthiest, nor the greatest in extent, was the most precious in his eyes, as it had been in the eyes of his father.

To Woburn towards the end of June the Earl and Countess returned. They had with them not only their two little boys, Francis and William, who this year were three and two years old respectively, but also the Earl's mother, Katherine, now Dowager Countess, and his youngest and only unmarried sister, Diana. The late Earl, remembering the happiness of those early years at Chiswick, had desired in his will that his widow should have the house there for her use during her lifetime. But the Countess declined the arrangement, perhaps because the memories of the past were to her too poignant. She preferred rather to remain with her son and his wife, and it was arranged that she and the unmarried girl should occupy one wing of Woburn Abbey.

There was every reason, quite apart from personal wishes, why they should all have been glad to get out of London. The smallpox epidemic was rising to its height and many deaths were occurring each week. Woburn seemed once again a place of refuge.

The abbey, hung like Bedford House in black, received them. Barely had they all settled down when a catastrophe occurred that caused the utmost consternation. They were not so safe from infection as they had supposed. The young Countess was seized with an illness which was speedily seen to be the dreaded smallpox.

Doctors from one or the other of the neighbouring towns were regular attendants at the abbey. But once the nature of the illness was proved beyond doubt, the Earl decided that a medical man must be fetched from town. He did not, however, call in either of those who had attended his father. The physician he chose was Dr. John Clarke, already a well-known man, who, four years later, was made President of the College of Physicians, in whose Reading Room his portrait, presented by his daughter, still hangs, showing a pleasant, genial man with white hair and a fresh complexion, whose attire, with plain cape and collar, seems to indicate that his sympathies were with the Puritan party. He was called to Woburn some time in June, but he did not get his fee until August. This was quite in accordance with custom.

August 1641. Paid to Doctor Clarke for his
pains going to my lady of
Bedford when she was sick
of the smallpox at Woburn,
as per warrant.   £20   0   0
Paid to a hackney coachman
that carried Doctor Clarke to
Woburn when my lady Bed-
ford was sick of the smallpox,
as per warrant.   £2   4   0

Happily, the fate which had befallen her father-in-law from the same illness was spared the Countess. She recovered, and as no other case of the disease occurred the family left again for London, where the epidemic was now abating, while precautions were taken to disinfect the abbey.

The disinfection was carried out by a process of fumigation on the strictly orthodox lines of smoking with a mixture of pitch and frankincense.

August 1641.—Paid to Anthony the porter, for pitch and frankincense to smoke the house and yard   5*s*.   0*d*.

This long continued the favourite method of fumigation, for some ninety years later Dr. Thomas Fuller, the great authority on eruptive fevers, was still recommending it in his *Exanthemologia*, published in 1730, although he added that sulphur was to be preferred as the sovereign remedy.

In any event, the Earl at least would have found it necessary to go to town again. There was still much to be done in the settlement of his affairs as the result of his succession to the title, and while he had been at Woburn, throughout the month of June, he had been taking stock of his resources.

On the 20th of May, just before the family had gone down to Woburn, Katherine, the Dowager Countess, had formally handed over to her son the keys of the great trunk which stood in Bedford House in the Strand and served as the family bank.

That trunk, still preserved, was and is an admirable specimen of the money chests of the day. Unlike many of them, however, it had not come from the workshop of an Augsburg or Nuremberg craftsman, but had been made in the Netherlands, probably for the father of the fourth Earl. The exterior is painted in the characteristic Dutch fashion, squares showing prim landscapes and flowers, roses and tulips. Inside, the beautiful design of the springs of the great double lock which fill the whole of the lid is Spanish in style.

The history of the money that was in the trunk when the keys were handed over and of that which was afterwards put in and taken out during the first year of the succession to the title is contained in a small, stout, parchment-bound book endorsed:

The account of all such monies as have been received for the right honourable William, Earl of Bedford, since the 20th day of May, Anno Domino 1641, at which time my lady Bedford, his mother, delivered the keys to his lordship of the trunk.

When the young Earl had opened the trunk he had found in it £1,557 14s. 1d. in all.

A good deal of this money had had to be taken out immediately. The bills for the late Earl's funeral, without the mourning, had come to two hundred and fifty-five pounds. This was less than half the cost—nearly seven hundred pounds—of the funeral of his great-grandfather, Francis, the second Earl, who had died in 1585. On that occasion, in order to meet the expenses, Sir Francis Walsingham, as one of the executors, had ordered the sale of all the magnificent furniture at Chenies. A simpler ceremony in later days required less drastic measures. The dues at Chenies, where the fourth Earl was laid among his ancestors, came to no more than seventy pounds, but a hundred and eighty-six pounds had to go to the College of Arms for conducting the funeral.

These two bills were paid immediately. Those for the mourning provided for family, servants and the houses came to just under five hundred pounds in all and were settled in instalments.

Paid to Mr. Brandwood at the Arm and
Sword in Paul's Churchyard, for baize bought
at my old lord's funeral as per bill, warrant and
acquittance thereon   £9   7   8
Paid to Alderman Garrett in part of his bill
for black cloth bought at my old lord's
funeral   £100   0   0

The young Earl had had, in fact, to be extremely careful
how he used his money and had not dared to pay out too
freely, even though arrears of rents to the amount of nearly
a thousand pounds had come in during the first few weeks
and had been added to the store in the chest. Tradesmen's
bills could be settled in part, but there were other claims
which had had to be met in full and at once. There had been
interest to be paid on certain loans, as well as a heavy payment due in respect of the fen enterprise; and sixty pounds
had had to go to the collector of the first two of the four
subsidies that had been granted by the Long Parliament the
previous December, with a gratuity of two shillings and
sixpence to the man who brought the letter demanding
the subsidy and another of one shilling to the collector's
clerk, who made out the receipt.

One way and another, therefore, the trunk had been
dipped into very freely during the two months which had
followed the taking over of the keys by the young Earl from
his mother. At the end of those two months, just about the
time when he returned to London, the Earl had appointed
an official who was to act as his principal steward, or, as he
was more generally called, receiver-general, and had handed
him the keys.

According to the accounts which this gentleman was
given with the keys, he should have found £825 7s. 5½d. in
the trunk. But the figures and the actual cash did not
agree.

July 1641.—Wanting of the monies in the
trunk which I stand charged with since the 5th
of this month, at which time the monies were
told and the keys of the trunk delivered to me £2   5   2½

Upon the receiver-general devolved all the responsibility
for the Earl's affairs, estate, household and personal alike.
He took control of and was accountable for all the money
that was put into and taken out of the trunk and his account
book is, in effect, a budget of the Earl's finances for the first
year of his succession to the title. Under the fourth Earl
the post had been held by Walter Wentworth, gentleman, a
relative of the Earl of Strafford. His successor was John
Trenchard, a member of the Dorset family long closely
connected with the Russells. He did not come as a novice to
the Earl's affairs, for he had already been employed by the
latter's father to help in the management of the estates in
the west. Now he took up his abode in Bedford House,
although his presence was constantly required at Woburn
also.

When the accounts for the six weeks during which the
Earl had kept the keys had been made up, the latter had
signed the book. He wrote 'W. Bedforde,' following the
older usage by which a nobleman invariably signed with the
initials of his Christian name as well as his title. After the
book was handed over to Mr. Trenchard, the Earl signed
it again at the end of the first six months. Then and thence-
forward he wrote himself 'Bedford.' He had dropped the
'e' from the termination of his name, which, however, had
been by no means always so spelt by his predecessors, and
had adopted the new fashion of signing by his title only, a
custom to which he kept, with very few exceptions, to the
end of his life.

The money that came in between 5th July 1641, when
the steward took the keys, and the same day the following

year amounted in all to just under £8,500. Except for the annuity of twenty pounds which had been granted to John, Lord Russell, on his creation as Earl of Bedford 'to support the dignity of an Earl,' it all came from the estates. But to separate the different items with anything like accuracy would require a detailed history of each piece of property. All that can be said is that sales of wood, malt, tallow, sheepskins, hay and other produce accounted for nearly a thousand pounds, while the remainder was rents and fines. It is just this practice of taking fines for the renewal of leases, with the consequent lower rents, largely adopted by the Earl's father, which makes it difficult to estimate what was the true rental of any estate. The difficulty is increased by the method of payment.

The income from the estates should have been paid in equal sums twice yearly, at Lady Day and at Michaelmas. Actually, the Earl received, as a rule, anything between a half to two-thirds of the amount due at each audit and then the arrears slowly dribbled in. At the end of each account there were always a certain number of rents outstanding, of which several were usually in the end marked 'Forgiven' in the account. All that reached the Earl represented clear profit since, before the money was sent up, each steward and each bailiff had deducted the costs of the upkeep of the manor or district under his charge, his own salary and the salaries of other employees, as well as any Crown charges, such as the tenths payable on the Tavistock estate, for these, too, were paid directly, on behalf of the Earl, from the districts on which they were imposed.

A substantial part of the money received by the Earl, something like two thousand five hundred pounds, came from the west, the Devon lands with the outlying property in Cornwall. In these counties Lord Russell, afterwards first Earl of Bedford, had added considerably to the original grant by purchase. In his day and in that of his son the western estates had been the principal source of the family income and they still represented a substantial part of it, although the turning-point had arrived and their importance was gradually to be eclipsed by the London property and that in the eastern counties.

Already the London property of Covent Garden and Long Acre was beginning to show a good return for the large sum of money which the late Earl had spent upon it. His son now received a rental from it of something rather under a thousand pounds as against the five hundred pounds which it had paid in the time of the third Earl, before the building developments.

The fourth Earl had sunk even more money in his property in the eastern counties, of which Thorney was the centre. Much money had here been invested and was still to be invested in the project of the draining of the fens, but when the fifth Earl took up his succession the time for the profits was not yet.

The remainder of the rentals came from scattered properties, one group representing the ancient Russell patrimony in Dorset, another, including Woburn, the residue of the grants to John, Lord Russell, the first Earl, and the last the very considerable dowry lands. Besides the great properties brought into the family by the first Countess, which had included Chenies and Thornhaugh, Katherine, the wife of the fourth Earl, now Dowager Countess, had been co-heiress with her sister of the Chandos property which lay mainly in Gloucestershire.

As the money due to the Earl came in, it was assembled at Bedford House in the Strand. That from the outlying property in the eastern or home counties was brought or sent over by the bailiffs who had collected it, but a more convenient and newer method facilitated the transference of the largest payments, coming from Devon and the neighbouring counties.

The estates in the western counties were managed by an official who was known as the steward of the west. He lived in the house at Exeter known as Bedford House, built by the first Earl. It had been necessary for this nobleman to reside for long periods of time in the west, since the Crown had relied upon him to keep order there, and both he and his son after him had kept high state at Bedford House in Exeter. Now that the family had somewhat turned their back upon the west, the house in Exeter, once magnificently furnished, had fallen into neglect, so that a dreary little inventory taken in the time of the third Earl shows a sad old building, with collapsed floors and almost every window broken. It had scarcely recovered its former glories, but at least it had been put into repair and was occupied by the steward of the west.

There to Bedford House, on the site still commemorated in Exeter by the name of Bedford Circus, came the bailiffs from the various manors for the audits at Lady Day and Michaelmas. Each brought with him his statement of accounts, showing what had been received and what expended, and handed over to the steward the surplus of profits. Once the latter had a sufficient amount in hand to make it worth while, he arranged for a bill of exchange to be drawn upon one of the London goldsmiths. The goldsmith selected was nearly always the celebrated Mr. Thomas Viner of Lombard Street. When the bill had been sent to Viner and received by him, notice was given to the Earl's receiver-general. The latter then proceeded to Lombard Street to fetch the money. He provided himself with bags, whi ch cost three shillings a dozen—the price never varied— in which to carry away the coins. They were heavy when full and, in order to convey them safely back to Bedford House, he usually hired two or three porters. The porters had to be bespoken before he reached Viner's establishment and the annoying part was that he was by no means sure whether the money could and would be handed over at once, or whether he would not have to wait for some hours.

November 1641.	Paid for going by water with Mr. Maxewell's men to receive a £1,000 in 'Lumber' Street.	6*d.*
	Paid for their dinners and my own, staying there all the morning before Mr. Viner could pay us the money and having much ado to make them stay.	3*s.* 0*d.*
	Paid to two porters for bringing this £1,000 from 'Lumber' Street to Bedford House.	3*s.* 0*d.*
	Received of Mr. Viner upon a bill of exchange from Mr. Snowe of Exeter.	£1,009 16*s.* 8*d.*

The delays in getting the money from Viner were no worse than elsewhere. The receiver noted again and again in his book that he had had to pay for his own dinner and for those of his assistants in the city as it was so late before the money was handed over. The waste of time and the annoyance of having to provide dinner for the porters were bad enough, but the primary cause of his anxiety to get the money handed over early was his desire to have it conveyed to Bedford House in daylight, in which he was far from successful. He constantly had to enter money paid to linkmen— the charge was fourpence a head—to light the little procession on its way. Very occasionally a hackney coach was hired, but porters were far more often made use of.

Once it was safely in Bedford House the money had to be counted:

November 1641.—Paid for a pint of sack and for Mr. Vahan's supper that helped me all day to tell the monies.   1*s.*   9*d.*

November 1641.—Paid for Mr. Vahan's dinner and supper the second day that he helped to receive the monies returned out of the west.   2*s.*   0*d.*

The greater part of the money was then put into the chest at Bedford House. A little went down to Woburn for immediate needs, sometimes carried by a servant on horseback, sometimes in a coach, but always with an escort of servants.

What was thus put into the chest had to cover the Earl's expenditure for himself, his family and his household. It likewise had to provide the annuities of one thousand and of five hundred pounds respectively with which he stood charged for his mother and his youngest brother, Edward. He was also aware that some time or other he would have to find a capital sum wherewith to make a substantial payment to his unmarried sister, Diana. The other sisters were off his hands, for they had had their dowries from their father on the occasion of their marriages. His brothers, all but the youngest, had also been provided for. But, unhappily, they had debts which the late Earl had asked their eldest brother to pay if he were able, without specifically ordering him to do so.

The annuities could and would be paid out of income, the more easily because the decision of his mother to live at Woburn Abbey was profitable to the Earl since she returned him almost the whole of her annuity in payment for the board and lodging of herself and her servants. The brothers' debts might also be settled, even though it might not be possible to pay them off entirely during the first year.

None of these liabilities, the annuities or the brothers' debts, provoking though the latter might be, constituted anything like a serious financial problem for the young Earl. Had he merely had to meet these in addition to his ordinary expenses, he would have managed well enough. His financial horizon was, however, darkened by two clouds, which, although one at least proved to have a silver, even, it might be said, a golden lining, oppressed his outlook during this first year of his succession.

His young sister, Diana, who had come back to the abbey with her mother, was now ripe for marriage and by her father's will her brother had been desired to provide for her a dowry of seven thousand pounds and to give her interest on it at eight per cent. as long as the whole, or any part of it, remained unpaid. This eight per cent. was the maximum interest allowed by the Act of 1625, which had sought to prevent usurious rates. The Dowager Countess was anxious for her youngest daughter to marry and the Earl realized that within a very short time he would somehow or other have to find the capital for her dowry.

A far more considerable sum of money than the dowry for Lady Diana had also to be found. The Earl's father had needed ready money, and a good deal of it, for his various projects, notably the building on the Covent Garden estate and the draining of the fens. This money had been borrowed, a little on mortgage but chiefly on bonds, also at eight per cent., in sums varying from one to two thousand pounds, from various friends, including such men as Lord Newport and Lord Feilding. When the son succeeded to the title there was a debt outstanding of nearly twenty thousand pounds, to which had to be added a debt of another thousand pounds which he himself owed.

There should have been a sum available which would have in part, although only in part, provided the money required. The Earl was still short, and likely to remain so, of the nine thousand pounds which should have been paid over by his father-in-law as his wife's dowry. He had chosen Anne in face of every kind of opposition and enough is known of his married life to make it quite clear that money counted little with him in comparison with her. Nevertheless, the lack of this nine thousand pounds, combined with the necessity of paying at least part of the dowry to his sister, not to speak of the urgency of getting rid of some of the outstanding bonds, forced him to enter into a series of elaborate financial transactions which cast a certain gloom over the book of the receiver-general, who, otherwise, had no difficulty in balancing his accounts, since the ordinary expenditure was based on the excellent principle that it should be less than the income.

This pressing necessity to harbour his resources, no less than the mourning in the household, dictated for the Earl an unostentatious year in which his household should be run on strictly economical lines.

From the chest the money was taken by the receiver-general as it was wanted. Some bills were paid directly by himself; others were settled by different members of the staff. A certain amount had to go to the Earl for his private use and the Countess had her allowance of three hundred pounds a year. Some of the general payments, such as those for provisions and wages, were made regularly, month by month, but the settlement of miscellaneous bills and fees continued to be made many months after they became due and, in the case of very large bills, by instalments stretching over a year or even longer, according as the rents came in to replenish the money, which might have sunk very low in the chest.

No very clear picture is left in this first set of accounts of the household staff, save for two principal figures, Mr. Dixy Taylor and Mr. Crawley.

Mr. Dixy Taylor was personal attendant to the Earl and his wife. He came from a family who were and had long been among the more important tenants of the Earls of Bedford at Woburn. From generation to generation one or more of the sons had entered into the Earl's service either on the estate or in the house. Dixy was destined to pervade the accounts for nearly half a century, until he was retired upon a pension. Other officials might come and go, but Dixy went on for a very long time indeed.

Taylor's colleague, Mr. Crawley, was responsible, under the receiver-general, for the entire administration of the household. He made all necessary purchases and presided over the staff. But he had nothing to do with the staff employed on any of the estates, not even at Woburn. The accounts for the estates, including the salaries and wages of all employed on them, were kept entirely separate from the household accounts, the receiver-general being responsible for both.

Of the members of the household below Dixy Taylor and Mr. Crawley, dim figures flit here and there, but it is only occasionally that one of them becomes distinct. There was Anthony, the porter, who did all the odd jobs, including the fumigating of the house, and was quite handsomely paid for doing them; there was Rose, a housemaid, who, in some mysterious manner, had five shillings in her pocket to lend the lord and master when he had sudden need of it; and there was Rolles, the coachman, who remained only a few weeks in the new Earl's service and then was retired, with a handsome present. How many they numbered in all it is impossible to say.

At the beginning of each month the receiver-general gave Mr. Crawley out of the chest a sum of money wherewith to pay salaries and wages. The total amount that Mr.

Crawley received for this purpose during the twelve months was something over two hundred and sixty pounds. But this figure is not any real guide to the numbers employed since to the salaries and wages for this year were added the legacies left to each member of his household by the late Earl and certain board wages and other expenses, which were incurred before the household was really set going again. Some of the payments were made very irregularly. The receiver-general and Mr. Crawley were clearly making brave efforts to distribute the money at their disposal as equitably as possible. But some of the servants had to wait a considerable time before they got their legacies.

Mr. Crawley also paid all the bills for the running of the household, which he accomplished on something like an average of thirty pounds a week. This covered the food, much more of which was bought outside than might be supposed, groceries, coal, wood and general household necessities. Unfortunately, no packets of detailed bills survive for his era, as they do for those of his successors. All that remains of his housekeeping accounts is a series of general figures set down in the yearly book. We can see that coal cost him a hundred and seventy pounds for the entire year, but not how much was bought or at what price.

If clothes had had to be bought, either for the family or for the liveried part of the household, either Mr. Dixy Taylor or Mr. Crawley would have bought them, or at all events paid the bills for them. But the mourning provided lasted every one for the year, which made for economy, although even so Mr. Crawley did pay out something under a hundred pounds. This was principally for the needs of the two little boys, who apparently wore out their suits very quickly, and for shoes and boots, always a heavy item. But one bill out of the ordinary was included here, marking the only occasion as far as the accounts are concerned, on which the Earl ever had to pay up on behalf of his father-in-law.

January 1641/2.—Given by my lord's command to a young man that was a silk-man in Cheapside and demanded money as due to him from the Earl of Somerset.   £1   o   o

Outside the house, the stables, the kennels and the mews where the falcons were kept cost two hundred and thirty pounds odd. Very little was spent on either the kennels or the mews during this first year and the expenses of the stables were reduced as far as possible.

The late Earl had left all his coaches and his horses to the Dowager Countess. Probably, since she was living at Woburn, she allowed her son to use as his own everything that was in the stables, and he had at least one coach and some horses of his own. Only in November 1641 did he make a new purchase and buy six coach horses for his own use from his neighbour, Lord Wharton.

November 1641.—Paid to the Lord Wharton, which was for six coach horses my lord bought of him, as per acquittance from Mr. Lightfoote, his man.   £150   o   o

The old coaches had to suffice for the whole of the year, until, in June 1642, more than a twelvemonth after his father's death, the Earl indulged in a new vehicle. His old coach was taken in part payment for it.

June 1642.—Paid to Prosser, the coachmaker, for a new coach for my lord, as per warrant and acquittance.   £32   10s.   0d.

Memorandum: he had my lord's old coach also into the bargain, worth about £5 0s. 0d.

Later on the travelling expenses were included in the stables accounts, but for this year they were reckoned separately. They came to something under a hundred pounds.

This hundred pounds covered the expenses of moving the family to Woburn, and back to London and down to Woburn again, after the smallpox case; and also the cost of the single journeys, usually up and down to London, taken by the young Earl himself and his receiver-general, with some of the servants.

The family travelled between Woburn and London, and back, in a coach. If the Earl went up by himself he also used a coach. The receiver-general rode—he had his own horse. The servants, when they were sent up and down, also went on horseback. The horses they rode, however, did not come from the Earl's stables, but were hired. A horse could be hired for the single journey between Woburn and London for eight shillings, with the addition of the expenses of baiting, usually at St. Albans, by the way.

September 1641.—Paid to Anthony, the porter, for the hire of a hackney horse, 8*s.* 0*d.*; and for his journey to Woburn, being sent by my lord.   13*s.*   0*d.*

On one occasion when the agent struck a bargain with a woman for the hire of a horse at sixpence less than the usual rate the result was not entirely satisfactory, for the lady did not keep the bargain and her pertinacity in demanding the additional sixpence wore out the master before it wore out the man.

August 1641.   Paid to Adam for the hire of a horse to carry a letter to my lord at Woburn.   7*s.*   6*d.*

Paid more to him towards his charges by the way.   1*s.*   0*d.*

August 1641.   Given by my lord's command to a
scolding woman that Adam
hired a horse of to ride to
Woburn: more than bargain,
got by scolding.   6*d.*

Hiring of both horses and vehicles was common. The
Earl himself, when he was in London, frequently went about
in a hired carriage. Little use was made this year of the
stables at Bedford House, probably on account of expense.
In town, however, the Earl was not, any more than any one
else, entirely dependent upon horse vehicles, for many of
his journeys were made by water, sometimes in his own
private barge, sometimes in a hired boat.

The barge was kept in Rayner's Yard on the river bank
almost exactly opposite Bedford House. The cost was not
extravagant, for the storage amounted only to one pound a
quarter and no more than £1 12*s.* 6*d.* was spent during the
year on repairs and painting.

As a rule, the Earl went to Westminster in this barge,
but sometimes a river boat would be hired for him. The
receiver-general, whose business frequently took him farther
both up and down the river, always hired a boat for himself.
The cost of the journey to Westminster was sixpence; that
to Chiswick, one of the most expensive journeys he made,
was two shillings and sixpence for the return fare, but all
charges were increased when the journey had to be made
against the tide.

June 1641.—Paid for going by water to Westminster from the Temple to show Mr. Maynard
the Bill and Mr. Attorney.   6*d.*

July 1641.—My charges going by water to
Chiswick to make a particular of the lands for Mr.
Attorney and for coming back from thence.   2*s.*   6*d.*

August 1641.—Paid for going by water to Mr. Hales at Hammersmith and coming back both against the tide.   4*s.*   0*d.*

Travel by water was by far the cheapest form of getting about and the Thames was still the great highway. But already angry murmurs had been heard from the watermen of London that their livelihood was threatened by a new fashion. They had viewed the hackney coach, on its first appearance in the London streets early in the century, with distaste and suspicion; when, in 1633, owing to the enterprise of a Captain Bailey, the first regular stand for these vehicles was seen in the Strand, they grew loud in their vociferations that this innovation spelt ruin for them. They were quite right, unhappily for themselves, in foreseeing what would happen, although the change over from water to street travel was only a gradual one. But to be able to secure a vehicle in the street instead of, as at first, hiring it from the stables was an encouragement to the drivers and a convenience to those who wished to obtain a carriage quickly. From one point of view it was too successful, for the numbers plying for hire increased so rapidly that within two years there was serious congestion in the streets, even to impeding the King and Queen when they drove forth. The consequence was an attempt to suppress the hackney coach by proclamation, but by this time far too many people had discovered how useful a vehicle it was. The Earl of Bedford had, for one; for him the stand in the Strand was particularly convenient since it was exactly opposite his own house and he frequently hired a hackney coach from it, the cost when he employed the vehicle for the whole day in town being 8*s.* 6*d.*

It must have been very pleasing to the watermen when, on occasion, they saw their hated rivals being prevented from travelling and their own craft once again triumphant.

December 1641.—Paid for going by water from Westminster when the tide overflowed the streets.   *6d.*

Entries for the hire of boats and hackney coaches were numerous in the accounts, for when the Earl and his receiver-general were in London, Bedford House was the scene of great activity. There were matters of import enough before the Long Parliament that year to take the Earl constantly to Westminster. He also had two pieces of business of his own which could only be carried through by private Acts of Parliament. The one was the settlement of the estates and the other the completion of a piece of work which had lain very near his father's heart, namely, the making of Covent Garden into a parish, now that it had its fine new church of St. Paul. The lawyers were frequently at Bedford House taking the Earl's instructions on both matters, after which they proceeded to Westminster to act as his attorneys there. Mr. Hales, the principal lawyer, seldom received less than two pounds for an interview and was frequently paid three pounds, and as much, or more, when he had to go to Westminster. There were other lawyers employed also and the receiver had to hand out considerable fees on his master's behalf; nor was he able to delay settlement, for the accounts show that the lawyers were almost alone in receiving the reward of their labours on the spot, instead of having to wait for them, as did even the worthy Dr. Clarke, and still more, the mercers and linen drapers.

June 1641.—Given to Mr. Hales by my lord's appointment when he came to Bedford House to read the Bill for settling the estate when it was fair written.   £3 *os.* *od.*

June 1641.—Given to Mr. Hales when he first attended the Lords' Committees at Westminster upon my lord's Bill.   £3 *os.* *od.*

July 1641.—Given to Mr. Hales for at-
tending the Committee in the House of Com-
mons upon my lord's Bill for settling his estate. £2 0s. 0d.

The lawyers went to and from Bedford House in a
hackney coach, of which the Earl paid the hire, and were
received by him either in the little waiting-room or in the
dressing-room attached to his bedroom. There is only one
occasion mentioned when the Earl himself, attended by his
receiver, went out to interview a lawyer in the latter's
chambers in Lincoln's Inn.

In all, rather over a hundred pounds went to the lawyers
for this year and a little less than a hundred pounds was
expended in fees of all kinds in connection with the proving
of the will, the settlement of the estate and the passage of the
private Bills through Parliament.

Besides moving about London, chiefly to Westminster,
the Earl paid various visits in the course of the year to the
Court at Theobalds or Waltham and also to friends. He
sometimes used his own carriage for these visits, but he
quite as often hired.

September 1641. Paid to the hackney coachman for carrying my lord
to Waltham with 6 horses
£1. 7s. 0d., whereof he
abated the 7s. 0d. for that
which was allowed him on
his last bill for the same
journey, being he waited
with his horses all day and
my lord put off his journey
till the next day.   £1 0s. 0d.
Given to the coachman and
postillion that carried my
lord to Waltham.   2s. 0d.

Presents given to the postillion and coachman were invariable items in the travelling expenses. Every journey and every visit, almost every time the Earl went forth, involved the expenditure of other small sums. Beggars were met by the way, to whom sixpence or a shilling might be thrown. Every one who opened a gate or door expected to be given a present, whether it was the self-appointed keeper who ran to open a gate directly he saw the coach, or one of the magnificent officers who guarded the Exchequer chamber or any other. If sixpence contented the former, the latter expected and received any sums varying from two to five shillings. Wherever the Earl went, whether to visit the King at Theobalds, on business to Westminster or elsewhere, or to walk for his pleasure in St. James's Park, his keeper of the purse had to provide the wherewithal for the presents.

September 1641.	Paid to a man that opened a gate in Theobalds Park as my lord came from Waltham to Woburn.	6*d.*
April 1642.	Given to the door-keeper in the Exchequer chamber when my lord was at the committee there.	5*s.* 0*d.*
April 1642.	Given by my lord's command to a poor man as I went with his lordship to Westminster.	6*d.*
	Given to the gate-keeper in St. James's Park when my lord walked there.	6*d.*
June 1642.	Given to the door-keeper in the Court of Wards when the Committee for Covent Garden sat there.	2*s.* 0*d.*

The Earl required yet more money for his personal use when he paid visits; for presents to servants in the house to which he was going and for the playing table of either dice or cards.

September 1641.—Paid to my lord at London when he went to supper one night with the Earl of Newport, per warrant.   £20   0s.   0d.

October 1641.—Paid to my lord when he went to lie at Kensington, for his own private uses.   £11   2s.   0d.

March 1641/2.—Paid to my lord for his own use when he went to Theobalds with my Lord Saye, as per his receipt.   £12   0s.   0d.

March 1641/2.—Delivered to Edw: Robbins to give my lord when he was at play.   10s.   0d.

May 1642.—Paid more to my lord on Whit Sunday eve when he went to Waltham.   £10   0s.   0d.

Besides what he thus took as pocket-money when he went away from home, the Earl at different times during the year asked for and received from the chest various sums of money for himself, which, with what was taken on the visits, amounted in all to about £262, concerning the expenditure of which the receiver-general had no details.

There is no evidence that on these visits the Countess ever accompanied the Earl. For the most part she remained quietly at Woburn. Once, however, when she was in London, she and her husband indulged in a ride in a new kind of conveyance that was now plying for hire, disliked as much by the hackney coach drivers as their own vehicles had been, and were still, by the watermen. The coach drivers detested the carrying-chair, while the watermen on the Thames hated both the hackney coach and the chair impartially. But the chair, thanks to the vigour of Sir Samuel Duncombe, whom Evelyn credits with its introduction on to the London streets in 1634, was making its way, and in the winter of 1642 when the Countess, Anne, was in town with her husband, two chairs were fetched to Bedford House in the Strand to carry them to the church of St. Clement Danes. The receiver could not have been there to hand out the money as usual, and the Earl had omitted to ask him for any, so that the five shillings which the chairs cost had to be borrowed by the lord and lady from the maidservant, Rose.

January 1641/2.—Paid to Rose, which she lent my lord to pay for two chairs to carry his lordship and the ladies to St. Clement's church.   5s.   0d.

The remaining items in the account book for the year can be put under the heads of repairs and so forth for the two houses, Woburn and London; illness; presents and alms-giving; amusements; and, finally, the inevitable miscellanea.

Not a great deal was spent on either house. The only purchase made was a quantity of household linen which was bought for Woburn Abbey at the first coming of the new owners there in May 1641, and cost sixty pounds. No furniture or plate was bought. The fourth Earl must have purchased new furniture when he rebuilt Woburn Abbey, although there is no account for it. But of gold and silver plate he had an excellent supply, which he had bequeathed to his eldest son. A little of this, but not a great deal, dated from the days of the first and second Earls. Both these noblemen, like most others of their day, had distributed the greater part of their plate by will among their friends.

A certain number of repairs had to be carried out both in Woburn and London, which amounted in all to £69 13s. 11d., the workmen employed being glaziers, bricklayers, masons, paviors and plumbers. The latter, who were wanted for Bedford House, duly anticipated their subsequent comedy rôle, and did not come when they were first sent for, so that Anthony had to be twice dispatched to call them. The piece of work on which they were to be employed was the most important carried out in this year, for this was the bringing into Bedford House of a water supply drawn from the pipes laid down by the corporation of London along the Strand.

November 1641.—Paid to Mr. Mitchell for drawing the order from the lord mayor and aldermen for the city water allowed my lord in his house.   10*s*.   0*d*.

A number of apothecaries' bills for medicines supplied to the household had to be paid. They came to over thirty pounds in all and doubtless included a certain amount of minor medical treatment, which the apothecaries were ready and eager to give instead of surrendering that function to a doctor.

Two cases of illness, however, after the smallpox, one of which may well have been serious in itself while the other was among the commonest of human ills, but serious enough in the opinion of the sufferer, did necessitate the calling in of a professional in each instance. Towards the end of the account book there is an entry dated May 1642, recording a payment to a Dr. Caleb Rawlin, or Rawling, who had undertaken to cure, for a considerable fee, some unspecified complaint which had attacked the 'little lord's legs.' The 'little lord' was the eldest son, Francis. It was the first sign of the ill health which haunted him throughout his life. Possibly the treatment was not completed at once; at all events, the fee was only paid in instalments.

May 1642.—Paid to Mr. Caleb Rawlin in part of the £40 which he is to have for the cure of my little lord's legs.   £20   0   0

The other patient was the Earl himself, and the entries tell their own story.

March 1641/2. Given to Sir Miles Sands his man
     that brought one to cure my lord
     of the toothache.   *5s.*   *0d.*

March 1641/2. Given to the man that cured my
     lord of the toothache.   *5s.*   *0d.*
     Given more to the barber again
     when he came to dress my lord's
     tooth at night, by his lordship's
     appointment.   *5s.*   *0d.*

March 1641/2. Given more to him that night Sir
     William Poole was with my lord. *5s.*   *0d.*

Presents and charitable donations filled a certain amount of space in the account book.

At the head of all the presents was a substantial obligatory gift, the customary New Year's present to the King, of which the amount was carefully regulated. This was sent up by the hands of Mr. Dixy Taylor.

January 1, 1641/2.—Paid to Mr. Dixy Taylor, which he carried for my lord's New Year's gift for the King.   £20   0   0

Gifts to friends were not many in the first year, but they did include a little gold and silver plate bought for presents at christenings and other festivals.

Alms, other than the pence given to the beggars who stood in the road or to others who came to the door of the inn where the Earl was known to be dining, were constantly bestowed and small sums devoted to these purposes were entered almost every week in the account book, besides more regular donations towards the relief of the poor generally, including the prisoners.

June 1641.—Given by your lordship's command to an old woman that claimed a pension given her by your lordship's father and said she was allied to the Dukes of Buckingham.　　　　10*s.*　　0*d.*

October 1641.—Given to the old woman that is my lady Bedford's almswoman, by my lord's command.　　　　2*s.*　　0*d.*

Amusements cost little indeed, for the reflection in the account book, in spite of the references to dice or cards when the Earl paid a visit, is of a year soberly spent. The most frivolous happening at Woburn was the arrival of the musicians who came to play before the lord and lady at the New Year.

Finally, a number of miscellaneous items, board wages of servants left in London, cartage, carriage of letters, clerical expenses and small, unidentified bills, came to rather over two hundred pounds.

All these requirements for his household and family during the year under review cost the Earl, in round figures, just over £4,400.

Taxation remains to be taken into consideration. Some of the taxes levied on the Earl were payments which had to be made on the different estates. These never came into the account book at all, for such were settled by the respective bailiffs. Direct taxation was paid by the receiver-general. In this year, after the sixty pounds which had been paid during the first six weeks for the third and fourth subsidies, the receiver had to find £94 11*s.* 6*d.* in all. This was made up of twenty-four pounds paid in November for the fifth and sixth subsidies, £60 11*s.* 6*d.* paid as poll money, and various small sums, amounting to something under ten pounds, paid in respect of homage, the livery tax, rates levied by churchwardens and so forth.

These payments brought the total of the Earl's own

expenditure to just over £4,570. The annuities and his brothers' debts accounted for another £3,400. That is to say, the receiver-general, between 5th July 1641 and the same date in the following year, had paid out, according to his account book, in round figures £7,900.

When he had received the keys from the Earl, the receiver had found £825 odd in the chest, always remembering the £2 5s. 2½d. which should have been there and was not. Another £8,500 had been received during the year from the estates and, besides this, the Dowager Countess had paid back on behalf of herself and her daughter for their board and lodging, £1,020 pounds. Since this amounted in all to £10,345, the receiver should have had a very satisfactory balance of money within the chest wherewith to carry on until the Michaelmas rents of 1642 should come in.

Actually, however, no less than over twelve thousand pounds in excess of the above had been paid out. Part of this had gone towards Lady Diana's dowry and part towards paying off some of the debts and meeting the interest on the remainder. Normally, at any rate for the dowry, the Earl might and probably would have raised the money entirely by means of mortgages and bills. He did, in point of fact, get a certain amount of money in this way, chiefly to meet the interest due. But, in view of the large outstanding debts which had already been raised by these means, it would obviously have been extremely imprudent to continue the process. Therefore, the situation was met in the main by sales of land.

Towards the end of 1641, the Earl had sent Mr. Trenchard on a visit of survey to the estates in the west, with which the agent was already well acquainted. As a result of this survey, nine thousand pounds had been raised. This cleared some of the debts and helped with the interest.

Then in March 1642, the Earl had several interviews with his lawyer, Mr. Hales, concerning the betrothal of his sister, Diana, to Sir Francis Newport. The marriage was arranged and it was agreed that the Earl should pay half the dowry immediately. Upon the rest he was to continue to pay the eight per cent. interest. Thereupon more land in Devon was sold. The process of transferring the money was, as usual, supervised by the receiver-general. Unfortunately, the counting of the money revealed the same kind of discrepancy between the figures and the actual cash which he had encountered before.

April 1642. Paid for our dinners when we received the monies returned out of Devon for my Lady Diana's portion, being five of us.   5s. 0d.

Paid to porters for fetching the money together from several places.   4s. 6d.

Paid to a carman for bringing the money from 'Lumber' Street.   2s. 0d.

April 1642. Paid which was short in one bag of the money which William Scott told for my Lady Diana, 1s. 6d.; and which was wanting in a bag taken upon trust, 4s. 0d.   5s. 6d.

April 1642. Paid to the Lady Diana Russell in part of her portion given to her by her father and being the first payment thereof, three thousand and five hundred pounds.   £3,500 0s. 0d.

On the whole, this year ended in triumph owing to careful finance: the young Earl had money in hand; he was paying his way; he had got rid of some of his liabilities and there was a good prospect that during the next few years the remainder would be cleared. The receiver strikes a lighter note at the very end of his account book with the entry that new liveries were to be bought for all the servants, including the bargemen, a sign that the time of mourning for the household was over. The clouds over the nation were, however, rapidly blackening.

CHAPTER III

SEVENTEEN YEARS: 1641 TO 1658

W HEN the accounts for the first year of the Earl's succession were made up in July of 1642 it was known that civil war was almost inevitable. Before the end of August the Earl of Bedford had received his commission as General of the Horse for the Parliament and had been sent down into the west country to oppose the Marquess of Hertford, who was collecting an army there for the King. On Sunday, 23rd October, of that year his silver banner, diapered with black and fringed with black and silver, was carried before him at Edgehill. The captain of his 67th troop of horse was one Oliver Cromwell.

But the Earl of Bedford had long been known to be one of the middle party of the peers. The trouble with the Russells, once said that remarkable woman Anne, Countess of Dorset, grandchild of the second Earl of Bedford, was that they disapproved at one and the same time of the character of the Stuarts and the politics of Cromwell. In the case of William, Earl of Bedford, his disapproval of the course that politics were taking was marked by his definite severance from the Parliamentary party before the end of 1642. In August of the next year he and Lord Holland, followed shortly after by Lord Clare, arrived at Oxford, where the King was keeping his court, to open up negotiations. The King had already left the city. Queen Henrietta Maria, who was still there, gave the three Earls an extremely cool reception. This, however, did not deter them from following the King

69

to Gloucester, where they offered him their services in the field.

The Earl of Bedford at least had to pay one penalty immediately for his change of party. In October of 1643 two Parliamentary commissioners arrived at Bedford House in the Strand in order to seize the goods and chattels of the owner to meet the payment of the fine of eight hundred pounds imposed upon him as a delinquent.

Looking through the list of the goods that were taken away, the thought comes that perhaps the Countess, if she were like other housewives throughout the centuries, might have been quite pleased to see a complete clearance of some old chattels. The removal of the dilapidated feather beds, the ancient skillets, the coverlets qualified by the commissioners as very much worn and many another household article of respectable age gave an excellent excuse for having everything new. All that was displayed before the commissioners' eyes was, of course, under such circumstances, whenever possible a medley of old and worthless things rather than those which were valuable and treasured. Certainly at Bedford House the visitors found neither gold nor silver plate upon which to lay their hands. But the fine furniture was there and that they carried off: the red velvet from the old Earl's bedroom, probably reeking with smallpox germs since it is known to have been in that room during his illness; the yellow damask from the young Earl's bedroom and dressing-room and the elegant stools and chairs from the Terrace Room and the Long Gallery.

A far more serious loss than the furniture was that of the wall hangings. The tapestries which were in the Terrace Room and some of the other sitting-rooms and bedrooms were valuable, although they were not the best that the Earl possessed. They were all taken down from the walls. Then, most unfortunately, the commissioners penetrated to the attics, where they found nineteen other pieces of tapestry of a better quality, which had been stored away in three trunks. They took these with the others.

The hangings were a real loss and presently there came a hint from no other than the Earl's father-in-law that the deprived owners had known how to compensate themselves. Somerset's house had been ransacked likewise, not by the Parliamentarians but by Royalist troops, and they, too, had carried off tapestries. Sourly the Earl of Somerset wrote to his Scottish relatives that he believed from the bottom of his heart that his daughter and son-in-law were the instigators of the whole affair, since he knew well that they had long since cast envious eyes upon those very hangings, even pretending, indeed, that they were Russell property which had been originally taken away by one of the Dowager Countesses. The letter, like all the others written by Somerset during these latter years of his life, was penned by an angry, an embittered and a disappointed man.

The battles of the civil war were lost and won and Woburn, standing as it did not far from one of the main roads leading out of London, grew accustomed to the sight of armies passing and repassing.

On Monday, 25th August 1645, King Charles himself arrived at the abbey and slept there for two nights. He had, although the future was mercifully hidden from his eyes, said good-bye to his Queen for ever. In April of the previous year Henrietta Maria had left Oxford for Exeter, it being considered that she would be safer farther west. At Exeter she had been offered the hospitality of Bedford House and in that house on 16th June 1644, her youngest child, Henrietta Anne, the future Duchess of Orleans, had been born. But when Charles came to Woburn Abbey in the following year, 1645, both the Queen and the baby daughter had left the shelter of the Earl of Bedford's western home and had reached France.

Two years later King Charles was at Woburn once more.

He arrived at the abbey on Friday, 23rd July 1647. There on the following Wednesday, 28th July, he received the delegates from the Army, who brought with them the document known as the Heads of the Proposals as a basis for the negotiations which the King, despite the advice of moderates around him, finally rejected. This, his third and last visit to the abbey, was also the longest, for he remained there at least for a week and perhaps for rather longer.

This royal visit was the last occasion for many years on which great state was kept at the abbey.

Until towards the end of the period of the Commonwealth the Earl and Countess lived quietly at Woburn with their growing family. Judging by the isolated bills that remain, the establishment kept up was probably simpler than had been the case even in 1641—certainly in so far as the number of servants was concerned. The burden of debt that was still, during the earlier years, on the Earl's shoulders would have forced him to a quiet style of living even if such had not been favoured by the conditions of the time and, more than this, by his own inclinations and those of his wife.

In 1641 the two little boys, Francis and William, had been the sole occupants of the children's rooms at Woburn and at Bedford House. During the next fifteen years seven more children were born to the Earl and Countess: four boys—Edward, Robert, James and George; and three girls—Anne, Diana and Margaret. Each girl had been given the name of one of her aunts, thus duplicating the family names, with much confusion resulting. The baby, Margaret, was born in 1656.

During these years a figure of great significance for the history of the family appeared at the abbey. When the elder children began to emerge from babyhood their father engaged a tutor for them. The Reverend John Thornton had taken his B.A. degree from Trinity College, Cambridge, in 1646. Almost immediately after this he came to Woburn.

As Edmund Calamy remarks, this gentleman 'lived and died a Nonconformist.' The predilections of the heads of many families, not only the Russells, more particularly those who afterwards, in the eighteenth century, were identified with the Whig party, were for tutors whose religious teaching would be definitely of the Protestant school of thought.

John Thornton was appointed at a salary of thirty pounds a year. He lived at the abbey and had his own room there as well as another at Bedford House. Officially he was tutor to the children and chaplain to the Earl. Unofficially he was given, or perhaps took upon himself, multifarious duties. The librarianship which he gradually assumed was suitably combined with his two other offices. But his activities also stretched to include those of secretary, of almoner and of medical adviser. In all of these things, however, he was always liable to be superseded, in other words pushed out of the way, by one of the other gentlemen officials, especially by Dixy Taylor.

In the schoolroom the tutor was supreme. Here he was never superseded.

It would be difficult to overestimate the importance of the part played in family history by such men as Thornton. At all times there must have been many tutors whose influence counted infinitely more in moulding the character of their pupils than did that of the father or mother. In the case of the young Russells father and tutor worked side by side in perfect unison, and it is not easy to say where the teaching of the one ended and that of the other began. There was no friction between the two where the schoolroom was concerned. The only occasions when any appeared was at such times when Thornton approached the Earl a little too confidently with a new remedy for the colic or rheumatism. The latter would then turn restive and refuse to be dosed.

The education of the children proceeded to a great

extent along the accepted lines, that is to say the foundations were religion and the classics.

Each child, when it was three or four years old, was given two *Bibles*, one in Latin and one in English, together with a *Catechism* and a *Book of Common Prayer*. A little later, usually, judging by the bills, when the boy or girl had attained the age of something like seven years, he or she was further presented with a copy of Baxter's *Sincere Convert*. This book was the keynote of Mr. Thornton's religious teaching, coloured as it was throughout, as might be expected, by the influence of the Geneva school. Other books were bought not for the personal possession of each child, but to be used in the schoolroom in common. Such were Nicholas Byfield's *Principles, or the Pattern of Wholesome Words* and the volume entitled *The Assemblies Pieces with Scriptures at Large*.

The secular side of the children's education was founded upon the Latin grammar, with at first such easy books as *Corderius*, or the *Dialogues of Mathurin Cordier*, and collections of sentences for practice in translation, including the *Anglicisms Latinised* of Willis. The Latin authors followed in their order of difficulty. This was all according to regular use, and for the two elder boys, Francis and William, Mr. Thornton did not depart from it. The younger brothers and sisters had, as is so often the case, their path of learning made easier for them.

In the sixteen-fifties new ideas as to education were in the air and Mr. Thornton at Woburn was fully aware of them. His approval of the principles then being enunciated and put into practice by Peter Comenius, Bishop of Moravia, came too late to be of advantage in the instruction of his two elder pupils. Comenius' primer called the *Vestibulum*, which embodied the author's theories for the better teaching of Latin, and his even more famous *Janua Linguæ Reserata*, or *The Gate of Languages Unlocked*, had both been published for some little time before Thornton introduced them into his schoolroom for the use of the younger boys and girls. When, however, the *Orbis Pictus*, an exposition of the Bishop's revolutionary view that the education of children could be helped forward by means of pictures and illustrations, was published at Nuremberg in 1658, Thornton immediately ordered not one, but several copies for his pupils and continued to repeat the order in subsequent years.

Expended in books, etc., from 10th September 1655 to 10th July 1661 as follows:—

	£	s.	d.
1655-1661.—For Mr. Edward, Mr. Robert, Mr. James, Mr. George.			
Imprimis a *Janua cum Indice Etymologico* for Mr. Edward.		5	0
A *Corderius* for Mr. Robert.		1	0
6 Oxford Grammars at several times (at 1s. 4d. apiece).		8	0
A Latin Testament for Mr. Edward.		2	0
Another for Mr. Robert.		2	0
Dictionarium Historicum for Mr. Edward.		6	6
Willis his *Anglicisms Latinised* for Mr. Edward.		2	2
A *Janua Linguarum* for Mr. James.		2	0
Another for Mr. George.		2	0
A Latin *Bible* for Mr. Edward.		7	6
Byfield's *Principles* (in common).		2	4
Carmina Proverbiala for Mr. Edward.		1	4
A *Phraseologia* for Mr. Edward.			8
A *Thomas Thomasius's Dictionary* for Mr. Robert.		11	0
A *Corderius* in English for Mr. James.		2	0
3 *Bibles* at 6s. 0d. apiece, for Mr. Edward, Mr. Robert, Mr. James.		18	0
A *Sincere Convert* for Mr. Edward.		1	6
Another for Mr. Robert.		1	6
The Assemblies Pieces with Scriptures at Large (in common).		4	6

	£	s.	d.
Brought forward	4	1	0
Two Lyford's *Catechisms*.		2	8
A *Bible* of the fair minion print for Lady Diana.		12	6
Another book for her entitled *The Wise Virgin*.		1	0
A *Janua* for Mr. George.		2	0
A *Justin* for Mr. Robert.		2	0
Pictus Orbis Comenii for Mr. Robert.		5	0
The Assemblies Pieces in Latin for Mr. Robert.		2	4
Small *Catechisms* at several times for them and for Lady Diana.		2	6
Paper and quills for them all for these five years.		3	6
	£5	14	6

Mr. Thornton had a high sense of duty and we must hope that he did not show too much favouritism in the school-room. There is no doubt at all from his letters which of the children he privately loved the most. For the character of the second boy, William—a character which, as the youth's tutor, he must have secretly felt to have been chiefly his own creation—he had an unbounded admiration. In Thornton's eyes, William was as nearly faultless a being as a man of the Puritan persuasion was likely to rate any one. But as for William's little sister Diana, she, of them all, not even excepting her brother, was the one nearest Thornton's heart, a place that she never lost. When all the other children had *Bibles* which cost either three shillings and sixpence or at the most seven shillings and sixpence apiece, little Diana had one of 'fair minion print' for which her tutor gave twelve shillings and sixpence, which looks like gross favouritism.

Women had little to say in the lives of the children, whether boys or girls. All their material needs were provided for either by Mr. Crawley or his successor, or by Dixy Taylor. One of these officials ordered the clothes:

suits for the boys made up by a Woburn tailor; dresses for the little girls made at home. If he did not actually supervise the latter process, all the bills went through his hands. All little necessities, combs, ribbons and so forth, were bought from pedlars.

April 1653. Paid to John Morrice for scurvygrass, or gittings, to put in the children's ale.   4*d*.

         For a bundle of stuff of my lady's to make clothes for the children.   4*d*.

May 1653. For tape, for black ribbon, for two fine ivory combs for the children, of the pedlar.   7*s*.   o*d*.

         For tape for the children, of the pedlar.   4*d*.

June 1653. Paid to Jones, the tailor, for work for diverse sorts of garments making for the children . . . and for some other things . . . according to my lady's knowledge which your honour saw.   £1   18*s*.   2*d*.

April 1654. To a barber for trimming Mr. Edward and Mr. Robert.   2*s*.   o*d*.

But the life of the little Russells, even in the schoolroom under Mr. Thornton, did not all centre round learning and books. The children had their balls, miniature horses and carts and plenty of sweet things.

April 1655. Paid to my lady Anne, which she did lay out when she went to see Mr. Dingley.   6*d*.

         For balls for my lady Anne.   6*d*.

May 1655. For   six   sweet   oranges   and
cherries for my lady Anne.   1*s.*   4*d.*

June 1655. To one that brought a cake for
my lady Anne.   1*s.*   0*d.*

Anne was then five years old and Mr. Dingley had
succeeded Mr. Crawley in the household. We do not know
whether the little lady spent her sixpence on a present for
him, or whether her journey to see him involved her in this
expense.

But Anne was not destined to grow into womanhood.
Two years later she was playing in the park with her younger
sister Diana. They saw berries, they picked and ate them,
and Anne died.

This was tragedy. But the Earl and Countess were, on
the whole, singularly fortunate in the health of their children
at a time when death was a constant visitor to nursery and
schoolroom. It was the more unfortunate that the only one
of the flock who should have caused them anxiety in this
respect was the eldest son, Francis, whose babyhood had
been overshadowed by illness and who had grown into a
boyhood in which it was only too clear there was no physical
strength. Even so, it had been decided to send him to
Cambridge and he had gone up to Trinity College in 1653,
whither he had been followed a year later by his brother
William. Both boys had been placed under the care of the
Reverend John Nidd, a close friend of Mr. Thornton. After
three years of college life they had been sent abroad with
tutors, remaining away from home another three or four
years.

In the meantime, the sober life led at Woburn Abbey
during the forties and the early fifties had not been for the
Earl without its material compensations. Interested as he
was in the education of his children, the latter were far from
absorbing all his energies and attention. When all was said

ANNE, DAUGHTER OF WILLIAM, FIFTH EARL OF BEDFORD

and done, the real love of his life was his estates, their development and their welfare. The result of the unremitting care that he bestowed upon his property was a measure of prosperity beyond his most sanguine hopes. The risks that his father had taken in borrowing money to finance the two great enterprises associated with the Covent Garden and the Thorney estates justified themselves. This was largely consequent upon the son's vigour in working out the projects.

The building in Covent Garden had been the first to show an excellent return and it was already paying well when the Earl had succeeded to the title in 1641. During the forties and the fifties the Piazza became the fashionable quarter in which to reside. Nor was there any difficulty in letting the houses in the adjacent streets. In the list of the Earl's tenants the names of peers jostled those of distinguished commoners. In 1647 Denzil Holles lived in one of the houses on the east side of the square, just in front of the church of St. Paul, with Sir Harry Vane only a few doors away. Opposite, on the west side, were the residences of the Countess of Peterborough and the Earl of Sussex. Between them came a fine array of some lesser lords and some baronets. On the north side of the square the Marquess of Winchester looked across to the garden wall of Bedford House.

It was a noble list of tenants and a correspondingly noble rental, which had risen by the sixteen-fifties to something over fifteen hundred pounds a year, at which figure it remained during the Earl's lifetime, although his practice of taking fines for the renewal of leases must be taken into account. For the moment the fruit and vegetable stalls had no particular significance. It was a good many years later, in 1671, that the Earl asked for and received, at a price, the royal patent of licence to hold a market 'within the Piazza at Covent Garden.'

The prosperity of this London property was not threatened even when taxation began to grow heavy, as it did during the latter years of the Commonwealth. The most alarming moment was when the Parliamentary commissioners proceeded to make a valuation of the property with a view to a tax upon the capital value. The Earl, however, here made a successful resistance. He entered a petition showing the money which his father had spent upon the building of the Piazza and the erection of St. Paul's Church. The first amount, he pleaded, was only now being partially repaid by the rents received. The £4,886 odd which had been the cost of building St. Paul's Church—the Earl was able, fortunately, to produce the original account book—represented, he said, pure benevolence, which ought to be taken into account.

The business of draining the fens was a much slower process than that of building on the Covent Garden estate and the rewards of the money and labour sunk in the enterprise were slower in coming. But when they did come they were substantial. The people of the fen country, in spite of the protests that they raised at the time, no less than the Earl of Bedford and his fellow adventurers, had all reason to be grateful to the Protector. The project was bound to be of interest to one of the Huntingdonshire squirearchy and Oliver Cromwell, like the Earl of Bedford, belonged to the ranks of those country gentlemen to whom a new experiment in agriculture was of great importance. The Protector may have interfered with the scheme, but he interfered to good purpose. Gradually, aided by the formation of a Company of Adventurers, the drainage scheme took shape and showed signs of success. The Earl's grandfather, William, Lord Russell of Thornhaugh, sometime Governor of Flushing, would have been pleased to see the result of his little venture in bringing across some Dutch workers accustomed to the drainage problems of their own country.

Before Cromwell had ceased to rule England it was clear that the financial results of the fen project would be highly satisfactory to the undertakers, of whom the Earl of Bedford was one of the chief.

The direct result of the increased income from Covent Garden and from the Thorney property, with other investments in the fen country, was that the Earl of Bedford was able, with the help of his own simple style of living, to consolidate his position and, what was of great importance to him, pay off the debts.

When exactly those debts were finally extinguished is doubtful. Perhaps the Earl was already clear of them towards the end of the sixteen-forties. It is certain that this was the case by the middle of the next decade. Then, and then only, did the expansion of the household begin, some time about the year 1658. It was hardly in full swing before signs appeared on the political horizon that England was about once more to acknowledge a King.

CHAPTER IV

THE RETURN OF THE KING

ON 10th February 1659, the Reverend Mr. Thornton, who was at Bedford House in London, wrote one of his interminable and, to say the truth, rather dull letters to his erstwhile pupil William Russell, who was then in Paris, but was preparing to return home. After the usual pages of admonitions for the young man's religious, moral and physical welfare, the tutor continued:

News I can acquaint you with little. Many hot spirits in the Parliament are against government by a single person, but I hope they will not carry it. Till that debate be determined, nothing will be done. And they are pressed to make haste and to forebear spinning out the time in long speeches (as they have hitherto done) lest the Dutch, who have a great fleet at sea, be too quick for us, for some great design is in hand.

Two months after the letter was written, Oliver Cromwell's son and successor, 'Tumble-down Dick,' thankfully allowed the heads of the Army to remove him from a position for which he had no liking and less aptitude. The months of confusion which followed gave General Monk and the exile who was waiting and watching their chance. On the 25th of May 1660, Charles, the second of that name, having dated the Treaty of Breda 'in the twelfth year of his reign,' stepped ashore at Dover.

The coming of the King in that month of May to take his own again changed the horizon for many who provided the luxuries of life. Purse-strings were opened, including those of the Earl of Bedford. That nobleman had already seen fit to begin an elaborate reorganisation of his household and had made several new appointments. Among them he had included one of a gentleman of his horse. This was opportune, since to welcome the sovereign with pomp and grandeur implied a cavalcade.

Many saddlers, tailors and others must have worked against time to be ready for the great day, 29th May, the royal birthday, when the King entered London. It was but three days since he had landed and a bare eight weeks since he had signed the treaty which had secured his return. That gave none too long for the preparations, even for the far-sighted individuals who had commenced theirs betimes. But enthusiasm for the Restoration swept all obstacles away and there was a brave show of brocade and velvet, gold and silver in the procession when the King came into his capital.

The Earl of Bedford rode among the noblemen, followed by his second son, William. His eldest son, Francis, was not present. The bills for the satin and brocade for the suits of the two gentlemen came to a hundred and twenty pounds. More than this went to the gold and silver workers who provided the embroidery, the fringes and the other trimmings. New riding saddles, too, had been bought. The Earl was mounted on a blue padded saddle, trimmed with gold and silver fringe, and gold and silver lace; William Russell had a green velvet saddle with a silver fringe and silver lace. The father and son were followed by the gentleman now in charge of the Earl's stables, Master Anthony Senhouse. He sat on a crimson velvet saddle with a matching silk fringe. Master Anthony was a proud man that day and had no reason to complain that his stables had gone short in the preparations, for he in his turn headed a group of the Earl's servants who had all been fitted out with new clothes.

1660.—Paid to diverse tradesmen for the several extraordinary liveries of his lordship's coachman, postillion, three grooms and six footmen, provided against the time of His Majesty's coming into England, viz:—

To the woollen draper—£44.7.0.; mercer—£12.14.0.; silkman—£74.0.0.; milliner—£19.12.0.; hosier—£5.14.0.; haberdasher—£4.15.0.; tailor—£75.0.0.; and cutler—£9.0.0. In all, as by the bills of the particulars thereof allowed by his lordship and the acquittances respectively given thereupon seen and examined appeareth.   £245 2 0

The hundred and twenty pounds for the silk brocade was only one item in the tailors' and silk mercers' bills sent in to the Earl that year, for he had more new clothes than he had had for many a long day and his entire wardrobe cost him £538 17s. 9d. For his Countess he bought a new set of jewellery, rubies and diamonds, at a cost of two hundred and fifty-five pounds.

Besides the fine new clothes, the coaches and the saddles and trappings for the horses, another entry stands out in the accounts. This was not for money spent upon a luxury, but upon a necessity. The King had ridden through London followed by nobles and gentry. Many of them, in the midst of their enthusiasm, must have wondered exactly what was their position relative to their allegiance to the Protector. Their difficulties were solved by the issue, for appropriate payment, of Letters Patent of Pardon. The Pardon issued to the Earl of Bedford, which absolved him from anything he might have done contrary to His Majesty during His Majesty's absence from the kingdom, is dated within a month after the entry into London, namely, on the 25th of June 1660. A few days earlier his lawyer had received the money necessary for the fee for the Patent itself and the other additional fees involved.

1660.—To several of His Majesty's officers and their clerks for their fees in passing the Patent for his lordship's Pardon, viz:

To Mr. Secretary Nicholas, with £1.0.0. to his clerk—£11.0.0.; the Clerk of the Signet— £3.16.8.; the Clerk of the Crown—£7.6.0.; the Clerk of the Hanaper—£11.13.4.; Mr. Attorney General, with £4.0.0. for the fees of two of his clerks—£9.0.0. In all, with 16s. 6d. for some necessary charges in prosecuting the dispatch of the said Patent.   £43 12 6

The security conferred was worth the amount, and the document itself, carefully preserved by the Earl's descendants, has the merit of being most pleasing to look at. Its pen-and-ink border, in a true Carolingian design of birds and flowers, is a most delightful one, even for a day when the ornamentation of Letters Patent was of very high artistic merit.

The Pardon secured, the coronation might be looked forward to with ease of mind. The date fixed for the ceremony was Monday, 23rd April, of the next year, 1661. This gave ample time for preparations, very different from the short space into which everything had had to be crowded for the entry into London. The latter had been a sufficiently fine spectacle. But its glories were now far outshone by those of the procession on Sunday, 22nd April, when the King, who, according to custom, had been lodging in the Tower of London, rode thence to Whitehall in readiness for the morrow's ceremony.

Much anxiety had been expressed as to the weather, which had been continuously bad. It was all the more satisfactory, therefore, that not only the Sunday, but the

Monday also were remarkably fine days—'the only fair days that we enjoyed of many both before and after,' wrote Thomas Ogilby, who had been entrusted with the preparation of the *Book of the Coronation*. The sun shone upon the returned King and the grand clothes could be displayed without any fear of damage, or the necessity of concealing them under frieze cloaks.

On his servants and equipages in the procession from the Tower the Earl of Bedford spent nearly a thousand pounds, and this did not include the cost of his own clothes. The bills for these that year again came to between five hundred and six hundred pounds, of which a substantial part was for what he wore on the great day. On that Sunday he rode upon a steed that had a rich footcloth, trimmed with gold and silver lace and fringe, and was followed by a group of attendants, headed by Master Anthony Senhouse in a suit and coat of chamlet, trimmed with gold and silver lace, and a plumed hat.

1661.—Paid for apparel and necessaries bought of sundry tradesmen and for workmanship done and performed for his lordship's use and service within the time of this account, part thereof being provided for the day of His Majesty's coronation, viz:

To the mercer—£82.7.6.; the silkman, for gold, silver and silk lace—£180.0.0.; woollendraper—£6.4.0.; tailor—£16.0.0.; milliner—£94.7.0.; haberdasher—£14.7.0.; for the falls of feathers—£11.0.0.; to the sempster and for holland—£96.2.0.; stocking-maker—£2.19.0.; shoemaker — £15.16.0.; periwigmaker — £16.0.0.; gownmaker—£10.10.10.; sword cutler—£4.16.0.; beltmaker—£6.0.0.; and for a black cloth suit, cloak, coat and stockings —£20.6.0. In all   £576 15 4

1661.—Paid to sundry tradesmen, artificers and others for wares delivered by them and workmanship performed for the especial accommodation of his lordship's attendants and servants with extraordinary apparel and liveries, and of the steed whereon his lordship rode, with a rich footcloth and furniture and also for the preparation of his lordship's coach in an honourable equipage to attend upon the King on the day of His Majesty's coronation, riding from the Tower of London to Westminster, viz:

To the mercer upon his four bills.	£60	16	6
The drapers upon their three bills.	£87	5	0
The lacemen, for gold and silver lace and fringe for his lordship's footcloth, and for the liveries, upon three bills.	£293	0	0
The milliners upon their five bills.	£82	10	0
The hosier on two bills.	£11	18	0
The haberdasher on three bills.	£11	12	0
The tailor on two bills.	£103	10	0
The sword cutler and beltmaker, for livery swords and belts, on three bills.	£23	17	0
For silk and worsted stockings, shoes, gloves, half-shirts, bands and bandstrings, hats and feathers for the pages and footmen.	£35	8	10
The coachmakers and coach-harnessmakers, upon eighteen several bills.	£131	5	8
And to the saddlers and bit-makers upon twelve bills.	£80	5	0

In all (with £35.10.10. for a suit and coat of
silk chamlet laid with gold and silver lace, and
for a plume of feathers for the gentleman of
his lordship's horse for that day, as by the
said bills of the particulars thereof allowed by
his lordship and the acquittances thereupon
given, seen and examined appeareth).   £921 8 0

Perhaps the fine costume and the well-dressed men and
boys behind him in part consoled Master Senhouse for
what had probably been a disappointment. The Earl of
Bedford's group in the procession required a coach to follow
the riders and a very special coach had been ordered, bespoken in Paris through the good offices of Lord Crofts, an
intimate friend of the Earl. In this carriage the leather
flaps in the window spaces had been replaced by glass panes,
a new fashion and one that was only just penetrating into
England. But if the Earl and his gentleman of the horse
had hoped to get the vehicle, which cost just over a hundred
and seventy pounds, into their stables in time to follow in
the coronation procession, they were disappointed. It
reached England indeed, but it was not passed through the
customs until early in June, when the coronation was a
thing of the past, and was then found to be somewhat
knocked about. The new windows, in particular, had been
their own undoing.

1661.—Paid for the charges of landing the
French coach and of the hackney coachman for
drawing it from Tower Hill—£1.16.0.; for the
repair of that coach—£4.6.6.; and for three
squares of Normandy glass for the same—7s. 6d. £6 10 0

Another coach had perforce to take its place in the line.
The procession, halting at intervals to observe the various

pageants prepared by the city and to listen to the verses put into the mouths of the performers, passed through Temple Bar into the Strand and so by the Earl of Bedford's house, before which labourers had been engaged to strew gravel.

April 1661.—To two labourers for spreading the gravel in the streets against the King's royal passage.   2*s.*   0*d.*

One of the many scaffolds for sightseers had been erected close by the house and there were seated the little children of Dr. Manton, of St. Paul's, Covent Garden, for whom the Earl had bought places.

April 1661.—Given for Dr. Manton's children's seats on the scaffold at His Majesty's royal passage. 6*s.*   0*d.*

The next day, St. George's Day, the sun again shining, the King went down the Privy Stairs at seven in the morning to his barge. He was rowed to the Parliament Stairs and, ascending these, proceeded to the Prince's Lodging to be robed.

In the meantime, his peers of the realm, lay and spiritual, and other great clerical and legal dignitaries had assembled, all in their official robes, in Westminster Hall. The peers and the clergy had had little use for their robes of late years, and those worn by the Earl of Bedford, for one, were not new for this occasion; they were his father's robes, which had been repaired and cleaned at a cost of five pounds.

The arrival of the King in the Hall was followed by the distribution of the regalia, which had been brought in solemn procession from the Abbey. The Earl of Bedford received from his sovereign the sceptre with the cross known as St. Edward's Sceptre. Carrying this, he walked in line with the Earls of Sandwich and Pembroke, one with St. Edward's Staff and the other with the Spurs, behind the Lord Treasurer and the Lord Chancellor, back to the Abbey. The way from the Hall had been laid with blue cloth, which had been supplied by the Earl's own parish of Covent Garden, twenty-four yards of it, at twopence a yard. This was not wasted after the ceremony, nor did it become a perquisite of one of the officials. On the contrary, a porter was dispatched from Covent Garden to fetch it and, being brought back, it was cut up and distributed among the poor of the parish.

The solemn ceremony of the coronation accomplished, the King, the nobles and the high dignitaries of the realm returned to Westminster Hall for the festal dinner. The King's table was placed apart, on the dais at the upper end. Towards the end of the meal, when that table was empty, for the King had left before the third course had been brought in, those still at table in the body of the Hall below were startled to hear the sound of thunder. The day, which had been so unwontedly fine, had ended in a storm. There came a change over the spirits of some of the revellers. Perhaps the stage of the dinner had been reached in which depression had begun to succeed exhilaration. Certainly Mr. Ogilby noted and put into his official account that, as the storm grew more violent, faces grew more gloomy and there were whispers that the thunder and lightning were signs of ill omen. Ogilby, however, upon consideration, did not share the apprehensions; the thunder and lightning were, he judged, good omens, in accordance with the best classical traditions.

> As soon as robed and sceptered, Jove aloud
> His signal favour thunders from a cloud.
> Successful lighting through Heaven's arches shines,
> Both at his coronation happy signs.

Whatever meaning was read into these manifestations of Jove, the crowd within Westminster Hall fared better than the crowd outside. It was not the first or the last time in England's history that the incompatibility of heavy rain with bonfires was demonstrated. But those who tended the fires and those who danced round them did their best to keep up the festivities, while the Earl of Bedford gave seventeen shillings towards the cost of the wine and beer which was shared out among all and sundry. At home he distributed, in honour of the coronation, handsome gratuities to all his household, beginning with ten pounds apiece for the chief officials.

CHAPTER V

AFTER 1660: THE FAMILY

AFTER the coronation in 1661 life at Woburn Abbey resumed its wonted course. John Evelyn, who wrote in his diary, in February 1662, that he was going home to be private a little, not at all caring for the life and hurry of the Court, was not the only one of that opinion. The Earl of Bedford, too, was all for a private life, by which he meant residence at Woburn Abbey, whence he could pass under review every detail concerning his estates, despatch orders for new trees and plants and inquire into, adopt or reject, new methods of agriculture.

The family in residence at the abbey were now much reduced in numbers. There was no separate establishment, for Katherine, the Dowager Countess who had remained at the abbey after her daughter's marriage, had died in 1657. The Earl had for companionship his wife and the two youngest little girls, Diana, who was eight years old in 1660, and Margaret, who was four years old in the same year. Their sister, Anne, lay in her tomb at Chenies. The sons, young men and boys, were scattered in different directions.

The eldest son, Francis, Lord Russell, was still wandering on the Continent, with a tutor companion, in search of the health that he never found. His lassitude of mind and body gave rise to the gravest anxiety in both the father and the tutor at home. Francis Russell was of those who found the world sadly out of joint and was too indecisive, too lethargic, too touched by what Mr. Thornton's theological instruction would have taught him was *accidie* to make any attempt to fit himself into his surroundings. The contrast with his younger brother, William, must sometimes have been a bitter one for the parents, even if the joy felt in the second also in part made up for the anxiety felt for the first.

William Russell, who had returned to England for the coronation, had spent his time abroad chiefly in Paris in order to learn the French tongue thoroughly, Mr. Thornton having warned him on no account 'to keep too much company with the English' in order that he might attain the greater facility in French. He had also taken lessons in dancing and fencing. His education might now be counted complete. But he had several trips abroad after 1661 in order to make himself better acquainted with foreign capitals.

In the meantime, the Earl had been debating the question of the education of his younger children, especially the four other boys who, in point of age, fell into pairs: Edward and Robert; James and George. For the two elder no drastic change in the usual system was proposed. The foundations of their education having been well and sufficiently laid by Mr. Thornton, they were to proceed on a Continental tour in charge of a tutor.

For the two younger boys, James and George, the Earl tried an experiment. Early in 1659, when they were about eight and seven years of age, they were dispatched to a private school at Twickenham kept by Mr. Fuller. Against their going Mr. Thornton provided each with a *Bible*, a *Sincere Convert* and a Latin testament and, upon the demand of their schoolmaster, he sent some other books after them, the *Orbis Pictus*, Mauger's *French Grammar* and the *Rudiments of Latin Grammar* written by the celebrated schoolmaster, Hoole—two copies of each of the books.

They remained at Twickenham for less than a year. In January 1660, when James was nine and George eight years old, their father decided to send them as boarders to Westminster, where Dr. Busby was using all his powers of argument to induce men in the upper ranks of society to entrust their sons to him. The fees for each were forty pounds a year, paid quarterly to Dr. Busby himself and receipted by him.

> *April* 1660.—Received this 7th April 1660 of the Right Honourable the Earl of Bedford, by the hands of Mr. George Collop, the sum of twenty pounds, being for a quarter's boarding of his lordship's two sons, to be due the 27th instant, I say received by me Richard Busby. £20 0 0

Besides this, Mr. Tublay, the scrivener, received £5 1s. 3d. for teaching the two of them writing during the first six months. It was necessary for Mr. Thornton to provide them afresh with *Bibles*, since each of them had contrived to lose the one he had had at Twickenham, and the tutor added a copy apiece of *Martial's Epigrams* and a *Nomenclature*.

> *Bought for them upon their remove to Westminster.*

	£	s.	d.
2 *Bibles* (those they had at Twickenham being lost there).		11	0
2 *Martial's Epigrams* at 1s. 6d. apiece.		3	0
2 *Nomenclatures*.		1	0

The remainder of the outfit for the two little boys, including some more books, was provided by the receiver-general.

> 1660.—For school books, paper books, wax lights, hats, hatbands, gloves, ribbon bands, stockings, shoestrings, knives, trunks, making up of linen and other necessaries for Mr.

James and Mr. George, with £6. 4s. 0d. for two
stuff suits and coats, £1. 4s. 0d. for two cloth
frieze coats and £1. 12s. 0d. for shoes for them,
and with £5. 14s. 0d. to the tailor for Mr. James
and £3. 2s. 6d. for the wages and some apparel
of his maid.   £35 10 0

Little James and George went up to Westminster School,
the first of a long line of their family who were to become
pupils there. At Woburn, the Ladies Margaret and Diana
still had the advantage of the instruction of Mr. Thornton.
But the new departure in the education of the brothers
pointed forward to the day when, the boys being sent to a
public school, the sisters would no longer share their education and for them the governess would replace the tutor.

The only sign of life that has survived from the little boys
themselves while they were at Westminster is a single letter
from James to his father.

James Russell to the Earl of Bedford.
Undated; written about 1660.

MY LORD,

I only acquaint your lordship that we are to act a play
very shortly and I thought it good to acquaint your lordship with it, for I was ordered by Mr. Lewis to put myself
in good habit, for there will be a great company of people
at the play and therefore a great company of the boys are
to have clothes against that day.

And so I rest your most dutiful son,

JAMES RUSSELL

In the autumn of that year, 1660, when James and
George Russell were thus plunged into the life of a public
school, their two brothers, Edward and Robert, who were
now about sixteen and fifteen years old, were sent abroad.

A tour in Europe for the purpose of education generally

95

embraced three stages. First came a sojourn at one of the university towns in France. Here, for very obvious reasons, such Protestant centres as Montpellier, Saumur and Nantes ranked in the eyes of most English fathers, including the Earl of Bedford, far before the Sorbonne, where boys would be exposed to what were, in their view, highly dangerous influences. But if the Sorbonne were suspect, a stay in Paris was always reckoned essential for the education of a young gentleman. No other town could, in the opinion of the day, offer such advantages for instruction in dancing and fencing and all other polite arts, including that of conversation. Therefore, a visit to Paris extending over some months, with all due safeguards that could be devised to protect the young man's moral and religious principles, was almost always included in the scheme. Finally, Italy and parts of Central Europe must be visited in order that a greater facility in foreign languages and yet more social experience might be acquired, combined with the advantages of sightseeing.

Francis and William Russell, who were sent to the Continent only after having had three years at Cambridge, spent most of their time either in Paris or in travelling between one capital and another. Their younger brothers, who had not been to an English university, were to go first of all to a university town in France for direct educational purposes.

The passports for the two boys, together with one renewed for their eldest brother, were procured in September.

September 1660.—Given by his lordship's command, viz:

Secretary Nicholas and his son for two passes for the Lord Russell and for Mr. Edward Russell and Mr. Robert Russell to travel beyond the sea. £12 0 0

A travelling tutor, Mr. Charles Rich, was engaged. He was an Englishman, whereas both Francis and William had had French tutors. Mr. Rich's salary was to be a hundred pounds a year in addition to his travelling expenses.

The steward of the household saw to the boys' outfits and passed the bills on to the receiver-general. Mr. Thornton provided reading matter in the shape of a pocket Latin dictionary, the *Vestibulum* of Comenius and the complete edition in one volume of the *Letters of the Sieur de Balzac*, a favourite purchase of his, often bestowed upon one of his pupils.

Thus equipped, boys and tutor set forth, the receiver-general having arranged for the hire of a vessel in which they were to cross the Channel, leaving from Rye, the favourite port of embarkation.

The tutor carried with him forty pounds in gold for immediate use. Besides this, four days before the little company left England, the receiver-general had arranged for a bill of exchange for two hundred pounds to be sent into France, so that money might be available on, or at any rate soon after, their arrival.

No stay was made in Paris, except perhaps to collect the two hundred pounds, which were payable in that town. Mr. Rich and his charges then proceeded to La Flèche, where they made a stay of three months. This was a little surprising in view of the Earl of Bedford's known religious opinions, seeing that the town was celebrated for the great Jesuit college called the Prytanée, which had been founded by Henry IV. The Fathers made a certain number of friendly overtures to the visitors, which created a certain amount of embarrassment for the latter.

Not one of the least desirable advantages in sending a young man abroad was that he should learn the etiquette to be observed in intercourse with distinguished foreigners, receiving them when they came to call, paying them visits of ceremony and, above all, it was to be hoped, profiting by their conversation. The most cheerful letter Thornton ever had from the eldest son, Francis, was after the young man had returned the call of the ambassador from Muscovy, whom he had met in Augsburg, and the latter had plied him with vodka, an entirely new drink to the young Englishman. But a visit from a Muscovian ambassador was one thing and one from a Jesuit Father quite another. On the whole, the young Russells appear to have managed the situation with admirable tact.

Edward Russell to the Reverend John Thornton.

LA FLÈCHE.
December 11, 1660.

SIR,

I received yours of the 16th of November, in which you give me to understand you are now at London, which will be much for our advantage in that I hope we shall hear so much the oftener from you. . . . You tell me my lord's dislike of the hand that I wrote to his lordship, which I shall endeavour to mend so soon as possibly Mr. Rich shall have got a writing master. In the meantime, you will pardon me, sir, if I write a few lines to you towards the attaining of a plausible style, which, as you say, cannot be acquired without often exercising my invention and pen. . . . Sir, I am sure you will find in these few lines little else but the affection that I bear to you. That time that I shall have to spare from doing of exercises I shall improve as well as I can. Although we have received several visits from the Jesuits and do return the same, yet we intend not to make any acquaintance with them.

Your affectionate friend and servant,
EDWARD RUSSELL

Shortly after this letter was written, and possibly on account of the information it contained, the boys and their tutor were desired to leave La Flèche and establish themselves in a centre where at one and the same time they would be in a more congenial religious atmosphere and yet be able to get first-rate outside tuition. The town chosen for the purpose was Saumur, the metropolis, since the Reformation, of Protestantism in France, with an excellent theological seminary which represented the more liberal side of French Protestantism.

To Edward Russell from the Earl of Bedford.
Undated; written early in 1661.

NED,

I received yours. I am much pleased with it, not only for your hand, which is much fairer than your former, but also and especially for your subject, it being handsomely composed and knit together. You may be assured that you cannot endear yourself to me by anything more than by your improvement; and you will find the benefit of it yourself more and more as your understanding ripens and you become to be engaged in action in the world. I am glad to hear you come on so well in your riding and dancing and take so much pains in these exercises. Continue but your diligence and you will soon attain your end. Difficulties will be mastered and imperfections wear away. You seem to be well pleased with your removal to so famous a university where your mind may be so much informed. I hope you will make good your words, and so lay out your time while you are there that it may appear hereafter you have lived in a university. Till you be able to understand sermons in the French tongue, it concerns you to spend most of the Sabbath especially in reading what good sermons or divine treatises you have with you, besides your Bible, and to get yourself well grounded in the main points of religion, wherein Mr. Rich will be still ready to help you. As ever you expect God should own you and save you, be sure to serve him in the first place and make conscience of all his commandments. Let me hear still from you; and be confident that while you continue to do well—as I pray God you may—you shall want no encouragement from

Your affectionate father,

BEDFORD

But neither Edward nor Robert were as well pleased with Saumur as was their father—or as their tutor had represented them to be—and had not been there long when their object became to cut short their stay there as soon as possible and to enter into the delights of a tour in Italy. Robert, always the bolder spirit, wrote to his father to this effect and did his best to enlist Mr. Thornton on his side:

. . . I pray you to speak to my lord about that which I have mentioned in his letter about our going into Italy, a place that everyone desires to see. As we go we shall see a great many famous towns. . . .

The reply from the Earl was very much to the point.

To Robert Russell from the Earl of Bedford.
Undated; written early in 1661.

ROBIN,

I received yours, and hope I need use no words to assure you that it was welcome: anything from you is so; especially when it comes accompanied with the good news of your hopeful proceeding in those exercises that you are to accomplish yourself by. Mr. Rich gives a very high commendation of you for your industry, activity and virtuous meditations, which makes me promise myself much comfort in you when you come home, and is in the meantime a sufficient motive for me to gratify you in any reasonable desire you can profess. That of going into Italy—which you seem to be so earnest in—I have taken into consideration and, for your encouragement, shall consent to the thing; only as to the circumstances of time I must deny you, since I cannot judge it reasonable for you to go this year for many reasons which I mention in my letter to Mr. Rich. No, the next year when you have spent a winter in Paris and attained some competent perfection in the French tongue and in your exercises you may be in some fitness for such a voyage, whereas should you go now it would set you back and hinder you every way; and you will confess so much yourself hereafter, when you have better considered of it, and be glad when you do go that you went not before. In the meanwhile, let it be your care to improve your time and opportunities to the best advantage that you may be capable to reap some considerable benefit by that voyage. I hope among your exercises you neglect not those of the mind, which are most considerable, and, above all, that you prefer those of religion, which is the one thing needful and relates to a better life. Be thankful for God's protection hitherto, seek him and serve him according to his mind, and you may be assured of his blessing, which is earnestly prayed for on your behalf by

Your affectionate father,

BEDFORD

The second letter from the Earl, addressed to the tutor, amplified the father's views that the boys must learn one language properly before proceeding to another and that the primary object of sending them to France had been for study rather than for enjoyment.

Although the wily Mr. Robert did not succeed in inducing his father to allow him to go at once to Italy for the sake of seeing the many famous towns on the way, he and his brother were by no means denied small expeditions in the neighbourhood of Saumur. They saw Richelieu and also Fontevrault, where the abbess, always chosen from the royal family of France, ruled monks as well as nuns, and where Henry II of England and the Cœur de Lion lay in their royal tombs.

LIFE IN A NOBLE HOUSEHOLD

Robert Russell to the Reverend John Thornton.

July 20, 1661.

. . . But the best of all our journey was that which we made to Fontevrault, where, by the favour of the lady abbess, we were admitted into the convent, which is a thing not done in an age, and she showed us the English Kings which are interred there and she commanded four of the sisters to show us all the convent, which they did, and led us into all their chambers and showed us all with a great deal of civility. And there is a convent of friars there which was founded upon the words that our Saviour said to Saint John: *Fili ecce Mater, Mater ecce Filius.* Therefore this is all that I shall trouble you with at this present. The news that you sent me of my brother William being sick of the smallpox did much trouble me, but I hope the worst is past. . . .

Finally, after six months at Saumur, they at last succeeded in wringing permission from their father to move to Paris. Fresh disappointment awaited them. Just as they were about to leave, Mr. Rich fell ill of low fever, which continued for some months, and then, just as he was recovering, Edward succumbed to the same complaint.

Robert Russell to the Reverend John Thornton.

SAUMUR.
August 31, 1661.

SIR,
Your last packet found Mr. Rich in his bed, being confined thereto by a fever which has continued on him sixteen days with some violence, which was occasioned by a rheum in his breast which he neglected, hoping by time and good government it would have gone away of itself. About five or six days after he began to be sick my brother found himself somewhat indisposed and his distemper proves to be a tertian fever, but very gentle and his fits not over-

violent. He has two very good physicians to have a care of him and wants no attendance that may be requisite. It is about twelve days that he has been sick and now there is many good appearances of his recovery and we are in hopes that before this letter comes to your hands he shall be able to walk abroad. The fever had left Mr. Rich eight or nine days, but venturing too soon out of his chamber to see my brother and staying up too late towards the evening with him has recalled his fever and hindered him from writing, as he did intend; but for all that he is, thanks be to God, upon the mending hand. It is generally a very sickly time through all France, but, praise God, I enjoy my health very well and hope shall so continue. Here has been of late a great resort of people by reason of the King's passing through this town to go into Brittany, whither he is attended with near forty thousand men. His going thither is thought to be to settle the gabelles of salt both in that province and in Poitou. And Mr. Rich desires Mr. Collop should know he has received the letter of exchange of two hundred pound, though with much disadvantage, having lost about three score crowns in it. When all are in health we purpose to stay at Blois about [a] month and so to Paris. In the meantime I remain,

Your most affectionate friend,

ROBERT RUSSELL

For Mr. John Thornton at Bedford house in the Strand, London.

Post payé jusques à Paris.

Robert was unduly optimistic. He proved to be the third victim of the tertian fever. The result of the successive illnesses was that the stay in Saumur was prolonged far beyond the boys' most gloomy expectations and it was not until the end of March 1662 that Robert was sufficiently recovered to permit a move to Blois on the way to Paris. They had now been abroad exactly eighteen months and during that time Mr. Rich had received for expenses one thousand two hundred pounds in addition to the first forty pounds in gold that he had carried with him. This one thousand two hundred pounds had been sent in instalments of a hundred or two hundred pounds at a time. It was all sent by bill of exchange arranged by the Earl's receiver-general and negotiated through a Mr. Charles Luce in London and a Monsieur Heusch in Paris. The tutor—it had to be the tutor, since no one under age could negotiate a bill of exchange—was then able to draw the money in whatever town he and his pupils had taken up their abode. Doubtless both Mr. Rich and the boys were well pleased to find money lodged to their credit when they arrived at Blois.

LONDRES *le 6me avril*, 1662.

A vue, n'ayant ma première, payes cette, ma seconde lettre de change, en Blois à Monsieur Charles Rich huit cent cinquante deux et son valeur de Monseigneur le Comte de Bedford et le passes à compte comme per avis de votre servant LUCAS LUCE.

A Monsieur Gerard Heusch à Paris.

At last in May 1662 the boys found themselves in Paris. There they remained for fifteen months, at the cost of another thousand pounds to their father, enjoying at intervals the society of their elder brothers as they passed to and fro.

The stay in Paris was not the complete success and pleasure that the young men had anticipated. Possibly, in view of the distractions of that city and the known liveliness of his pupils, Mr. Rich held the reins somewhat tightly. At all events, letters of reprimand and admonition from the Earl and from Mr. Thornton were tolerably frequent. Even when the boys were behaving themselves—in one instance at least they were accused of great incivility to a visitor, a heinous offence in the eyes of the father—they were reproached for not writing home as often as they should have done. This called forth a sharp remonstrance from Edward. 'I have sent several times to you both,' he wrote to his father and his former tutor, 'by the post and by others that I could name that went from Paris, though, as it seems, they [the letters] never came to your hands.'

At last the boys made peace with the authorities in England and, after the restraints of Saumur and the disgrace into which they had fallen in Paris, they were on the tiptoe of expectation at being allowed to make the long-promised tour in Italy. Unlike their two elder brothers, Francis and William, who constantly crossed and recrossed the Channel, Edward and Robert did not return home, even for a short visit, before going farther afield. The arrangement proposed was that they were to have six months in Italy and then return to Paris for another winter of instruction.

The tutor and his pupils reached Rome in August 1663. Some doubt had been felt, as well it might be, that the climate of Rome at that time of year would prove extremely trying. This was not the case, for Robert reported, 'We were never more in health and the heats, which maybe have been represented to you as insupportable, are here almost passed over without any incommodity to us.'

The young gentleman had, however, another grievance in which he saw an opportunity of turning on the home authorities.

The great disquietness we have proceeds from the want of our monies, which as yet we hear nothing of, though we are very much behindhand and are put to inconveniences. We are very much pleased with Italy and had purposed to have petitioned my lord to have given us leave to reside at Florence and Venice next winter, but finding ourselves so much neglected at this distance we shall with the less regret leave it. . . .

Robert's reproaches had reason in them. His letter is dated 10th August and when he wrote the bill of exchange had not yet even been despatched from London. Actually it is dated 17th August. A considerable space of time must, therefore, have elapsed before it arrived and could be cashed, during which the tutor and the boys had to put up with some inconvenience.

Possibly the annoyance of waiting for the letter of credit prejudiced the boys and their tutor against Rome. They also let fall one or two remarks to the effect that they did not care to be in a place where every one was of a contrary religion to them. When the order came to leave Rome and make their way northward by Florence and Bologna to Venice, all three were frankly delighted. Venice was the Mecca of many another young Englishman besides themselves. Its attractions on this occasion shone all the brighter because they were far better served by the post, perhaps because the authorities at home had taken Robert's words to heart. Not only did packets of letters await the travellers in Venice, but one of them contained the all-important bill of exchange.

October 1663.—To Mr. Rich by a bill from Mr. Jacob Luce, charged on Mr. John Dryveston, to be paid at Venice 597 ducats. £140 0 0

The ducat was still, as it had been when it was first issued in 1284, one of the most beautiful coins in Europe. Then, famous for the fineness, purity and weight of its gold, it had been worth nine shillings and sixpence in English money; but now it was somewhat fallen from its high estate and the Russells paid something just over four and eight-pence in return for each of the Venetian coins.

A considerable amount of money was sent out from London during the stay in Venice. This was not only to meet the ordinary expenses, which appear to have run to much the same amount as they did elsewhere. Additional bills of exchange were forwarded in order that purchases might be made.

Glass and lace from Venice were high in favour in the great houses in England at this time. Both of them could be and were bought in London, but the visit of a member of the family to the Italian city nearly always called forth orders for buying on the spot. Already in the previous year the Earl of Bedford had had a fine consignment of glass especially ordered for him in Venice and dispatched to him at Bedford House. Now the tutor and the boys received instructions to purchase lace for both the Earl and the Countess. Edward and Robert, in their letters home, were quite smart enough to leap upon this order as an excuse for prolonging the stay in Venice—'Having received orders to buy laces for my lord and lady, whereof one we sent by the post . . . did force us to make some longer stay in the search after them.'

The laces bought and sent away, the little party would have proceeded northward, according to the Earl's express commands, but it was now late in the year and the weather was broken. Why not prolong the stay a little further?

Edward Russell to the Reverend John Thornton
at Bedford House, London.

VENICE
November 30, 1663.

. . . We were, by reason of my lord's express commands, for some time unresolved what to do, but since in the opinion of all we are thought to have done most advisedly in staying, for almost these twenty days since there has fallen such continued rains that they have made the ways in these parts almost impassable, and about the Alps we should have found them far worse; and besides, riding so many days in perpetual storms, to omit other accidents, could do no less than much endanger our healths. We hope the stay of some few months caused by an unavoidable necessity will not be displeasing to my lord. So soon as eight or ten days of the carnival are over, which begins the 2nd of January, we shall not fail with the first fair weather to begin our voyage.

Had the Earl foreseen the continued difficulties that were to interfere with travel, he might have issued orders that, bad weather or good, boys and tutor were to attempt to cross the Alps. Even the young gentlemen themselves might have shrunk, had they known it beforehand, from the idea of prolonging their stay in Venice not for some weeks, but for more than a year. Yet that delay actually occurred.

The Turkish leader, Achmet Kiuprili, had crossed the Danube at the head of a great Turkish army. He had ravaged Moravia, Silesia and Hungary and was threatening Vienna. Under those circumstances, Mr. Rich thought it well to keep his pupils where they were. The lion of St. Mark was, it is true, as ever, roaring defiance to the East and the Turkish navy was besieging Crete. But that siege, which had begun in 1645 and continued for twenty-five years, did not affect the amenities of Venice for the visitors. The marching armies in Central Europe were, the tutor decided for the boys, another matter.

Even so, one member of the family was watching the armies with interest. The Earl's eldest son, Francis, in the course of his peregrinations in search of health, had arrived in Germany to drink the waters—there was scarcely a known spa in Europe unvisited by this young man, for whom waters were always being recommended. In the midst of his melancholy, the sight of soldiers going and coming did arouse him to a certain enthusiasm. 'We thought to have been gone before this time,' wrote his personal servant from Ratisbon on 23rd May 1664,

But the French brigade not coming so soon as was expected has been the reason of our stay, for his lordship has seen pass the Germans and he has a desire to see the French also, which are daily expected here. . . . The German troops are most of them passed by here to go to the general rendez-vous in Hungary, where they count of a hundred thousand men to assemble, but most of them new raised men. Here are daily abundance of the French gallants pass by here to go to the army and a great many more which come this week with the French brigade. The nine thousand Italians which were expected from the Pope on their march to the frontiers of Germany mutinied for want of pay and are most of them returned back into Italy.

The moving of the German and French troops was more significant for the future than the writer of the letter realized. Later he and his young master moved to Schwalbach for the latter to try the waters there. An undated letter written from that spot was sent to Mr. Thornton reporting:

We have had this last week good news out of Hungary, that the Imperial army has gained a second victory of the Turks, in which were five bashaws killed and five thousand men, three thousand of which was of the best janissaries. Of the Emperor's side they say was killed but two thousand men, amongst which were six Earls, one of which was the Earl Fugger, general of the foot, but it is thought the losses are equal on both sides. The French are much commended for their valour in the last battle, on whom fell the hardest service, and had four of their chief officers killed and seven hundred soldiers. The confirmation of this battle is expected more fully by the next post. When we come to Strasburg, which is four days' journey from hence, I shall write to you again.

The battle of which the first news had thus come was the decisive conflict in which the united forces of Emperor and French King had defeated the Turkish army at St. Gotthard on the Raab. Following that victory came the truce of Vasvar. But troops of disbanded soldiers constituted as great a menace, or even greater, to the security and peaceful ways of others than the armies had done. Not until May of 1665 did Mr. Rich receive his last bill of exchange for Venice. At the end of that month he and his charges at last crossed the Alps and made their way through Germany towards Antwerp.

They did not at once return to England, but spent some months in both Brussels and Paris. The final bill of exchange, payable this time through Lord Berkeley, was sent to Paris in April 1665. There the four brothers, Francis and William, Edward and Robert, met once more. A ship was sent to meet them and the two younger boys landed in England in May 1666, after an absence of six years.

May 1666.—To Monsieur Jerolt for Lord Russell, Mr. William Russell, Mr. Edward and Mr. Robert, by bill for diet when first come out of France, by Mr. William's order.   £17   0   0

The entire cost, reckoned by the bills of exchange sent out to Mr. Rich, for those six years' travel was just over five thousand pounds. This included the money sent to Venice for the buying of the lace.

During these years Mr. Thornton had continued to teach the two girls. But work in the schoolroom with the tutor was supplemented by instruction in accomplishments from teachers who were brought from London. These included a French master for that language—in which Mr. Thornton was evidently not an adept—a dancing master and a music teacher. For dancing and music the Countess of Bedford sometimes shared with her girls. She had several lessons at different times in dancing and in two successive years, 1677 and 1678, had some instruction in playing the guitar.

By the time their brothers had returned, Diana, the elder of the two girls, was fifteen, and so of marriageable age. In 1667 a match was arranged for her with Sir Greville Verney. Leaving home did not mean that she abandoned her friendship with one whom she continued to address as her 'best friend,' Mr. Thornton. She wrote to him constantly. He was the recipient of all her confidences and in return freely gave his advice, whether on matters of mental, moral or physical import. 'I . . . do begin to hope you are a true prophet,' wrote she when she had already been a wife and mother for many years, 'for I find myself very much out of order, but cannot yet call it being with child, although I am sick all day long.' She was then Lady Alington, for Sir Greville had died in 1668, after only a year of married life, and she, after seven years of widowhood, had married again.

Diana was the only one of the Earl's children who married young. Francis never married. William was already thirty when, two years after his sister's wedding, he ordered, or rather his man ordered for him, in 1669, the fine clothes which are recorded in a bundle of bills to make ready for his marriage to Rachel, Lady Vaughan, who had been Lady Rachel Wriothesley and co-heiress to Thomas, Earl of Southampton. The marriage settlement brought to the Russells, as Lady Rachel's share in her father's inheritance, the manors of Bloomsbury and St. Giles, with a house and a small estate in Hampshire. How notable an acquisition it was no one could guess. It was a century and more later before the Russells woke up to the fact that this property implied anything more than a convenient residence when they wished to come up to town. Had the choice been left to them in the seventeenth century, they would have preferred the great country estate of Beaulieu, which Lady Rachel's sister took to the Montague family.

The other brothers and sister waited much longer than William and Diana before they entered into the state of matrimony, except George, whose scapegrace career was, it is to be feared, no credit to the school which had educated him.

CHAPTER VI

AFTER 1660: THE HOUSEHOLD

THE Restoration accelerated, but did not inaugurate, the expansion of the establishment at Woburn Abbey. That had commenced at least two or three years earlier with the improvement in the Earl's financial position. Life still went on in the house in a stately calm. There was but little change in the tastes of the Earl and Countess. But their household was becoming far more highly organized. Departments which had been only vaguely differentiated in earlier accounts began to acquire more shape and substance, with a new official at the head of each and a number of men under him.

Shortly before the Restoration the Earl appointed a new receiver-general in the person of Mr. George Collop. Collop, a member of a Dorsetshire family who held one of the Earl's farms in that county, had been a student of Staple Inn and in 1653 had been admitted a bencher of Gray's Inn. In taking a Dorset man, the Earl was following a custom long established in his family. His predecessors had invariably appointed a man from the west country, whence they themselves had sprung, to be their chief official. Not, however, previously a man of Mr. Collop's type. The receivers-general before him had been the sons of country gentlemen of some position, personal connections or friends of the Russell family. Mr. Collop was the son of a small tenant and certainly had his own way to make in the world.

Collop had first a salary of fifty pounds a year, which,

after ten years in the Earl's service, was raised to a hundred pounds a year. A married man, he had a house on the Covent Garden property. There his family lived, but he could not have enjoyed a great deal of family life. When he was in town he had his own office room in Bedford House, but he was far from being always there. His presence was constantly required at Woburn Abbey, where a room was also kept for him. Visits to the outlying property were an important part of his duty and a great part of his time was spent either in riding eastward into the fens or westward to inquire what was happening on the Devon estates. On these journeys he was allowed, as his predecessor in 1641 had also been, as long as he was travelling, board wages for himself and his servant, usually two shillings a day for himself and one shilling for the servant, besides the expenses, such as the fodder for the horse, which were incidental to travelling. He did not, however, have to provide his own lodgings once he had reached his destination, for in the west he was put up in Bedford House in Exeter and when he went to the fens he stayed in Thorney Abbey, where in 1662 the Earl furnished a room especially for his use.

1662.—For four pieces of 'perpetuana' at £1. 18. 0. the piece, and fifty-six ounces of silk fringe at 1s. 7d. the ounce, bought and sent to Thorney towards furnishing of Mr. Collop's chamber there (besides £26. 14. 1. paid in Mr. Batten's account this year for more stuff and other materials bought at Peterborough, and for the upholsterer's workmanship, to complete the furniture of the said chamber). £12 0 0

Collop's beautifully kept account books cover every year until his own death in 1682. For the estate business he had the assistance of a separate staff, headed by a surveyor, but he was personally responsible to the Earl for the whole. Even without the supervision of the estates his work was heavy enough, for it amounted to the financial responsibility for what was now a large and elaborate household. He was not, of course, without help. In particular he had a principal assistant. This was Mr. John Dawson. He had appeared at the abbey in the fifties, when he had acted as assistant to Dixy Taylor, buying everything for the children and a great deal for both the Earl and the Countess. From the time of Mr. Collop's arrival onwards he was that gentleman's principal clerk. Dawson undertook the work at Woburn when Mr. Collop did not come down, on the latter's instructions, and also carried on the negotiations with that gentleman when he was in town.

Mr. Collop prepared the accounts, both for the household and for the estates, and they were then checked by the auditor. The latter's salary began at thirty pounds a year and gradually rose until in 1670 it was sixty pounds, at which figure it remained. Former Earls of Bedford had had their auditor also, but his work had been almost entirely the checking of the estate accounts. To have the household accounts fully audited by the same official was something of an innovation.

Another official associated with Mr. Collop represented an entirely new departure. During the earlier years of his succession William, Earl of Bedford, like his predecessors before him, when it was necessary to seek legal assistance, as it so often was, had employed a lawyer for the particular piece of business in hand. From the latter years of the Commonwealth onward he had attached to his staff a lawyer.

Mr. John Fox was appointed to this office about 1658. He received a salary of twenty pounds a year, which was in the nature of a retaining fee. Each piece of legal business he undertook for the Earl—and there was much undertaken

—was rewarded by a substantial payment. Moreover, of all the officials, Mr. Fox was the one who did best in gratuities, acknowledgments, as he himself wrote, of the pains he took in going about his lord's affairs.

He did not take those pains in vain. As long as he was lawyer only his salary was never increased, which is not, perhaps, surprising considering the amount he accumulated in fees and presents. When, however, in August 1682, Mr. Collop died, still in his master's service, Mr. John Fox stepped into his place and at the same time continued to act as legal adviser. No new lawyer was appointed. To the end of his life Fox kept both offices, enjoying the salaries of both and the handsome perquisites of the one associated with the law. Small wonder that when he died, in 1697, the London gossips reported to one another that the 'steward to the Duke of Bedford' had died a man of incredible wealth.

Two other individual figures of importance stood out among the officials. The one was Mr. Thornton. The other was the gentleman of the chamber, sometimes called the gentleman of the privy purse, who was in close personal attendance upon the Earl.

Dixy Taylor, who had been summoned from the homestead of the Taylors twenty years earlier, now filled this office. Probably the work he did was much the same as that which he had done before, but, as with all the other officials, his sphere was now more clearly defined and he was required to keep detailed accounts. Those accounts he kept for thirty years after the Restoration in a clear, recognizable hand, becoming more and more the trusted personal and confidential official. He lived in the abbey at all events at first, although later, when he had taken a wife, he may not have done so. His salary was twenty pounds a year. Apparently this was never raised, but he received many presents.

The receiver-general, the tutor and chaplain and the

gentleman of the privy purse were the officials in the abbey in closest personal contact with the family. This is true even of their relationship with the Countess and her daughters. The Countess had her gentlewoman, with an assistant who also acted as maid. But in the accounts they are figures of little significance. It is quite clear that the ladies of the house relied much upon Dixy Taylor and his colleagues.

The remaining principal officials were those who were responsible for the running of the different departments, both inside and outside the house, having for the most part a staff under them. All of them were to some extent subject to the receiver-general in that all their accounts had to go before him. He also paid the salaries and at the beginning of every month dispensed to every one who was entitled to it the money, called imprest money, which was needed for current expenses.

Within the house, after 1660, the steward was supreme, with a clerk of the kitchen and a house bailiff as his seconds. But this was the end of a process of evolution. The household had originally been run by a kind of 'Jack-of-all-trades,' of whom Mr. Crawley, in 1641, had been typical. He had managed everything with the assistance of some underlings. During the early fifties, when the Earl's family was growing rapidly, the activities of this official had been transferred to two men who worked side by side. The one was an acaterer, who supervised the household, and the other a clerk of the kitchen, who was responsible only for that department. Some time between 1658 and 1660, probably in the earlier year, a full-blown steward of the household was appointed, an innovation which the expansion of the household was doubtless making necessary. He took the place of the acaterer and assumed, at all events at first, a considerable amount of authority over the clerk of the kitchen. The first steward to be appointed was William Baker, gentleman. He and the other stewards after him received a salary of forty pounds a year. He was also given an assistant, a house bailiff, who had twenty pounds a year. Both of them lived in the abbey.

The steward had under him all the household staff, both men and women, in so far as they were employed indoors. But a principal part of that staff, the footmen, belonged partly to the house and partly to the stables. Therefore they came under the authority of the steward in the first instance and that of the gentleman of the horse in the other, a highly complicated arrangement which, it is not surprising to find, led to considerable friction. The steward, on the other hand, had full control of the porters and watchmen whose functions lay chiefly outside the house.

The footmen were eleven or twelve in number. Their wages varied from two to six pounds a year. They waited on the lord and lady in the house and accompanied them when they drove or rode forth, besides undertaking all kinds of personal service, such as carrying presents to other land-owners, or taking their master's clothes up to town. Two or three of them, those who received the higher wages, were in closer attendance upon the family than the others and among them there always stands out conspicuously one man, Clem Robinson, clearly the trusted factotum, although his official status, according to the steward's list, was no higher than that of his comrades. Clem it was, however, who went to London and on other jaunts far more frequently than any of the others and who, on occasion, was dignified in the accounts with entries all to himself.

Being livery men, the footmen had their clothes supplied to them. But these did not concern the steward of the household. The liveries were reckoned as part of the stables equipment and were ordered and paid for by the gentleman of the horse.

Below the footmen were the little boys who acted as

pages and were, like their betters, partly employed in the stables. They received no wages, but they were clothed and fed and hoped for promotion one day. Being on the stables' list, their liveries, like those of the footmen, were supplied by the gentleman of the horse, but the housekeeper was often told to buy them extras in the way of clothes or to wash those they had. Sometimes they were given a present of money and some of them at least were taught accomplishments.

1663-1664.	For teaching the page on the flageolet.	£2	10s.	0d.
May 1670.	To Mistress Abigail for two shirts for the little page.		7s.	0d.
July 1670.	To Mr. Freiston for two periwigs for my lady's page, by direction from Mr. Taylor.	£2	0s.	0d.
November 1681.	To the page, paid for twice cutting his hair.		1s.	0d.
December 1681.	To the page for scouring his clothes.		1s.	0d.
February 1682.	For three pair of stockings for Lady Margaret's page.		10s.	6d.
	For a hat and case for him.		11s.	0d.
	For shoe buckles, buttons for his cuffs and a comb.		3s.	4d.
March 1682.	To the page, pocket-money.		10s.	0d.
May 1682.	For two pair of stockings for the little page.		7s.	0d.

The masculine element provided the greater part of the household service. Only some seven or eight women in all were regularly employed. At their head was a house-keeper, but she was subordinate to the steward and, except when she is mentioned in the account books as engaged in doing fine needlework, of which she did a great deal, she is not a very imposing figure. The other women had at least the merit of having charming names. But Betty Buskin, Lydia Long, the laundry-maid, and she who was called by the excellent title of 'Alice-about-the-house' are chiefly conspicuous for the amount of medicine they were given by doctors and apothecaries, whether it was taken of their own free will or not.

The women were often given clothes. But it is not clear whether they received them in the regular way of service, or whether they took the form of presents. It almost appears that it was half and half.

November 1670.—To Abigail towards a night gown.   £1 10 0

July 1692.—Laid out for a manteau and petticoat, it being two years since I had any.
ANN UPTON.   £6 17 0

The bills show how varied was the ability to write among the servants, both men and women. Ann Upton, who was the housekeeper, wrote quite a good hand. This had not been the case with her predecessor, who had not been able to write at all. Among the maids in one year there would be two or three who could use their pens. A few years later perhaps none of them could do so. The footmen had some advantage in this respect. At all times three or four at least could not only sign their names clearly in giving a receipt for their wages, but were also able to make out a good bill in their own handwriting to give the receiver-general for any money they had expended on their master's behalf. The others made their mark on the steward's wage list, or affixed it to a bill that he made out for them for any money they had spent. There was a good free school in Woburn, which had been re-established and endowed by the second Earl of Bedford and this a certain number of the servants had doubtless attended as children.

No women were to be found in the kitchen. There the men reigned supreme, with the clerk of the kitchen at the head of the staff. After him the chief personage was, of course, the cook, who had to help him a heterogeneous collection of scullions and turnspits. Some of them were paid low wages, varying from ten shillings to two pounds a year. The others, mainly little boys, 'Tom-in-the-kitchen,' Little Dick and their companions, had no wages, but were fed and given presents of clothing.

Presents, either in kind or in money, formed a consider-able part of the Earl's expenditure on his household. Every one, from the highest official down to the least of the little boys in the kitchen, looked for gifts, and he or she was an unfortunate man or woman indeed whose resources were not considerably augmented in this way. The Earl dis-tributed gratuities in money always at Christmas and on such special occasions as the coronation, and all shared in them, beginning with the receiver-general. There was, too, always the pleasant prospect for an employee of a present being given for special services rendered. Those of the men who went to and fro on errands to friends of the Earl were, of course, in an especially favourable position, since every journey implied a present from the person to whom they had been sent. The long list of such presents given by the Earl to those who brought anything to Woburn shows how much money, in a great household, was expended in that way.

This matter of presents given and clothes supplied makes it very difficult to see exactly what were the comparative resources of the officials and the servants in a household such as that of the Earl of Bedford. A further complication arises out of the questions of board wages and residence either within or without the abbey. It is quite clear that what sometimes seems to be an extraordinary discrepancy in salaries can be accounted for by the fact that the salary was in some cases the only payment made for services, while in others it was accompanied by all kinds of allowances. This applies to the higher and lower officials and the ordinary members of the household alike. No doubt the line of demarcation, where residence in the abbey was concerned, was, roughly speaking, between the married and the unmarried men.

It is not easy to say how many benedicts were included in the staff in any given year. But at all times a certain proportion of both the officials and the servants did not live in the abbey, but in houses or cottages on the Woburn estate. Mr. Collop lived in Covent Garden, but his office made him an exception. Other indications show that most of those who thus lived outside the abbey were married men. Some of them paid rent; some did not. A number of them, but by no means all, were given board wages, which varied from twenty to fourteen pounds a year, according to the status of the recipient.

The miscellaneous group of men who worked outside the abbey but were considered to belong to the household comprised the porters and the watchmen. The porters kept the gates. Their wages were from three pounds to four pounds a year and they were supplied by the steward with gowns, hats, shoes and stockings.

1669.	Paid for six yards of broadcloth at 10s. the yard to make a gown for the porter at Woburn.	£3 0	0
	Ten yards of orange baize to line it.	£1 0	0
	For making it.	£1 18	0

The watchmen, who watched through the night and were responsible for seeing all the lights out—a most necessary precaution—had wages of one pound or two pounds a year, but they had many perquisites besides, for they undertook many odd jobs, each of which was paid for separately.

1684. To John Bradnock, being his lordship's
gift to him yearly to see all candles put
out every night.   £2   o   o

And to him more for killing rats and
mice, etc.   £1   o   o

1687. To John Bradnock, being his lordship's
gift to him yearly to see all candles put
out every night.   £2   o   o

And to him more for heating the oven
and helping to bake.   £1   o   o

The watchmen had no regular livery like their companions the porters, but they, too, like the women in the house, were often helped out with their clothes. Most often the present took the form of a pair of shoes; doubtless they wore out many. At another time the above John Bradnock was given some green cloth to make a coat and an extra ten shillings to pay the tailor to make it up.

Rooms in the outbuildings of the abbey were allotted to the watchmen and there was a porters' room in the abbey itself. When, as sometimes happened, they lived in a cottage in the park, they had board wages in common with the others.

The above comprised the permanent staff considered as belonging strictly to the household. But there was always a floating population of casual workers brought in to take the place of some servant who was sick, an unhappily frequent occurrence, or for additional labour in an emergency. If the women were, as was certainly the case, in a minority among the regular employees, they had their revenge when casual labour was wanted. By far the larger number of those who constantly came up to the abbey to do an odd day's, or even a few hours', work were represented by 'old Susan' and her companions, some of whom were not so old. A few men came also, but they were lost among the crowd of women and in most cases were clearly either very old men or those who, for some reason, were incapable of regular work. One woman at least let out her husband regularly and received the wages for him.

The rate of pay for this casual labour varied much. Unfortunately, the steward, in distributing sixpence here and a shilling there up to as much as five or ten shillings, did not trouble to set down how many hours' work it represented, or what the kind of work was. But the money, together with the perquisites in the shape of food, must have been an agreeable addition to the women's own resources.

Outside the casual workers, the number employed on the permanent staff remained wonderfully constant for the forty years between 1660 and 1700 and the figures of the salary list were almost as steady. In 1664 the entire salary list for all officials and servants, inside and outside the house, amounted to six hundred pounds. Thirty years later it came to seven hundred pounds. This increase was due neither to a change in the number employed, nor to a general rise in wages, for the extra amount represented almost exclusively the rise in the salaries of certain of the officials and men who had been for many years in the Earl's employ.

These annual wages included those payable in the two departments outside the house, the stables and the garden. All went through the hands of the receiver-general.

Finally, the staff at Woburn Abbey, that is to say the

permanent part of it, were also, with certain exceptions, the staff for Bedford House, moving up and down with the family.

In the London house the only permanent employees were a housekeeper, a watchman and a gardener.

CHAPTER VII

THE KITCHEN AND ITS CLERK:
1653 TO 1667

THE appointment of a steward of the household in 1658 or thereabouts must have been something of a blow to the clerk of the kitchen, who had been working alongside the acaterer as an equal. But matters presently righted themselves.

The line of demarcation, of course, was not quite clearly marked, any more than it was among other of the Earl's officials. Sometimes the acaterer or steward appears to have been buying something which the clerk ought to have bought and *vice versa*, not to speak of the occasions when a third and sometimes most surprising person would suddenly be entrusted with a purchase.

The clerk of the kitchen was, as a general rule, responsible from the beginning for the supplies of butcher's meat, game, fruit, vegetables and dairy produce.

An astonishing quantity of all of these was purchased outside. The bills for what was so purchased were all entered up in a kitchen book. This book was signed every week by the Earl and every week the steward gave the clerk a sum of money by way of imprest for the next week's purchases.

Besides this kitchen book, the clerk also kept a book for petty cash. All the more important kitchen properties, copper cauldrons, great wooden tubs and many pots and pans and the like, were ordered by the steward, usually from London. The clerk, however, provided himself with the numerous mops, besoms and cleaning materials that he required, as well as with the many yards of coarse cloth which he bought nearly every week to turn into bags and dusters. All these went into the petty cash book. He also dealt with the pedlars who supplied such articles as thread, needles and tape for the use of the maids. Like other members of the household, he required to have pence on hand with which to reward messengers who brought goods to the abbey. The petty cash book, like the kitchen book, was signed every week by the Earl.

The remainder of the provision for what both men called in their books the diet of the household was made by the steward. His multifarious duties always included, as far as actual food supplies were concerned, the buying of groceries and all special delicacies, not a few of which were imported from abroad. During the earlier years he was also responsible for buying the wheat which was required for grinding into fine flour in the mill in Woburn Park, and had likewise to make certain purchases of live stock.

The kitchen authorities could and should, it might be supposed, have at all times relied to a great extent upon supplies from the Earl's own estate, or estates. But at first surprisingly little of anything whatsoever came from the various bailiffs. Later developments enabled some of them to do better and to become of more use to the clerk of the kitchen at Woburn, but never to the extent of precluding the necessity of buying a good deal in the way of provisions outside.

Woburn itself was very far from being the estate which supplied the most foodstuff. On the contrary, it produced very little. The accounts of the bailiff, together with a survey made by Sir Jonas Moore in 1661 and the other survey taken at the death of the Earl in 1700, point to the fact that, outside the gardens, the Earl reserved for his own use only the well-wooded deer park. Otherwise the demesne was divided into holdings for tenants. There was nothing in the shape of a home farm.

One substantial contribution, as far as the meat supplies were concerned, the park did indeed make. This was venison from the deer that roamed there. For the purpose of killing for food, deer had a great advantage over other animals in that during the cold weather they could forage for themselves. Hence the frequency with which venison was perforce eaten in the winter months.

Other than the deer, rabbits and an occasional hog were all that the clerk of the kitchen could rely upon to come from the Woburn bailiff for the meat larder. He could look for no dairy produce whatsoever. On the other hand, the greater part of the fish which appeared on the Earl's table came out of the Woburn ponds.

As for the gardens, comparatively little came from them during the earlier years. Here there was a notable change later on.

Another estate, distant from Woburn, made, especially during the later years, far more generous contributions to the food of the household. From the first a certain number of supplies were drawn from Thorney, the estate in Cambridgeshire which had been the nucleus of the scheme for draining the fens. As time went on that property was gradually turned into a source of food supplies of all kinds, beasts, birds, fish and, to some extent, corn.

The first Earl of Bedford, receiving the grant of the site of the dissolved abbey of Thorney, with certain of its lands, had attached but little value to what he received. Less than a third of the whole estate was culturable land. The remainder was a swampy waste of fen ground, overgrown with sedge, reeds, willows and alders. No one would have been more astonished than the first owner could he have foreseen that this piece of property was destined to become the seat of a great enterprise in land development peculiarly associated with the title he had taken. He would have been equally surprised could he have seen the consignments destined for the sustenance of those at Woburn which towards the end of the sixteen-sixties began to travel regularly from one abbey to the other.

The accounting for all that was brought in, either from Woburn or from Thorney, or on occasion from one of the other estates, was carried out in a very irregular fashion. The cost of transport when anything came from the more distant estate was usually given, although by no means invariably so. Only very erratic attempts were made in the bailiff's books to estimate the value of what had been delivered to the clerk or the steward. Consequently the account books of the clerk and the steward do not represent the true cost of living in the Earl's household any more than they show how much food was actually consumed.

On the other hand, the books do indicate how much was at different times spent on food outside the estate produce and the varying relations between the two sources of supply. They also reflect the change in the style of living which was from time to time adopted, according to the Earl's income and the exigencies of his household.

The housekeeping at Woburn in the Earl's lifetime, or that part of it for which the account books have survived, passed through three epochs. Until the end of 1657, or the beginning of 1658, the keynote might fairly be said to be simplicity and economy. Then came ten years of increased expenditure which corresponded with the numerical expansion of the household. Finally, from about 1668 onwards, the style of living was on an altogether more splendid scale.

For the economical years prior to 1658 only three complete account books of the clerk of the kitchen have survived, for 1653, 1654 and 1655, with a few single bills in addition.

I   129

During this time the clerk had to provide for a household staff of forty odd, as well as for the family. For that purpose he spent on food for the three years, in round figures, £280, £260 and £310 respectively. His petty cash book came in each year to something between thirty-five and forty pounds.

During these three years the prices of the food purchased varied but little, while the numbers in the household remained fairly constant. But the clerk's money—as can be checked by bills also surviving from other years—was never anything like equally distributed over the fifty-two weeks. The reason for this was that he sometimes received from a bailiff or the steward of the household quite substantial additions to his larder; at other times he got nothing at all. Thus, in one week he might pay out four pounds and in the next as much as ten pounds. In almost every case the meat larder was the department responsible for the difference. In the first instance the clerk's heart might have been gladdened by the arrival in the kitchen of the carcasses of perhaps an ox and a couple of sheep or a pig; and in the other he might have had a dozen rabbits at the most.

The rabbits probably came from Woburn, although such was not invariably the case. The cattle, sheep and hogs might or might not have come from Thorney. That estate never at any time failed to send some provisions, but what was sent throughout the Commonwealth period was scanty compared with the generous supplies that arrived later. During these three years birds and hogs appear to have been the chief contribution. In 1654 a note says that pigs for killing have been sent to Woburn and adds that the journey was a hard one. This was doubtless true.

How many cattle were sent over at this time is doubtful. There are indications that none of the estates was able during the sixteen-fifties to supply beasts for slaughtering. The clerk, however, was not left entirely disconsolate, dependent upon the killed meat he bought in the markets. He yet received carcasses of animals, for which he himself did not have to account. They came from the steward, who had bought the animals alive and had entered them in a special book as 'provision for my lord's diet.'

The markets attended by the steward for this purpose, as for many others, were those at Woburn, at Leighton and at Luton. When the cattle from the two more distant markets reached Woburn—the drover who brought them from Leighton got anything between fourpence and eightpence—they went to the town shambles, which were kept up by the Earl of Bedford. There they were slaughtered, usually at a cost of sixpence a head, by a man called Hawkins the butcher, evidently quite a well-known figure in Woburn, and thence the carcasses were carried up to the abbey for the meat larder.

Generally speaking, the amount spent in this way seems to have been anything between forty-five and fifty pounds a year. The cost of each animal, depending upon the weight and quality, varied with every entry. No indication is ever given of the weight, and of the quality only sometimes the remark that the beast was fat.

A live hog, too, was sometimes bought in the market— in 1665 a hog at Leighton cost £1 6s. 0d. The estates, however, did better in the matter of hogs than they did with the other animals. Even Woburn itself sometimes managed to supply a few.

Whatever thus came in in the shape of meat, including the staple venison, there was never sufficient for the entire needs of the household. The clerk always had to buy additional meat, besides the other articles of food for which he was responsible.

The week beginning 11th April 1654 was one of those when the expenditure was at its lowest, for the clerk had received a bullock which weighed sixty-eight stone, two sheep and a calf. The meat bill was, therefore, a small one.

	£	s.	d.
Meat.			
A quarter of mutton.		4	6
A side of veal.		7	6
10 stone 4 lbs. of pork.		19	3
1 pig.		2	10
2 calves' heads.		1	10
	£1	15	11
Poultry, etc.			
4 capons.		8	6
12 pigeons.		5	6
		14	0
Dairy Produce.			
20 lbs. of butter.		10	0
Eggs.		3	0
		13	0
Fish.			
Crayfish.		1	10
Fruit.			
A peck and half of apples.		1	9
Miscellanea.			
Bread.		1	6
2 pecks of oatmeal.		2	8
Yeast.		1	8
12 lbs. of candles.		5	0

At the foot of the bill the clerk added that he had used six bushels of fine flour from the general store. The bread he had bought additional to this was probably coarse bread bought for the servants' hall, for in other weekly accounts he specified it as such.

There is no mention at all of any vegetables or fruit, whether from the garden or bought.

The week beginning 20th March of the next year, 1655, showed a contrast of expenditure. In that week all that the clerk took into the larder was one sheep, its provenance not stated. Consequently, he had to spend £9 12s. 0d. in all.

	£	s.	d.
Meat.			
27 stone 2 lbs. of beef at 1s. 8d. a stone.	2	5	5
1 breast of veal.		1	10
A side and a neck and breast of mutton.		10	4
1 pork weighing 12 stone.		18	6
2 gammons of bacon weighing 16 lbs.			
3 quarters at 1s. 0d. a lb.		16	9
Tripe.		1	8
Sheep's feet.			6
1 neat's tongue.			10
	£4	15	10

	£	s.	d.
Poultry, etc.			
5 tame pigeons.		4	7
18 wild pigeons, 6 at 6d., 6 at 5d. and 6 at 4d.			
apiece.		7	6
3 pullets.		4	8
7 chickens, 5 of them 1s. 2d. a piece, 2 at 1s.			
apiece.		7	10
4 hens.		4	6
2 capons.		4	2
A cock for broth.		1	2
	£1	14	5

£   s.   d.

Dairy Produce.

9 lbs. of butter, 5 lbs. at 8*d.* a lb., 1 lb. at 9*d.*,
   3 lbs. at 6*d.* a lb.   5   7

1 lb. of butter for oatcakes.   5

15 lbs. of butter at 6*d.* a lb.   7   6

Milk.   2   7

Eggs.   3   0

New laid eggs.   7

Eggs.   1

                                      19   9

Fish.

3 lobsters.   2   0

4 salt fishes and a side.   4 10

6 flounders.   1   8

                                      8   6

Fruit and Vegetables.

6 oranges and 3 lemons.   6

Asparagus.   4   0

Onions.   2

Herbs.   1   8

                                      6   4

Flour, etc.

3 bushels of coarse flour.   8   0

Bread to the pantry.   2   4

Bread for the kitchen.   1   0

                                   11   4

Besides the bread bought for the kitchen and pantry and the coarse flour, the clerk had used the same amount of fine flour as before, six bushels, and in addition he had bought a peck of pease flour, a peck of oatmeal and a quantity of oatcakes.

At this juncture the supply of condiments in the house, which should have been kept up by the steward, must have run short, for the clerk had to buy some mustard and a barrel of salt, clearly for emergencies.

Some of these provisions were bought, as the live cattle had been, at one of the neighbouring markets. The clerk patronized both the weekly market held at Woburn and that at Luton. But neither of these was his principal shopping place. Leighton Buzzard was pre-eminently the market which not only he, but also others at Woburn, attended. A note of the payment of the expenses either of one of themselves or of someone they had sent to Leighton had to be entered every two or three days in the petty cash books of both clerk and steward.

The killed meat mainly came from these markets. The exception was bacon. A good deal of this at all times came direct from Essex. It travelled by carrier's cart first to Bedford House in London and thence in another cart to Woburn. A rare entry is one which records a gratuity being given to a porter who brought four stone six pounds of pork from Smithfield.

For his poultry and his dairy produce the clerk went to many scattered purveyors. All three markets were visited, sometimes all of them within the one week, and the clerk's attentions were by no means confined to any one seller. Nor did he here rely entirely upon the markets. On the contrary, at all times he bought some poultry and a great deal of dairy produce in the neighbourhood of Woburn, usually, as the names of the purveyors show, from the Earl's own tenants.

Every few weeks one or more of these tenants would sell a chicken or a fat capon, or several of each, for use at the big house. The average price they received worked out at the same as was given in the markets. At the New Year those who thus disposed of their poultry made presents to the house. In return they received a gratuity—usually a shilling.

What was presented this New Year.

		£	s.	d.
1654.	Presented by Robert Rewburt 3 pullets; given to the maid.		1	0
	Presented by Goodman Hackins 1 turkey; given to the maid that brought.		1	0
	Presented by Goodman Hill 2 capons.		1	0
	Presented by John Gayles 2 capons; given to the maid.		1	0
	Presented by Stephen Whitbread 2 capons; given to his maid.		1	0
	Presented by Mrs. Plumor 4 capons; given to her maid.		1	0
			6	0

Partridges were sometimes sent over from the Chenies estate, which had been celebrated for them even in the fifteenth century, long before its heiress had married John Russell, first Earl of Bedford. Occasionally a few ruffs and reeves would come from Thorney. With them perhaps would be a number of those birds called knots and dotterels whose simplicity, not to say stupidity, allowed them to be easily snared. They had at least the distinction of adding an expressive word to the English language.

On the other hand, snipe and larks were bought in the markets. In the week beginning 6th December 1653, eighteen larks and three snipe were bought for one and ninepence and, later in the week, two snipe, a teal and a cock cost two shillings and fourpence.

The butter from the market was usually bought in lots of about twenty pounds—an average of thirty pounds of butter in all in the week was the usual supply. The non-market people sold in much smaller quantities. In the week beginning 13th September 1653, the clerk collected thirty pounds of butter from six different tenants, which was a very fair average. All these six tenants received the uniform price of sixpence a pound, which was precisely what was being paid in the market, where a few pounds were also bought that week.

This price of sixpence a pound was exactly the same in the spring of the two successive years. It must, however, be taken only as an average price, for many bills show that butter bought on the same day would often vary in cost by as much as twopence or threepence a pound. In 1654 an especially expensive butter appeared several times in the clerk's book. This was called 'the butter from Hackney.' It cost tenpence a pound and in the weeks—only a few in all— in which it was bought, it was distinguished from the other butter which came from the market and from the farmers by the latter being referred to by the clerk in his book as 'the ordinary butter.'

The cost of eggs varied greatly, for the prices, as is shown in the above account, depended in part upon the age of the eggs, since they were subject to the time-honoured division of being either 'new-laid eggs' or merely 'eggs.' They were bought in much the same way as the butter, either in a great quantity from the market, or in smaller quantities from many farmers' wives.

All the farmers' wives supplied cream as well as eggs and butter, each lady selling her quota of a pint or a quart as the case might be. In the autumn of 1653 the regular price was threepence a pint. Two years later, in the spring, it was fourpence-halfpenny or fivepence. Sometimes milk would be sold with the cream, but more often this commodity came from the markets. Unfortunately, in all the numerous entries for the purchase of milk at Leighton or elsewhere, no quantities are ever set against the three shillings, four shillings or five shillings that were expended.

How much fruit and how many vegetables were grown in the gardens at Woburn at this time is a moot point. Some there must have been. But the clerk's accounts show plainly what a great quantity of each was bought outside for the table. Artichokes, spinach, turnips, beans and peas were bought in the markets, as well as salads, herbs and potherbs. The summer saw the purchase of cherries and strawberries as the autumn did that of apricots, quinces and apples. Among the vegetables, artichokes were singularly unvarying in price, always costing threepence apiece. Quinces in October 1653 were seven for a penny. A peck of apples in December of the same year was a shilling. Unhappily, these details are a rare occurrence, leaving the reader of the account book in doubt what quantity of either fruit or vegetables the clerk obtained for his money.

A little of the fruit, chiefly apples, was sometimes bought from the tenants. More came from farther afield. Entries in the steward's book—for this belonged to his department —show that he frequently had to pay Mr. Gilbank, the gardener at Bedford House, for fruit that the latter had bought for the diet of the Earl. Doubtless Gilbank purchased it, or some of it, from the stalls under the walls of Bedford House. Then it travelled down to Woburn by carrier's cart in baskets or sacks.

The first marked alteration in the character of the bills came in 1658. In any case it might have been expected that they would have been higher this year. The year of the Protector's death was marked by the high prices consequent on high war taxation. For many persons it meant a lower standard of living, and not a few of the Earl's fellow peers were feeling the pinch. So little did the Earl of Bedford do this and so well had he husbanded his resources during the previous years, that he found himself now, when most people were retrenching, able to live on a more important scale than before.

The changes in his household staff in that year included the kitchen. A new clerk, Mr. James Clendon, was appointed at a wage of twenty pounds a year as against the fourteen pounds which the clerk before him had received.

Clendon was the man who made the office of clerk of the kitchen in the Earl's household once more really important, for he ultimately succeeded in creating a kitchen department for himself that was parallel with and not subordinate to that of the steward of the household. This only came about gradually. But from the beginning Clendon had much heavier and more responsible work than had had the clerk before him. With the increased numbers on the staff, he had to provide for many more mouths at the tables of the servants and officials than his predecessor had done. At the family table there were fewer changes. The boys and girls were, indeed, fast growing up, but this counted less as far as the provisions for the household were concerned than it might otherwise have done since at this time and over the next ten years the sons were much away from home, either at school or at the university, or abroad.

As a consequence of the bigger quantities of food which it was necessary to buy and also the higher prices which it was necessary to pay for it, it is not surprising that when Mr. Clendon brought his account book for the year to the new steward it showed he had been spending very much more than his predecessor had done. His kitchen book for 1658, he buying exactly the same sort of provisions as had been done before, came to five hundred and forty pounds in all as against the former maximum of three hundred and ten pounds. The total of his petty cash book for the same year amounted to sixty-eight pounds.

As far as the prices were concerned, the most marked change was in the case of meat.

In March 1653 a stone of beef cost one shilling and eightpence. The price remained the same in the same month of the two successive years. In 1658 it was two shillings. During the three earlier years the cost never rose above one shilling and tenpence and frequently fell to one shilling and sixpence a stone. In August of 1654 it was actually only one shilling and twopence a stone, but this seems to have been unusual. In 1658 two shillings represents the minimum price and very often two shillings and twopence or two shillings and fourpence had to be paid. So also with mutton. The average price of a side of mutton rose between 1653 and 1658 by as much as half a crown or three shillings. In 1653 and for the next few years a calf's head could often be bought for eightpence or ninepence; it was never necessary to give more than a shilling. There were few occasions indeed in 1658 when Mr. Clendon could enter in his book that he had bought a calf's head even for a shilling; many were the weeks during the year when he had to expend just double as much for one head.

No comparison can usefully be made between the earlier and the later years for the prices of poultry and eggs. Both showed great variations at all times, not from year to year, or even from week to week, but very often at a single buying.

The minimum price of butter, on the other hand, had risen from sixpence to sevenpence-halfpenny in the spring of 1658.

With more to buy and prices up, an economy might have been effected by a simpler style of living, had economy been necessary. Actually, there was an improvement on what had gone before. Either because the Earl felt he could now afford it, or because they were more easily obtainable, certain delicacies began to appear with far more frequency than hitherto upon the table at Woburn. This was especially the case in the fish and vegetable courses.

The staple fish supplied for the Earl's table out of his

own resources had been in the past, and for that matter continued to be, the fresh-water fish, pike and perch, which came from his own ponds in the park at Woburn—the only notable contribution besides the venison that Woburn made towards the food supply. Besides these, the inevitable sides of salt fish, with flounders, herrings and whiting, had always been bought. The appearance of anything else in the shape of fish had been during the earlier years a rare occurrence. Very occasionally a barrel of oysters would be sent down from London. Once or twice over three years a pair of soles or a dish of smelts was provided. Three lobsters which cost eightpence apiece, in March 1655, were another rarity. Salmon was once mentioned and then as a present from Lady Acton.

The marked feature of 1658 and the subsequent years was the recurring mention in the bills for fish of what had been rarities in the earlier years, even though prices were now much higher. Lobsters, which now cost one shilling, one and twopence and even more apiece as against the earlier eightpence, were purchased with frequency. Salmon was in the same case. During 1658 it was constantly bought by the clerk. One entry shows a whole fish costing eighteen shillings; a chine was sometimes entered at 4s. 0d., or a jowl at three shillings. Trout, which before had appeared but seldom, often came into the accounts.

Provision for a week in Lent made by Mr. Clendon in March of 1661 offered a good deal of variety, even of luxury, in the way of fish, for, besides the inevitable salted fish, there were included fresh cod, a quartern of smelts, twenty flounders, a chine of salmon, two pairs of soles and, finally, four quarts of oysters, the total cost being £2 18s. 0d. Of this the four quarts of oysters cost six shillings, and no single item appeared more frequently in the lists, for the family at Woburn Abbey were great oyster eaters. Barrels of oysters, usually at the cost of two shillings a barrel, came regularly from Colchester to Bedford House in the Strand and then were dispatched by carrier's cart or special wagon to Woburn.

The total amount of the clerk's bills not unnaturally increased with the improvement in the fish course. In the same way, bills for vegetables went up by leaps and bounds in the spring months when asparagus, instead of being an almost solitary entry as it had been in 1655, was bought and eaten freely each week while it lasted. During the spring and early summer of 1658 the vegetable appeared on the Earl's table in unprecedented quantity. Possibly it was an unusually good year for its growth. Certainly it once more appeared somewhat early upon the table according to modern reckoning, although not quite as early as it had done in 1655. The first week in which it was now bought was that beginning 20th April, when two hundred heads, or, as Mr. Clendon called them, sticks, cost four shillings. The next week the price was slightly down, for three hundred and fifty heads were bought for six shillings. There was a much greater drop by 4th May, when nine hundred heads were secured for thirteen shillings and sixpence. The price, however, went up and down with remarkable rapidity, for there followed in weekly succession six hundred heads for thirteen shillings and ninepence, next a great rise, when eight hundred cost as much as a guinea, which in its turn was followed by a drop to eleven shillings for six hundred and twenty-five heads. As it appeared surprisingly early, so it disappeared, for after the 1st of June no more asparagus was bought that year.

The accounts for 1658 show clearly that the Earl of Bedford had embarked on his more elaborate style of living two years before the return of the King. What the Earl would have done had political events run a different course between 1658 and 1660 is an idle question. On the other hand, it is not easy to see how far the restoration of a Court at Whitehall influenced him in continuing the expansion of the household. It is certain that, in spite of that expansion, life at Woburn continued to be extremely quiet until towards the end of the sixties. No royal visit was paid to Woburn. There was remarkably little entertaining, probably because two of the daughters were married and for the greater part of the time all the sons were away.

Only in one respect did the return of the King affect the social life of the Earl and Countess of Bedford and this touched on London rather than Woburn. Little as the Earl and Countess loved the Court and seldom as they went there, they did use Bedford House in London to a much greater extent after 1660 than they had done earlier. As a rule, the greater part of the household only migrated once a year, as before, but the migration was on a bigger scale and the stay in town was sometimes prolonged. The clerk of the kitchen then had to make provision for those who were in town as well as for those who remained at Woburn. This always meant a definite increase in his bills.

The clerk now had to make other provision for Bedford House also. After the Restoration, whether because of the changed social life in London or because of family arrangements, the married daughters and the sons travelling to and from the Continent began to use Bedford House for a night or so much more frequently than they had done hitherto. Always after such a visit Mr. Clendon at Woburn received an account from Mrs. Bruce, who was resident housekeeper at Bedford House, telling him what she had spent on the diet of the visitors. Then he had to transmit the money to her. This also was a new departure, for formerly, on the occasions when a member of the family had been at Bedford House for only a night, the cost of the visit was paid either by the receiver-general or by the steward and did not go through the clerk's accounts.

Given these circumstances, it is not surprising that the

bills under Mr. Clendon's rule, inaugurated on a note of increased expenditure in 1658, continued to rise.

The two heavy years were 1663 and 1664, when the total amount came respectively to £735 and £758.

The bills for these years show that, while much greater quantities were bought weekly of meat, poultry, dairy produce and fish other than the home supplies, the prices for all these remained much as they had been five years earlier. A stone of beef in the local markets showed no other variations than between two shillings and two and twopence, sometimes forward, sometimes back. The price of butter showed variations between sixpence-halfpenny and ninepence, sometimes clearly according to the quality, sometimes according to the season of the year. There was little difference in what was paid for game and fish.

The case of fruit and vegetables was otherwise. Here in some instances at least there was a definite rise in prices. Artichokes, for example, which formerly for a long period had been sold at threepence apiece, never appeared at that price again. Now they cost fivepence, sixpence or sevenpence and sometimes even more.

Fruit, too, cost more. Here, however, comparison is not entirely satisfactory owing to the clerk's inveterate habit in the earlier years of setting everything down in a lump, sum and not troubling to state quantities. The method of the later years was far better. At least from 1663 onwards Mr. Clendon set out his fruit and vegetable bills in detail.

The bill for the week beginning 21st June 1663 came to £2 3s. 8d. The cheapest thing the clerk bought was really the asparagus, which was evidently continuing much later this year. He only gave sixpence for his bundle, but he does not say how many heads it contained. This was counterbalanced by the high price of artichokes, which were ninepence-halfpenny apiece.

	£	s.	d.
Fruit.			
Pippins.		1	0
A pound of Duke cherries and a pound and a half heart cherries.		5	0
2 quarts of gooseberries.			6
4 baskets of strawberries.		4	0
White and red currants.		1	8
A basket of raspberries.		1	0
8 pounds of cherries.		5	4
Oranges and lemons.		1	6
	£1	0	0
Vegetables and Herbs.			
3 bushels a peck and half of peas.		9	4
10 artichokes.		7	10
Cucumbers.		3	6
Carrots and turnips.			8
Asparagus.			6
Lettuce, sorrel and parsley.		1	0
Onions and potherbs.			10
	£1	3	8

Altogether, at this point Mr. Clendon was taking very much more interest in fruit. Perhaps the growth of orchard and garden lore had something to say to this. At any rate, his gooseberries, apricots, cherries and so forth were no longer the mere gooseberries, apricots and cherries that they had been earlier, but had delightful adjectives attached to them. 'Amber' gooseberries, 'great' apricots, and 'carnation' cherries all make the lists of fruit read very pleasantly.

The high-water mark of the clerk's purchases for 1663 was in the week beginning 19th July. Then the fruit bill was a noble one.

	£	s.	d.
5 baskets of red raspberries.		5	10
3 baskets of strawberries.		4	6
8 dozen and half pears.		8	6
10 dozen white plums.		10	0
6 dozen red plums.		6	0
4 dozen Morocco plums.		8	0
10 dozen Newington peaches.	1	0	0
4 dozen great apricots.	1	4	0
4 pounds of carnation cherries.		8	0
Lemons and oranges.		5	6
6 pounds of cherries.		1	9
Pears.		1	3
Currants.			10
Codlins and gooseberries.		1	10
Plums.		2	3
	£5	8	3

As if this were not enough for the dessert, Clendon added a quantity of fruit delicacies calculated to make the mouth water. These put another £3 12s. 0d. on to the bill.

	£	s.	d.
A pound of dried currants in bunch without stones.		8	0
A pound of dried cherries with raspberries in them.		6	0
A pound of apricots.		12	0
A pound of currant paste.		6	0
2 pounds of orange pills.		10	0
A dish of marchpane.		6	0
2 pounds of candied cherries.		8	0
2 pounds of candied currants.		8	0
A dish of white apricots.		5	0
A dish of white cherries.		3	0
	£3	12	0

This must have been a time of high festivity, with important visitors—perhaps the return from abroad of some of the sons—for all the other bills for this week are on the same lordly scale.

The accounts for the year 1664 follow on the same lines as those for 1663.

Then came a remarkable drop of something over a hundred pounds in the year. Mr. Clendon's total for the year 1665 was no more than six hundred and six pounds against the seven hundred pounds odd in the two previous years. There can be no doubt that this had been deliberately brought about. It was the year of the Great Plague. It was also one of financial crisis. The amount of money the Earl of Bedford had to spend dropped with what must have seemed alarming rapidity. He was far too shrewd not to endeavour to counterbalance this and must have given definite orders for a general economy in the running of the household. This was the more easily done because few, if any, of the Russell family went to town in that year and little or nothing, therefore, had to be provided for Bedford House in the Strand. When in the summer the disease broke out with great violence in Woburn itself, a quiet style of living became both natural and desirable, although the increased doctors' and chemists' bills and the nursing of those members of the household who caught the infection in their turn made a drain upon the Earl's pocket.

No return to expenditure on the scale of previous years was made in the next year. The year of the Great Fire resembled that of the plague which went before it in that it was one of difficult finance. The income of the Earl of Bedford showed some signs of recovery which were ultimately justified. But he was no taker of risks and it was not until half-way through 1667 that he allowed anything like an expansion of the bills once more.

CHAPTER VIII

THE KITCHEN AND ITS CLERK:
AFTER 1667

THE third and final period of the accounts, during which the expenditure was on a far more impressive scale than anything that had been known hitherto, may be said to have commenced towards the end of the year 1667. Then the Earl must have realized that the financial depression of the two previous years had begun to pass away, and that his own resources had made a complete recovery.

It is true that the enhanced figures for this particular year can to a great extent be accounted for by the expenses attendant upon the wedding of Mr. Thornton's pet, Lady Diana, to Sir Greville Verney. But that was the starting-point of a scale of spending which mounted rapidly.

During the next year, 1668, the total amount spent by the clerk of the kitchen rose to eight hundred and seventy pounds. Three years later, in 1671, it reached what looks like the astonishing figure of £1,465 and, although this was the apex, nevertheless the figures for 1688 and 1689 were respectively as much as £1,379 and £1,239.

These figures are at first sight amazing when compared with those for the earlier years. They become less so when an inquiry is made into what they actually covered. Then they can be seen to include the expenses at various times not of one household, but of several, all occupying either Woburn Abbey or Bedford House.

After Lady Diana was married to Sir Greville Verney, and particularly during her young widowhood, she frequently returned to the abbey on a long visit. She continued to do so after her second marriage in 1675. Her brother William followed the same practice. He, with his wife, Rachel, was constantly at the abbey. Both son and daughter brought with them, when they came, a number of servants and, later, their children. The charge, however, on their father was by no means what it appears. They were in reality paying guests. The total of the clerk's book for the year includes the cost of their entertainment and that of their retinue, but on the credit side is entered the amount handed over by each visitor as a contribution towards the expenses.

At the end of March 1671, William Russell, two years married, brought his wife to the abbey, with a number of servants. They remained until September and William, still Mr. Russell, for his elder brother was yet living, handed over £259 to the steward, who transferred it to the clerk of the kitchen.

1671.—Received of Mr. William Russell for the diet and entertainment of himself, his lady and retinue from Lady Day, 1670, to the 9th of June then next following at £8 the week—£88; and of him more from the said 9th of June to the 30th of September following at £11. 5s. 0d. the week, abating £9 for three servants after the rate of £1. 10s. 0d. the week for six weeks—£171. In all   £259 0s. 0d.

Evidently, therefore, the cost of the entertainment of each servant was reckoned at ten shillings a week.

While William Russell was still at the abbey Lady Diana Verney arrived there with her little son. She also had a company of servants with her and in her turn handed over £230.

These handsome payments reduced the cost to the Earl for his household to £1,038 for the year.

An examination of the books for the next twenty-nine years tells the same story. Not only married sons and daughters, but also relatives-in-law came frequently on long visits to the abbey accompanied by many followers. All of them paid over a substantial sum to the Earl's steward, who in his turn credited the clerk of the kitchen with so much in respect of the visitors' diet.

As against this, the Earl himself made similar contributions when he went to stay with any of his children. He visited them, however, much less frequently than they came to him and it is not absolutely clear whether what he paid was or was not reckoned in with the expenses of his own clerk to the kitchen.

Quite apart, however, from these visiting households who paid their own way, the Earl's own household was a much more expensive matter than it had been hitherto. Single sons and daughters living in the abbey were liabilities and not assets as far as the clerk of the kitchen was concerned. Both Robert and James Russell, prior to their rather late marriages, lived either at Woburn Abbey or at Bedford House. Their brother Edward was often called away by his military duties, but he, before his marriage—also a late one—used his father's house as his regular residence. The youngest brother, George, also made his appearances at Woburn in the intervals of being despatched abroad by his father owing to his incorrigible habit of getting into debt. None of these, nor yet the unmarried daughter, Lady Margaret, paid anything out of their allowances for their board, nor for that of the personal servant, or servants, by whom each was attended. Only later, as each married and came on visits, did he or she contribute to the household expenses as the elder brother and sister had done.

At the same time, the presence at the abbey of these unmarried sons and the arrival of married sons and daughters implied a good deal more entertaining.

WOBURN ABBEY CIRCA 1630 TO 1752

Lastly, during the later years certain of the grand-children, notably the children of William, Lord Russell, after his execution, and the little son and daughter of the ne'er-do-well George, more or less lived at the abbey and had establishments there of their own, the expenses of which fell upon their grandfather.

As a consequence of this expansion of the family life, the scale of living at Woburn Abbey became far more elaborate than heretofore and the bills of the clerk of the kitchen for these later years kept—when the contributions of the visitors were deducted—to a steady average of something between nine hundred and a thousand pounds.

This rise of two to three hundred pounds over the previous period was in the main spread out over the cost of feeding the extra numbers in the house, the additional entertaining and, above all, the increased use of the London house. No universal rise of prices can be detected. Where variations occurred, the increased cost of one article of food was often offset by the lower price of another. Nor, as far as the kitchen was concerned, was there any marked change in what was served at table.

Comparisons, however, become somewhat difficult since alterations in the management of the Earl's estates now had their repercussions upon the clerk of the kitchen and his books.

At Woburn the decision of the Earl in 1671 to improve his gardens and orchards gave much more home produce to the kitchen. Cherries had always been grown in profusion, but now 'mascelline' apricots, fine violet musk peaches and Roman nectarines were added to them. The vegetable seeds and plants bought from the gardens of other gentry, from market gardeners, or from the seedsmen in the Strand, gave forth their increase. Clendon and his successor, Simon Wilde, could call upon the Woburn gardener in a way that had not been possible earlier and no longer had to journey so often to Leighton Buzzard or Luton markets.

They did not entirely desert those markets. At all times some fruit and vegetables continued to be bought. Especially was a certain amount of fruit still sent down from London. But the bills for these things were not what they had been previously.

No difference occurred in the matter of buying dairy produce, which continued to come from the markets or from the tenants.

A far more significant development than that of the gardens and orchards at Woburn, although perhaps no more interesting to the Earl of Bedford himself, took place elsewhere.

The improvements on the Thorney estate which so greatly increased its value for agriculture can be dated from the estate books as beginning shortly after the Restoration. After the Earl, in 1662, had arranged for his receiver-general to have a room at Thorney especially furnished for him, it is clear that that official spent, as he was expected to do, a considerable amount of time on the eastern estate in order to supervise the work that was being done there. The ancient abbey itself was partly rebuilt. A new gardener was engaged and bills for plants and fruit trees sent to Thorney began to appear at intervals alongside the similar bills for Woburn. But far more important than these things was the development of the estate itself under a new bailiff.

The result was that Thorney presently began to supply Woburn with produce on a scale which made what had been sent before seem a mere trickle.

Corn was sent over. It is doubtful how much, if any, corn had been grown at Thorney hitherto, at any rate before the Restoration. A great deal was being grown during the sixties and seventies, especially after 1673, when a big new granary was built. From this time onwards it appears that the greater part, if not all, of the corn required at Woburn for grinding was supplied by the Thorney estate instead of being bought as hitherto.

Thorney also provided Woburn with oats, hempseed and coleseed. Hemp had long been grown in the eastern counties. But the coleseed, from which, when crushed, the oil called colza could be extracted, had been introduced into the district by the Flemings. The ground proved to be particularly favourable to the growing of the seed and many notes show the great quantities which were transferred from Thorney to Woburn.

Later generations would have seen in the growing of corn at Thorney the most natural use to be made of the estate. For their part, they thought of the land as far more suitable for arable purposes than for pasture. Such was not the view of the seventeenth century. The corn that was grown at Thorney and sent to Woburn was merely one among other products. The natural resources of the fen country ensured a supply of birds and fish, while, as the estate itself was improved, the breeding of cattle began to rival in importance the growing of corn.

Bullocks for slaughtering were being brought over to Woburn from Thorney during the sixties. From at least the middle of the seventies onwards they came in great numbers.

Sometimes the steward at Woburn signed the receipt for the animals on their arrival there.

June 13, 1681.—Received from Francis Underwood, Esquire [bailiff at Thorney], by the hands of Thomas Vesey, six fat bullocks.
July 27 following.—Received six fat bullocks.
September 6 following.—Received seven fat bullocks.
October 21 following.—Received eight fat bullocks.

All the abovesaid fat beasts received at Woburn Abbey for the use of the right honourable William, Earl of Bedford, by me

RANDOLPH BINGLEY

153

This was, on the whole, unusual. Possibly the clerk of the kitchen was out of the way on this occasion. Normally, the latter undertook the entire business and carried on all the negotiations. James Clendon, who wrote an excellent hand, constantly corresponded with the Thorney bailiff.

James Clendon to Colonel Underwood, then bailiff of Thorney.

WOBURN ABBEY
This 31st July 1674.

HONOURED SIR,
These are that there was received at Woburn Abbey for his lordship's use five bullocks before we did come into the country, and now this 30th of July received by Thomas Vesey six bullocks more by me, who desires to remain,
Your humble servant,
JAMES CLENDON

Similarly Clendon's successor in the kitchen, Simon Wilde, wrote the letters and signed receipts for the animals.

June 1, 1694.—Received 6 bullocks.

July 20.—Received 7 bullocks.

September 6.—Received 6 bullocks.

October 18.—Received 6 bullocks.

In all 25 bullocks of Mr. Thomas Vesey, for the use of his grace the Duke of Bedford. I say received per me
SIMON WILDE

That the clerk of the kitchen should do all this was the more natural since the cost of getting the beasts over to Woburn had to be borne out of his money, not out of that of the steward.

It was usually possible to set down that the cattle, on their arrival at Woburn, were fat. They had certainly needed to be in good condition before they started, for the journey to Woburn was an arduous one. This was testified to, if testimony were needed, by the bitter complaints of the drovers who had to traverse the remarkably bad roads of the long stretch of country between the two pieces of property. To drive the bullocks from Thorney to Woburn implied a dreary trudge of at least four days for man and beast. That was reckoned the normal time for the journey. Often longer was required. The expenses for the four days' travel were always set down either as 14*s*. 0*d*. or 14*s*. 6*d*.

July 1694.—Paid in charges to Woburn with
7 bullocks 4 days driven.   14*s*.   6*d*.

Even given these payments, however, the clerk of the kitchen was still on the right side of his accounts, for the charge for bringing the beasts over came to considerably less than the cost of live cattle at Leighton market.

Whether in the long run there was any pecuniary profit to the Earl of Bedford in this particular use of the Thorney estate is questionable. Obviously at this time a good deal of money was being spent on the Cambridgeshire property, quite apart from the matter of the draining of the fens. The latter enterprise was profitable indeed. How far the development of the estate for produce saved the Earl money is another matter.

All the beasts that came over from Thorney did not come from the Earl's own estate. From the sixteen-seventies at least onwards the bailiff of Thorney constantly visited the markets or fairs at Wisbech and even at Setchey, over the Norfolk border, to buy cattle for the clerk of the kitchen at Woburn.

November 1691.—Received then of Mr. Peirson the sum of forty-five pounds for twenty Scotch runts which I bought at Setchey fair and delivered them at Woburn for the use of the Right Honourable the Earl of Bedford. £45 0 0

THOMAS VESEY

Pasturage in this eastern district was indeed reckoned excellent in the seventeenth century, seeing that the cost of getting the animals over to Woburn had to be added to the cost of purchase. In spite of this, the Cambridgeshire and Norfolk markets tended to oust Leighton Buzzard and Luton.

There are some signs that the month of November, in which the cattle at Setchey were bought, and the previous month were those during which at all times the greatest number of beasts were sent over to Woburn from Thorney.

This is what might be expected, since the meat would be needed for salting down for use during the winter months. At this time notable advances had been and were still being made, chiefly owing to the introduction of new roots, in the methods of feeding animals throughout the winter. Nevertheless large numbers still had to be slaughtered soon after Michaelmas because of the difficulty of keeping them alive during the approaching winter months, and the households still relied largely upon salted meat until the spring should come again.

However good the pasturage, however valuable the corn land, the real richness of the fen country around Thorney, when all was said and done, lay in the fish with which its streams teemed and the birds and water-fowl which flourished amid the low-growing trees and bushes and in the swampy places. Excellent as doubtless were the fat bullocks sent over from Thorney, the birds and fish which came thence were even more excellent. Long afterwards, when the laments of the local fishermen and bird-catchers over the draining of the fens had died out, since those who lamented had had perforce largely to change their occupation, the naturalists, in their turn, raised cries of despair at the complete disappearance in some cases and the partial disappearance in nearly all of the unique birds and butterflies which had once haunted the marshy regions. As a naturalists' paradise and the breeding-place of birds destined to become rarer and yet more rare, the district had little or no appeal for the men of the seventeenth century. As a feeding-ground of delicately fleshed birds which could be elegantly dressed for the table and which appealed to all gourmets it was of very great importance indeed.

Already in the earlier years a few birds had been regularly sent over from Thorney to Woburn. During the later years the flocks of ruffs and reeves which ornamented the fens and marshes were drawn upon monthly, or even weekly, to make a second course for the Earl's table at Woburn.

July 1681.—Received then of Francis Underwood, Esquire [bailiff at Thorney] the sum of eight pounds in full for eight dozen of ruffs delivered to Mr. James Clendon at Woburn Abbey for my lord of Bedford's use. I say received. £8 0 0

The mark of ROBERT LAXTON

This one pound a dozen was the usual price paid for the birds, although occasionally as little as fifteen shillings a dozen was given. So acceptable were they on the Earl's table that the bailiff at Thorney was sometimes hard put to it to get sufficient for the purpose and made a comment that he had had to send out a special order for them to be brought in.

The other birds brought in by the fishermen were chiefly the knots and dotterels, with occasionally some quails or a brace of fat swans. Like the bullocks, the swans that came from Thorney were never anything but fat.

The Thorney bailiff—Mr. Ralph Peirson succeeded Mr. Underwood here—gave anything between sixteen and eighteen shillings a dozen for the knots and dotterels.

> *October* 1689.—Received then of the right honourable William, Earl of Bedford, by the hands of Mr. Ralph Peirson, the sum of eight pounds for ten dozen of knots at 16*s*. 0*d*. per dozen delivered at Woburn 4th instant. £8 o o
>
> The mark of ROBERT LAXTON

The arrival of quails from Thorney was always welcome, but their appearance was much sparser than that of the other birds and it was only occasionally that the bailiff was able to procure them. Even then he seldom succeeded in getting as many as the clerk of the kitchen, waiting for them at Woburn, hoped to receive. 'Only nineteen quails received,' exclaimed Simon Wilde, then clerk of the kitchen, in a letter written to the Thorney bailiff on 20th September 1692, 'but,' he went on in a moment of softening, 'my lord hath ordered that you should give Richard Ashby fifteen shillings for them, for they were very good.'

The swans were sometimes bought, but the bailiff was fond at all times of making a present of a brace to the Earl.

The birds, often in company with other produce, travelled to Woburn in a basket on the back of a horse or in a cart. The journey took as long as did that of the bullocks with their drover, for a man with one horse or two, or with a cart, never accomplished the distance in less than four days. In autumn or winter, when, as he sometimes put in his bill, the ways were worse than usual, he might need as much as five days.

July 1695. To Robert Laxton for four days, himself and horse, carrying a brace of fat swans to Woburn which were presented his grace by Mr. Peirson, at 3*s.* 0*d.* per day.   12*s.* 0*d.*

More to him for five days, himself, two horses and a cart, carrying of golden pippins, two hampers and six bushels of hempseed to Woburn for his grace's use at 5*s.* 0*d.* per day in the latter end of October last, the ways being very bad.   £1   5   0

£1   17   0

The presence in their midst of such a customer as the Earl of Bedford's bailiff was valuable to the fen men, who got good prices for the birds they brought in. Once the birds were being brought across regularly, they accounted for quite a considerable proportion of the spending money of the clerk of the kitchen at Woburn, especially when the cost of getting them to his kitchen was taken into consideration.

The fen men could also reckon upon selling fish to the bailiff. It appears from the Thorney accounts that the Earl had one or perhaps more fishermen regularly attached to that estate. On the other hand, his bailiff undoubtedly bought fish from the fen dwellers generally. These fish, or at any rate most of them, were not bought for immediate eating purposes. Before that fate overtook them, they went into the ponds in the park at Woburn. The supply of pike and perch in those ponds was very largely kept up by the fish which were sent over from Thorney with great regularity.

This method of renewing the Woburn fish supply was not a cheap one. The fish fetched good prices and to get them over to Woburn was quite an expensive process. They did not come by road but by water—an easier, but much slower mode of progress and costing considerably more. The expenses of the men who accompanied the fish had to be reckoned for at least fourteen days from the time when they left Thorney and, reaching Barford, gained the Ouse, whither they came up to Bedford, to give up the fish there to the men who had been sent to meet them, and so returned to Thorney. Sometimes the seeds, hemp, colza or oats came over in the same fashion.

The clerk of the kitchen was not required, since the fish did not come immediately to him, to pay either for them or for their journey. Both charges had to be met by the bailiff of Woburn, who carried out the entire transaction with his brother bailiff at Thorney.

In March 1691, this Woburn bailiff bought sixteen pike for the Earl at a cost of £9 7s. 0d.

March 1691.—Received of the right honourable William, Earl of Bedford, by the hands of Mr. Ralph Peirson, the sum of £3. 10s. 0d. for 7 pikes of 26 inches at 10s. 0d. apiece; and £3. 12s. 0d. for 6 of 28 inches at 12s. 0d. apiece; and £2. 5s. 0d. for 3 of 30 inches at 15s. 0d. apiece; in all £9. 7s. 0d. in full for the said 16 pikes, which were delivered to Richard Wych, his lordship's fisherman, on the 15th instant for his lordship's use. £9 7s. 0d.

JOHN PHILLIPS

The fish having cost just under ten pounds, their journey to Woburn cost the bailiff another seven pounds odd. This included five shillings for the messenger who went ahead, presumably by road, to warn Woburn of the arrival of the boat at Bedford.

A bill of charges for carrying the pikes from Thorney to Bedford.

	£	s.	d.
March 1691. To Richard Wych, my lord's fisherman, for to bear his and the two watermen's charges to Bedford and the watermen's charges back again.	4	18	0
To Robert Sanderson and Edward Cherriton, the two watermen that went with Richard Wych, for fifteen days apiece, at 1s. 0d. per diem each of them, £1. 10s. 0d.; and given them to bear their charges to Crowland, 6d.; in all	1	10	6
To Robert Laxton for the use of his boat, his journey being fifteen days at 6d. per diem.		7	6
Paid for a line 50 yards long for the fisherman to draw the boat and trunk.		6	0
Paid for charges to Woburn to carry news of the fish.		5	0
	£7	7	0

These were at all times the regulation prices for pike according to the inches they measured. The sums paid to the watermen and for the use of the boat seem never to have varied.

When, therefore, the clerk of the kitchen wanted fish from the ponds, he applied to the Woburn bailiff. On the other hand, the meal for the feeding of the fish came out of Mr. Clendon's kitchen store.

Thus Mr. Clendon's view was now extended beyond Leighton and Luton markets to include Thorney and his friends the bailiffs there. He himself grew in magnificence along with the household. His reign over the kitchen at Woburn continued until the Michaelmas of 1690. Then he surrendered the reins to his successor, Simon Wilde, after a service of thirty-three years, and retired, whether because of old age or sickness, on a pension of £20 a year. This pension was equal to his former salary, but he must, in his retirement, have somewhat missed the fleshpots of Woburn.

Simon Wilde belonged to a family whose name was already well known in the Earl's service. When he became clerk in 1690 he surrendered nothing in the way of either independence or importance. The friction between the clerk and the steward which is evident during the earlier years, at a time when the steward obviously considered himself enormously the superior of the clerk and certainly attempted to interfere in some of the latter's activities, was past.

Except as a matter of prestige, the stewards had little cause to grumble at this. The supervision of the Earl's household was no light matter and they had plenty to do on behalf of their lord. Nor were they entirely divorced from kitchen affairs, since to the end the clerk of the kitchen had to look to them for the purchase of all groceries; for the enormous supplies of salt which were always needed for the household; and for coal.

CHAPTER IX

THE STEWARD OF THE HOUSEHOLD

Mr. Henry Baduley was acaterer of the household at Woburn from some time in the early fifties until 1658. Unfortunately, he left very few papers behind him. Most of his activities have to be inferred from a few scattered documents and the mention of his name in the books of the clerk of the kitchen.

Next followed the epoch of Mr. William Baker, who was no longer called the acaterer, but the steward. His rule continued for ten years. In 1668 he was succeeded by Mr. Randolph Bingley, who was still at Woburn in 1700.

The steward was a most active individual in every sense of the word in pursuit of his master's business. Where the clerk of the kitchen was static, the steward was peripatetic. The farthest from home the clerk ever got was to Leighton Buzzard or Luton markets. Even so, he often sent underlings to make his purchases for him. The bailiff's men, and not he, went to Bedford to meet the boats which brought the fish from Thorney. The steward, on the contrary, was for ever flitting up and down to London and even farther afield, although the errands on which he went varied from epoch to epoch.

One particular purchase undertaken by the steward in the sixties, but not apparently later, was the buying of the wheat that was ground by the windmill in Woburn park. He left only one piece of information as to whence he procured this wheat. He gives the name of the man from whom he bought it, namely, William Griffin, but he does not say where the latter dwelt.

It seems quite clear that throughout Baker's time of office all wheat required was bought outside. This had almost certainly been the case in the days of his predecessor also. But the wheat accounts of the acaterer and of Mr. Baker for the first five years of his office are either missing or very inexact. For the final five years between 1664 and 1668 the latter left behind him a precise account of the quantity of wheat he bought and the prices he paid for it.

In 1664 Baker bought in all one hundred and fifty-three bushels of wheat, for which he paid £35 7s. 5d. The minimum rate for the year was four shillings and threepence and the maximum five and eightpence a bushel. The following year the maximum price was again five shillings and eightpence, but the minimum was a penny less at four shillings and twopence. One hundred and seventy-five bushels were bought. The next two years saw a big drop in prices. In 1666 the minimum price was only two shillings and threepence and the maximum no more than three shillings and ninepence. Perhaps this accounts for the big purchase of three hundred and twenty-one bushels, for which the steward paid £51 3s. 7d. At all events, he never bought as much either before or after. In the following year, although the price was still low, he bought only a hundred and eighteen bushels at a minimum price of two shillings and eightpence and a maximum of three shillings and eightpence. This cost him altogether £20 18s. 9d. In 1668, his last year, the price was back again at a minimum of four shillings and fourpence and a maximum of five shillings and threepence. That year one hundred and twenty-five bushels were bought for £34 0s. 10d.

It seems quite clear that this wheat provided the kind of flour which the clerk of the kitchen, in noting down how much he had used of it, always qualified as fine. At all times it was supplemented by the coarse flour, which was bought already ground, and by a great quantity of rye.

This coarse flour, rye and oats were bought to the very end of the Earl's lifetime. The accounts for the buying of corn disappear as a whole after 1668. Only here and there is mention made of a little being purchased. The date of this alteration in the accounts coincides almost exactly with that of the completion of the great new granary at Thorney. Hence the inference that after 1668 the eastern estate was supplying Woburn with most of the corn that was wanted.

One principal set of orders which always went through the steward dealt with groceries. Between July 1658 and June 1693, which are the dates of the first and the last surviving bills, the Earl, or his steward for him, patronized only three grocers in chief, all of whom lived in London. The first was Mr. Carter; the second was Nathaniel Child and partner; and the third Mr. Ashfield. All three of them sent in their bills either quarterly or half-yearly.

Those bills seldom amounted for the whole year, from first to last, to less than twenty-five pounds and often ran up to thirty-five pounds or even more.

Bought of *Ansell Carter, grocer*.

		£	s.	d.
July 1658.	Sugar 100 lbs. at $8\frac{1}{4}d.$ lb.	3	8	9
	Sugar 28 lbs. at $10\frac{1}{2}d.$	1	4	6
	Sugar double refined $31\frac{1}{2}$ lbs. at $2s.\ 0d.$ lb.	3	3	0
	Smooth sugar 3 lbs.		4	0
	Raisins sun 50 lbs. at $5\frac{1}{2}d.$	1	2	11
	Blue currants 50 lbs. at $6\frac{1}{2}d.$	1	7	1
	Case nutmegs 2 lbs.		13	4
	Cloves 1 lb.		8	0
	Large mace.		8	0
	Large cinnamon.		3	7
	Large ginger 1 lb.		1	9

	£	s.	d.
Rice 2 lbs.			8
Barley 4 lbs.		1	8
Prunes 6 lbs.		1	3
White candy 1 lb.		2	6
A box.		1	6
Jordan almonds 1 lb.		1	6
	£12	14	0

Prices were high in the year 1658. Thirteen years later, in 1671, when the Earl's custom had been transferred to the grocers Nathaniel Child and partner, they were definitely down.

Bought of Nathaniel Child.

		£	s.	d.
October 28, 1671.	2 cwt. sugar at 6d. per lb.	5	12	0
	2 boxes and cords.		4	0
November 2.	1 lot double refined 4 lbs. 2 oz. at 1s. 3d. per lb.		5	1½
November 3.	1 lot double refined 3¾ lbs. at 1s. 3d. per lb.		4	8½
November 7.	1 lb. powder sugar.		1	0
December 11.	1 lb. raisins.			4
December 13.	2 lbs. currants at 6d. per lb.		1	0
	2 lbs. sugar at 8d. per lb.		1	4
December 18.	½ cwt. currants at 6d. per lb.	1	8	0
	½ cwt. Malagas at 2½d. per lb.		11	8
	¼ cwt. sugar at 8d. per lb.		18	8
	40 lbs. prunes at 2d. per lb.		6	8
	½ cwt. raisins at 4d. per lb.		18	8
December 23.	½ lb. large mace at 16s. per lb.		8	0
	½ lb. cloves at 14s. per lb.		7	0
December 24.	½ lb. ginger at 1s. per lb.			6
December 28.	1 lb. sugar at 4d. per lb.			4
	¼ lb. sugar candy.			3
January 7, 1672.	1 lot refined 6 lbs. 6 oz. at 9d. per lb.		4	9½

		£	s.	d.
February 19.	½ cwt. new currants at 6*d.* per lb.	1	8	0
	½ cwt. raisins at 4*d.* per lb.		18	8
March 14.	1½ lbs. blue figs at 1*s.* per lb.		1	6
		£14	2	2½

In spite of a definite drop in the prices of certain groceries, the steward was nevertheless spending from the late sixties and early seventies onwards a great deal more money in the course of the year than hitherto. The first and simple reason for this was that which had also made the clerk of the kitchen require more money. The household was ordered on a more elaborate scale and there were more mouths to feed. Quite apart from this, however, the steward found himself, as the years went on, more and more committed to expend money on newly introduced luxuries, the cost of which more than counterbalanced any small savings in other directions.

In the year 1685 a notable addition was made to the list of items in the grocer's bill. In that year Randolph Bingley ordered from the grocer Ashfield one pound of coffee powder at three shillings. Thereafter similar entries appeared regularly in Ashfield's half-yearly or quarterly accounts.

But coffee was by no means a new drink at Woburn in 1685. The family there had been drinking it for at least fifteen years. The novelty was in its appearance in the grocer's bills. Hitherto it had not been bought from a grocer, nor had it been ordered by the steward.

John Evelyn had remarked in his diary that one Nathaniel Conopios, out of Greece, was the first he ever saw drink coffee. That incident took place in Balliol College in 1636. Thirty years were needed, according to Evelyn, to accustom the English people to the drink. The estimate was fairly accurate as far as the household at Woburn Abbey was concerned, for everything indicates that coffee did not appear there much before 1670. Then during fifteen years it was bought at intervals in extremely small quantities. The official entrusted with the purchase was Mr. Dixy Taylor as gentleman of the privy purse, a fact which has some significance when it is seen by his bills that the supply was always laid in not for the common use of the family, but for some one particular person. Dixy usually bought a shillingsworth at a time, but whither he went for it and how much or how little he got for his shilling is never stated. He did, however, make other purchases in connection with it, for with the coffee arrived the special little china sets in which it was served. In 1670 Dixy procured for the use of the master of the house a coffee-pot, a china dish and coffee. He paid £1 2s. 2d. for the whole, but did not separate the items. A little later on in the year, however, he bought a 'little coffee-pot' for sixpence and a china cup to go with it for one shilling and sixpence. This pot and cup, or dish, were the regular form of the set. After the Earl had had his, which was speedily followed by one for the Countess, many others were bought, so that in time most members of the family and some of the household seem to have acquired his or her own set. The frequent renewal of the sets was doubtless due to the fate which befalls most china.

The transference of the coffee to the general grocer's bills in the eighties marks the moment at which the quantity drunk at Woburn during a year began to rise slowly, but very steadily. In 1685 two or perhaps three pounds were bought, a sufficient contrast to the very small quantities procured earlier. The following years showed the extension of this item on the grocer's bills until in 1693 Mr. Ashfield was supplying the household with anything from two to three pounds, either the powder or the berry, in a month.

The increase in consumption must have been due to a growing taste for the drink, for it was certainly not due to a lowering of the price. On the contrary. The cost of a pound remained at three shillings until 1689. Customs duties were, however, being increased and in that year it jumped first to three shillings and sixpence and then to four shillings a pound. It remained at four shillings until 1690, but by 1692 it had risen to five shillings and in 1693 the last of the grocer's bills recorded a price of six shillings.

Tea, unlike coffee, never got into the grocer's accounts at all during the Earl's lifetime, although during the later years, from 1685 onwards, plenty of it was drunk at Woburn.

Tea stood in the accounts in a class by itself. It was bought neither by the steward, nor by the gentleman of the chamber, although the steward checked up the bills for it and handed over the money to pay them. The purchase was made almost invariably either by the man called Dawson, who was assistant to the receiver-general, or more frequently by his wife. Eliza Dawson often went to Bedford House in those later years to help the housekeeper there and she may well on those occasions have been given a commission to buy the half-pound or pound of tea which was sent down to Woburn. It came always from one man, Mr. Richards, but the bills give no inkling as to who he was or where he lived.

Every purchase of tea was, just as had been the coffee, at first earmarked for some particular individual and the resemblance was continued in that each member of the family acquired his or her own little tea-set. The entire family were, however, more extravagant in their drinking of tea than they ever were in the matter of coffee. Not only was the former beverage very much the dearer of the two, but they drank a good deal more of it.

In 1685, the year of the first bill, the total cost of the tea bought came to just over ten pounds. The highest price then given for a single pound was twenty-five shillings and the lowest twenty-three shillings. Subsequently the prices varied very greatly. In 1687, when altogether nearly fifteen pounds were spent, one kind of tea at least cost three guineas a pound, but others again only twenty-five shillings. In 1692, when the customs duty was very high, a number of small bills mention tea at three guineas a pound.

The china sets that came to Woburn along with the tea were very much more expensive than those provided for the rival beverage. In that year of 1685 when tea was apparently first bought for Woburn, Lady Margaret Russell received a set of tea dishes, bought for her by her father's steward at a cost of £1 14s. 0d. How many dishes were comprised in the set is not mentioned, but three years later she had another set of six of which the cost was twenty-four shillings. The steward also bought for her in that year of 1688 a tea salver for five shillings. A year or two later a teapot cost £2 3s. 0d.

These individual tea-sets were presently supplemented. As more tea was drunk at Woburn, so was the china cupboard enriched. The East Indiamen who called at China ports on their way home began during the eighties and nineties to carry fine collections of ware especially ordered by noble patrons. The Earl of Bedford was not among the least of these and before his death in 1700 Woburn had acquired tea tables from India as well as several sets of teapots and cups from China.

One kind of tea, however, and one only, fell directly within the province of the steward. Such tea was that from the Dutch West Indies, imported directly from Holland. It cost, as a rule, £1 16s. 0d. a pound.

To send to meet the tea at the docks, to settle for its purchase, pay the customs dues and then to have it brought to Bedford House, whence it went to Woburn, was work to which the steward was well used. At least from the time of the Restoration onwards a certain number of delicacies were regularly imported from abroad for the table at Woburn Abbey. They were as a rule expensive delicacies and when the cost of transport was added payment for them meant a considerable charge on the steward's bills. To get them safely into England and down to the abbey also involved him in a good deal of work.

In particular, hams were frequently imported from Westphalia. The Earl had eaten these hams long before the Restoration. Already in 1653 the clerk of the kitchen had noted that he had received, presumably through the steward, some Westphalia bacon, and there is at least one other entry a little later to the same effect. He did not say whether or not this bacon was imported direct or bought in London. Later the hams certainly came direct and they arrived not as single hams, but in dozens—four dozen of them in 1671.

A bill of the charges of the four dozen of West-phalia hams sent from Monsieur de Famars to the Earl of Bedford.

	£	s.	d.
March 1671. To Monsieur de Famars for the 4 dozen Westphalia hams as he paid in Westphalia.	10	8	9
Charges in Holland paid by Monsieur Gerard Baen.	2	10	8
Charges of letters.		10	0
	£13	9	5

These particular hams were bought—in what town it is not known—from Monsieur de Famars by the private servant of Francis, Lord Russell, who at that time was in Westphalia with his master. The presence abroad of a son or servant of the Earl, or for that matter a friend, was often the occasion of an order being given for some special delicacy to be bought and dispatched to England.

The steward seldom stated in his final accounts whether he paid money directly over to some agent for the hams, or whether he negotiated through a bill of exchange.

Another arrival for the Earl at the Port of London was on occasion fish, which had travelled even farther than the hams had done, since it came from Newfoundland.

November 1676. To the shipmen that brought
the fish from Newfound-
land.   6*s.*   o*d.*
To a waterman to the ship.   1*s.*   6*d.*
To porters for bringing the
fish home.   1*s.*   6*d.*

Confectionery sometimes came from France. Anyone visiting Paris could be required to buy and bring back with him, or to send, some of the sweetmeats, or perhaps some *confiture*, for which the French confectioners were famous. The *confiture* in particular often came in this way. Fifty shillings' worth of it was sent over in 1671, coming from the establishment of Monsieur de Villair. Monsieur de Villair also supplied candied or dried fruits—oranges, lemons, apricots and cherries. A bill for these in 1673 came to over four pounds.

Some confectioner's bills, although endorsed 'Delivrés pour monsieur le Comte de Bedford' and also receipted in French, may very well have not come from Paris, but may represent French confectioners established in London, especially where, as is sometimes the case, the items have been written wholly in English, or in a mixture of the two languages. The tradesman, whose real name was Etienne Emery, by which he signed his receipts, but who was known to the Earl of Bedford's staff by the simple and convenient title of 'Monsieur,' sent in several of these bills.

Monsieur's bill for sweetmeats.

		£	s.	d.
December 1673.	4 pounds of machepain biscuit tartlets and conserve.		16	0
	5 pounds and 6 ounces of all sorts of sweetmeats.	1	7	0
	4 pounds of oranges and lemons.		16	0
January, 1673/4.	2 pounds of sweetmeats.		10	0
	2 pounds and halve oranges and lemons and zingo roots.		10	0
	1 pound of biscuit.		4	0
	1 pound and halve of pistaches.		7	6
	2 pounds and a quarter of chocolate amandes.		9	0
		£4	19	6

The journeys from Woburn to Bedford House and from Bedford House to the Port of London were not particularly lengthy, although no doubt they often involved troublesome business. But two of the steward's most important purchases throughout the year, salt and coal, took him farther afield into Huntingdonshire.

A considerable quantity of salt had to be laid in every year, particularly for the preserving of meat for the winter. The quantity of salt used at Woburn for this and general purposes was wonderfully constant throughout the whole forty years; nearly always a regular seven and a half quarters, or sixty bushels, in the year. The price was no less constant than the amount, for it almost always remained at sixteen shillings a quarter. Once or twice, notably in 1671, it sank a little below this, to fifteen shillings and fourpence a quarter.

The steward always bought his salt at St. Neots. The convenience of this town, standing as it did upon the Ouse amid a network of waterways, was obvious as a centre for trade between the east coast and the home counties, particularly Bedfordshire. Whence the salt reached St. Neots the steward did not say. He was only interested in the price he had to give for it at St. Neots itself. It may have come from any of the coastal towns engaged in the white salt trade, most probably from King's Lynn. The steward had it loaded at St. Neots into wagons sent especially to fetch it—the charge of two shillings and eightpence a quarter for loading added considerably to the price—and thence it was slowly conveyed to Woburn.

The steward went into Huntingdonshire for other purposes than to buy salt. A far from unimportant part of his duties at Woburn was to see that not only the abbey, but also Bedford House, was kept well supplied with all that was needed for lighting and heating—coal, charcoal, wood and oil.

A considerable part of the coal used at Woburn Abbey came, like the salt, from St. Neots, for that town was as well placed for the coal retail trade as for the salt. Once again the steward, since the coal was actually bought at St. Neots, not merely ordered and then delivered there, did not trouble whence the ships which had brought it to the east coast, thence to be transferred again by water to St. Neots, had come. His concern was, as for the salt also, for the price he had to give and the labour—the very considerable labour—of getting it to Woburn. He did, however, invariably, until the end of the time, divide his supplies into the categories of sea coal and Scotch coal.

Considerable quantities of both kinds of coal were needed for use at Woburn Abbey and also at Bedford House. Since the steward knew perfectly well, as did also the receiver-general, to whom he rendered his accounts, and the Earl of Bedford, who approved them, what at this time was meant by sea coal, it was unnecessary for the steward—

however much later generations may regret this—to mention whether the name still referred, as it originally had done, to coal taken from outlying surface crops on the north-east coast, or whether it had been transferred to coal mined under the sea, or even to sea-borne coal. In any case, one point stands clear, that the sea coal came from north-east England and that large quantities of it arrived at St. Neots, whence it was retailed.

In 1664 the steward set forth his purchase of coal at St. Neots thus:

1664.—For 55 chaldron at 17s. 6d. the chaldron, bought at St. Neots, with £25 paid for the carriage thereof from thence to Woburn Abbey at 10s. the chaldron, and with 8s. 4d. for loading and wharfage at 2d. the chaldron.   £73 8s. 4d.

The steward does not say whether this was the Newcastle or the London chaldron, between which there was a considerable difference in weight. In any case the cost of the carriage to Woburn, which he reckons here at ten shillings a chaldron, raised the cost to a very considerable extent. Normally the charge appears to represent the cost of getting the coal across the country in wagons. Not unnaturally an opportunity was sometimes taken to send it at the same time as the salt, which was an economy of time for the man who had to buy both and saved his lord's pocket. On some occasions at least, however, the coal came by the Ouse, to be landed at Bedford and fetched thence by the Earl's wagons.

This sea coal did not entirely suffice for the needs of Woburn. Every year a quantity of coal from the Scotch mines was also laid in at the abbey. This was not bought at St. Neots, for it was coal that had come up the Thames to the Port of London. One single bill at least shows that the steward sometimes went to Durham Yard on the Thames to buy this coal off a coalman whose name was James Hutton. This was highly convenient, for Durham Yard was almost immediately opposite Bedford House in the Strand. Hence charges for carting the Scotch coal to Bedford House were low, but it then had to be sent to Woburn either by carrier or, more often, by the Earl's own wagons. In 1664 four tons of Scotch coal were bought in Durham Yard at a cost of twenty-four shillings a ton.

Bedford House was always supplied with coal bought at one of the yards on the river bank. As a rule, however, the kind of coal that went into the cellars of the London house was described not as Scotch coal, but again as sea coal. Fifty chaldron of this were bought in 1664 for Bedford House at a cost of eighteen shillings a chaldron. Fourpence was paid on every chaldron for wharfage and carriage charges.

The next year, 1665, was a repetition of the previous year. Precisely the same quantities of different kinds of coal were bought for the two houses and exactly the same prices were given. This was far from being the case the year after.

The troubles of the coal trade in 1666 are well reflected in the accounts of the Woburn steward. The Dutch War, with the Dutch fleet endeavouring to intercept the coal vessels which sailed from Newcastle, had given the Hostmen of Newcastle, who now were colliery owners as well as middlemen, an opportunity of which they had not been slow to take advantage, first to raise prices and then, when legislation was attempted to deal with this, to suspend operations in the mines. Whereas two years previously the steward had only had to pay seventeen shillings and sixpence a chaldron at St. Neots, he now had to give throughout the year a number of different prices which began at nineteen shillings and ended with twenty-eight shillings and ninepence a chaldron. The loading money remained at twopence a chaldron and he continued to pay another ten shillings for every chaldron that was conveyed to Woburn.

The steward laid in no Scotch coal at all in this difficult year, either because it was not to be easily obtained, or because he, or his master for him, did not choose to give the price—at one time nearly six pounds a ton—to which it had risen at the Port of London. But he was bound to buy some of the usual sea coal for use at Bedford House—that which he bought at St. Neots went, of course, to Woburn—and for this he had to give two different prices on the river bank which averaged two-thirds as much again as he had given in the previous year. He got forty-two chaldrons at thirty shillings and eightpence a chaldron; for another ten later on he had to pay thirty-three shillings and fivepence. It cost him £7 18s. 6d. for the loading and wharfage charges, and for the men who brought the coal to Bedford House.

The next year, with the troubles somewhat abated, the price of Scotch coal at the Port of London had gone back to twenty-four shillings a ton and because of this, or because he had been woefully short in the preceding year in the quantity he had laid in, the steward ventured upon as much as twenty tons. Sea coal, however, with the troubles in the neighbourhood of Newcastle not yet completely settled, remained at a very high price. He bought none this year at less than thirty-four shillings and sixpence a ton and on one occasion at least had to give thirty-six shillings and threepence, double the normal price of two years previously.

After 1667 there is a hiatus in the accounts, except for isolated bills. When the complete books begin again, in 1684, the days of Scotch coal at twenty-four shillings a ton have vanished. In that year the steward had to give the two prices of thirty shillings and thirty-five shillings. In 1685 the price was thirty-three shillings and thereafter fluctuated round about thirty-one to thirty-two shillings until 1691, the last year of the accounts, when the steward actually succeeded in buying five tons at twenty-six shillings, but as against that had to give thirty-four shillings for another five.

The steward kept his prices for Scotch coal very fairly exact. It was a pity he did not do the same in the case of the sea coal. After 1667 he abandoned his former excellent habit of detailing the price per chaldron, whether at St. Neots or at Thames-side, and merely made a fine, broad statement to the effect that he had laid in so much sea coal at St. Neots for Woburn, so much at the Port of London for Bedford House 'at several prices,' together with expenses for wharfage, porterage, placing the coal in the cellar and including, he would often go on, the carriage of some salt and some deal boards 'with loading money for all from St. Neots to Woburn.' By setting down a round sum for the whole here he successfully prevented any attempt being made to disentangle what he had actually given, out of all these items, for a chaldron of this coal and even more successfully hid what was being spent on coal in general by the Earl for the whole year.

That the coal bills went up steadily there can be no doubt; nor was this entirely due to rising prices. As in every other department of the household, the use of coal was more lavish in the last thirty years of the Earl's life than it had been previously.

All this time much charcoal was also bought and used, as a rule anything between two hundred and two hundred and sixty sacks, although sometimes the number sank a little below this. The prices throughout the forty years fluctuated between one and eightpence and one and tenpence. In 1666, the troubled year, the price remained, as it had previously been, at one and eightpence a sack.

The final provision for heating was wood, 'besides,' as the steward wrote, 'his lordship's own provisions of fuel arising of windfalls and otherwise brought out of the park at Woburn this year not valued.' No other wood than windfalls came from the estates—the trees had to be carefully preserved; apart from anything else, seasoned wood might at any time be wanted for the needs of the Navy. Therefore, any wood other than windfalls for use for the fires and ovens at Woburn Abbey had to be bought and was bought in great quantities.

These purchases comprised faggots and billets. Anything round about thirty thousand billets—the number varied between twenty-six thousand and thirty-two thousand—and thirty loads of faggots were used every year. They added considerably to the expense of fuel for the house. In 1666 twenty-six thousand billets at eighteen shillings a thousand cost the Earl £23 8s. 0d. in all. At the same time, twenty-seven loads of faggots cost fourteen pounds. Twenty-two years later billets cost thirty-one pounds and faggots just under eighteen pounds.

After the heating, the lighting. Candles appeared in due course in the grocer's bills and were a tolerably heavy expense. Oil cost less. A certain amount was extracted at Woburn from the colza seed sent over from Thorney. The remainder came from an oilman, always the same man called Daniel Doddridge, although the place where he dwelt is not mentioned. His bill seldom came to more than six or seven pounds in the year.

Finally the steward, who supplemented what the clerk provided for the household to eat, was himself responsible for what they drank.

Every appurtenance for the brewing of beer was naturally kept at Woburn and there is frequent mention in the bills of the arrival of vats, coppers and so forth for brewing purposes. Malt was bought by the steward. But the hops came mainly from the Earl's own estate. This was something that Woburn Park could and did produce, and the picking and drying of the hops always offered several days' casual employment to men and women, chiefly the latter.

The women who were thus employed were always set down in the bills as widows, goodwives or merely by their names, in which latter case they were presumably spinsters. Most of them were undoubtedly either tenants of the Earl, or the wives or daughters of tenants. The flat rate for their labour was fivepence a day.

The amount of beer brewed at the abbey by no means sufficed every year for the needs of the household. A considerable quantity had to be bought outside. Between July 1675 and March of the following year Thomas Cross, the brewer, supplied a hundred and thirty-four barrels of ale and beer—the two, as was usual, were distinguished from one another—at a cost of £52 9s. 6d. Between March and June 1681, the same brewer sent to Woburn seventy-seven barrels, for which the charge was £27 13s. 0d.

Such bills were numerous for the last thirty years of the Earl's lifetime. With them went another set. The lord and lady of the house did not as a rule, if ever, drink the home-brewed product, nor yet that supplied by Mr. Cross, the brewer. The steward bought beer and ale for them both and for some at least of the sons and daughters of the house quite separately, endorsing these accounts 'Beer for my lady's drinking' or 'Ale for my lord.'

Mr. Jenkinson the brewer's bill for ale for my lady.

	£	s.	d.
1675.—3 firkins of small ale.		9	11¼
2 firkins of strong ale.		8	7½

Mr. John Cross, the ale brewer's bill, to bottle for my lord's drinking.

	£	s.	d.
1676.—10½ barrels of ale.	£5	1	1½

This ale or beer supplied for the family was regarded as the special property of the individual for whom it was bought. When the household broke up on the death of the Earl—then Duke of Bedford—in 1700, some members of the family at least, in removing their possessions from the abbey, took their own special casks of beer with them also.

What applied to the beer applied also to the cider. A great deal was made at Woburn; some was bought. The apples for the making thereof were frequently brought over from Thorney. Occasionally, especially during the later years, they came from the orchards at Woburn. Very often a quantity was purchased.

	£	s.	d.
October 1670. For 91 bushels of apples at 1s. 8d. per bushel.	7	11	8
For 13 bushels of the same apples at 2s. 0d.	1	6	0
To five men for beating and pressing.		16	0
To six women for picking the apples.		6	11
For carriage.		3	6
	£10	4	1

The other cider which was bought came always from the same man, called Walker, who sold cider both by the hogshead and by the bottle. In 1682 Mr. Bingley, the steward, paid him five pounds for a hogshead. This was the usual charge. In 1693 some was ordered for Bedford House and this was delivered in bottles.

Cider for Bedford House.

	£	s.	d.
June 1693. Six dozen and seven bottles of cider at 6s. 0d. the dozen.	1	16	6
For straw 6d.			6
To the watermen and porters.		4	0
	£2	1	0

The clerk of the kitchen had nothing to do with all this, except that he was required to note down in his book how much beer, ale and cider had been consumed in the household each week and how much remained.

The filling of the wine-cellar was another and much more serious matter. There is every reason to believe that the clerk was never allowed to meddle with that at all, not even to mention what wines had been served. Here the steward reigned supreme.

CHAPTER X

THE WINE-CELLAR

'A NOBLE wine-cellar indeed, worthy of a great nobleman!' was the exclamation of a great modern authority on the history of wine when he read the list of wines brought to Woburn from the Restoration onwards. Nothing would have been more gratifying to William, Earl of Bedford, could he have heard this encomium.

Good fortune attended the Earl in the matter of his wine-cellar as elsewhere. He had the felicity and privilege during his lifetime of learning to know two great wines, novelties in the seventeenth century, which, within a very short time, were to rank highly in the estimation of English gentlemen. The one was champagne; the other was port.

Neither of these two wines, the elegant champagne or the majestic port, figure of course in the early and pre-Restoration accounts. They were reserved for the days when the King had come into his own again. Champagne and the Restoration were not unfitly closely connected.

Not that there was any lack of variety in the staple wines served at Woburn, as elsewhere, in the younger days of the Earl. Spain and the Canaries supplied the drinks known as sack, sherry, Malaga or Canary.

Hear me as if thy ears had palate, Jack,
I sing the praise of sack.

*

Sack will the soul of poetry infuse,
Be that my theme and muse.

183

But, even though it was still pre-eminently the theme of drinking songs, sack had many rivals, particularly on the tables of the gentry. Wines came to England, as they had long come, from Bordeaux and from Burgundy. Others were imported by way of Holland from the Rhine valley. Florence and even the Levant and the Greek islands were drawn upon for the luscious Malmsey.

Unfortunately, the Woburn wine bills for the greater part of the period of the Commonwealth are scanty and few and far between. The earliest belongs to July 1653. Then a puncheon of 'claret wine' travelled to Woburn by carrier's wagon. With it came twelve dozen stone bottles packed in a great flasket, or bottle case.

A gross of corks, costing four shillings, was ordered to come with the bottles. The use of the cork to stopper the bottle in place of the piece of oiled hemp formerly employed had been known in England for some time, perhaps as far back as the end of the previous century, and was now beginning to be fairly common. The corks, however, were conical corks, only placed loosely in the bottles, which continued for the time being to be made in the bulbous standing-up shape common in earlier days. The wine drawn into them from the barrels was, therefore, still perforce drunk as new wine. The excellence of matured wine was not and could not be recognized until the arrival of the cylindrical bottle that could be laid on its side, with a cork driven right in flush with the neck.

Whence the claret of 1653 was procured the bill does not say. The puncheon might have had many adventures before it was placed in a carrier's cart to be brought to Woburn, for the purchase of wine in the seventeenth century was by no means a uniform matter.

Wine could be bought from a regular wine merchant. It might, on the other hand, be procured at a port, usually the Port of London, direct from one of the merchant adventurers, whose ships often traded in other commodities as well as wines. Sometimes it was purchased abroad, often in Paris. In this case it not infrequently happened that the purchaser ordered a great deal more than was sufficient for his own needs. He then disposed of the remainder to his friends. This might be and often was an act of pure kindness undertaken for convenience' sake. There was no need for half a dozen people to have the trouble and nuisance of getting wine across the Channel when one of the number was willing to undertake the business for them all. The purchaser did not look to make a profit and only his servants benefited, since they received a handsome gratuity when the wine was distributed to the various houses. On the other hand, many impoverished gentlemen carried on a regular trade of the kind, looking for and receiving a commission for their services.

But in all the different ways whereby wine might reach a gentleman's cellar, much depended upon the import laws in force at that particular moment. Trade rivalry sometimes led to the enforcement of a limitation in the amount of wine that might be brought into the country, or to a total prohibition of wine from certain districts. High customs duties, very necessary in the eyes of the government at a time when customs and excise were so important a part of the revenue, meant further regulations. Both kinds of legislation called forth earnest and on the whole successful attempts to circumvent them.

One way of getting over the difficulty of importing any wine concerning which a regulation had been made was strictly legitimate and was itself a source of revenue. Licences were issued, at a price, whereby the licensee could not only import wine for his own use, but also extra quantities to dispose of to his friends.

Other methods were more questionable. The import regulations were in the nature of an open invitation to wine pirates or smugglers to do their best, and a very good best it sometimes was. In the case of a naval war the activities of these gentlemen were redoubled.

There must have been more wine ordered for Woburn in 1653 than the puncheon of claret, which is merely recorded in a single bill. But it is perhaps not without significance that in November the clerk of the kitchen was reduced, to his own great annoyance, to sending out to buy a pint of white wine, which cost eightpence, and another of sack at a shilling, which he needed for kitchen purposes and which he ought to have been able to obtain easily from the steward. The fact was that these were difficult and disheartening days for wine merchants in England, as for all drinkers of wine. The Navigation Act of 1651, aimed at the maritime supremacy of the Dutch, had effectively killed the trade in Rhenish and had considerably damaged that in French wines. Both kinds of wine, but that from the Rhineland in particular, had been mainly imported in vessels of Dutch nationality. When, as a result of the Act, the Dutch war broke out, it was difficult to import wine in any vessel of any nationality. A great deal of such wine as did get into England at this time was, in fact, pirated wine. During the war it became a peculiarly meritorious action for wine pirates to seize unwary vessels and empty them of their wine barrels.

Did the Earl of Bedford buy any of the wine which had entered England in this manner, he might have reflected that he was acting in accordance with family tradition. His ancestors had been merchant squires of Dorset. In the fourteenth century the ships of Stephen and Henry Russell had carried wine between Bordeaux and England. They could have told their descendant exactly the sort of dangers that a wine-carrying vessel ran from pirates and could, if necessary, have supplied him with many a useful hint not only how to evade them, but how one might oneself best seize a wine vessel of another country. Stephen Russell, in particular, in common with many another west country noble and squire, had been a past master in the gentle art of replenishing his own wine supplies out of an enemy vessel.

The conclusion of peace with the Dutch in 1654, shortly after Cromwell had taken the title of Protector, encouraged the wine merchants to hope that their trade was about to revive. But their optimism was somewhat damped a little later on by Parliament taking the opportunity of increased drinking of wine to put on increased customs duties, and within the next year or two making matters worse, at all events according to the view of the wine trade, by fixing maximum prices at which wine should be retailed.

No other bills prior to the year 1658, save the solitary one for claret, remain to show how the wine-cellar at Woburn fared under these conditions. But with 1658 the history of the cellar really makes a commencement. In that year the steward was able to purchase a very fair amount of wine of different sorts. In the first place, he bought eight dozen bottles of Rhenish wine, which cost one pound a dozen, and sixty-five gallons of Canary at eight shillings a gallon. The last were bought from the wine merchant, Mr. John Do. He also laid in a supply of wine from France, which he procured from the well-known merchant adventurer of London, Mr. James Houblon. The latter's fleet of ships brought many goods up the Thames, but always included among them were barrels of wine. Houblon now sold the Woburn steward first a puncheon of Burgundy and then a puncheon of what was written down on the bill as 'Paris' wine. Possibly this was wine made from the grapes from one of the vineyards then flourishing on the slopes of Montmartre or Mont Valérien, wine which later generations cannot hope to taste. It may, however, have been another cask of Burgundy or even wine from Orleans sent to Paris by river and sold in that city.

February 1657/8.—Received the 19th of
February of the right honourable the Earl of
Bedford, by the hands of Mr. William Baker,
the sum of sixteen pounds for one puncheon of
Burgundy wine and five shillings for a double
cask. JAMES HOUBLON. £16 5 0

April 1658.—Received the 1st April 1658,
of Mr. William Baker, the sum of fourteen
pounds, being for one puncheon of Paris wine
sold to his excellency of Bedford. I say,
JAMES HOUBLON. £14 0 0

The merchant signed himself James Houblon. Mr. Pepys
and also the steward of the Earl of Bedford, when he made
up his accounts, indifferently referred to him either by that
name or as Hubland.

This James Houblon, with his two brothers John and
Peter, represented, as did many other merchants in the
city at the time, a family who had fled to England from
religious persecution on the Continent. The grandfather,
Pierre Houblon, was a Fleming who had arrived in England
when the Duke of Alva was attempting the destruction of
Protestantism in Flanders. His son, called by his fellow
merchants *Pater Bursae Londinensis*, had become English in
all but name. In 1658, the grandsons were rapidly rising to
eminence. They, too, were highly esteemed, especially for
their financial acumen, by their fellow citizens of London.
Nearly forty years later, in 1694, James Houblon and his
brother Peter were made directors of the newly founded
Bank of England. A higher office was reserved for their
younger and even more brilliant brother, John. He became
the first governor of that institution.

Both Evelyn and Pepys highly appreciated the entertainment given to their friends by the Houblon brothers. At no
table was one likely to get a better supper than at one which
they had spread for their friends and furnished with rare

wines brought from France and elsewhere. 'A splendid entertainment' was the verdict of John Evelyn the night he supped with Mr. James Houblon at the house 'furnished *en prince*' in Winchester Street in the city.

At Woburn in this year of 1658, when wine was coming over in Houblon's merchant ships, something new occurred in the bills. For the first time, twelve dozen bottles were ordered which were specifically said to be of glass.

April 1658.—Received of Mr. Thomas
Cross in full for twelve dozen of glass bottles,
the sum of two pounds fourteen shillings.
Received per me, THOMAS HARTLY.   £2 14 0

After this, glass bottles generally appear in the accounts alongside the older variety of stone.

Whatever other wine the steward succeeded in getting, the cellar at Woburn must yet have been restricted, as so many cellars were, during the time of the Commonwealth. No wonder that the poet Cowley expressed his feelings upon the Restoration and return of His Majesty with the ecstatic exclamation, 'With wine all rooms, with wine the conduits flow!' The vision was only partly realized. To drink wine was, in the eyes of perhaps the majority of the population, a good and laudable thing. The disagreeable feature was the high price asked, since Parliament, seeking a source for increased revenue, speedily seized upon the customs duties on wine. On top of this, in different years came a series of regulations aimed at keeping sometimes the wine of France and sometimes that of Spain out of the country.

One consequence was that licences to import wine were eagerly sought after. In the year of the Restoration a wine licence was held by the Countess of Bristol, who had been Lady Anne Russell, sister of the Earl. Her brother took advantage of the fact to buy a quantity of wine through her both in this year and the next.

October 1660.—Received this 5th October 1660, of Mr. George Collop, by the hands of John Dawson, the sum of three score pounds to be transmitted into France for wine for the use of the Earl of Bedford. I say received, ANNE BRISTOL. £60 o o

August 1661.—Received this 20th August 1661, of Mr. George Collop, by the hands of John Dawson, thirty pounds for a tun of wine, to be sent for, for the use of my brother Bedford. I say received, ANNE BRISTOL. £30 o o

Having secured this wine, the Earl's steward resold part of it to relations and friends of his lord, including the Countess of Carlisle and the Earl of Salisbury.

In 1662 the Earl of Bedford had a wine licence himself.

1662.—To the Lord Treasurer's servant, his fee for a licence for the import of wine. £1 4 0

Matters did not get easier, nor wine less expensive, as time went on. Rather the contrary. Nevertheless, the stewards in many families could point with much greater pride to their cellars than hitherto and the steward at Woburn was no exception to the rule. His account for wines put into the cellar for the year 1664, the first complete account that exists, is very different from any mere mention of an odd puncheon of claret or another of Burgundy.

In that year of 1664 he was allowed to spend over a hundred and twenty pounds on stocking the cellar and he must have got a good deal of satisfaction out of it. Ten pounds went on claret, one tierce or barrel for five pounds and thirty-nine gallons more which cost another five pounds. Rhenish wines came to only four pounds. But the steward's best efforts were reserved for the Canary wine, of which he bought 157 gallons. This cost him, it is true, less per gallon than it had done six years previously, for the highest price he paid was seven shillings a gallon and some cost only six shillings. Nevertheless, in all he spent fifty pounds in this way. Next he added two dozen bottles of Greek wine, the white variety, which came not from Greece, but from Syracuse and cost three pounds.

The amount the steward spent on wine would alone have made 1664 a notable year for the cellar. It was rendered far more so by the two final purchases, both products of the French vineyards. Sixty-two bottles—it came in bottles, not in a cask—of white wine were added to the cellar which the steward wrote down as 'Shably' wine, the first time this name, as far as Monsieur André Simon, the wine authority of to-day, has any knowledge, appears in a wine account book. The sixty-two bottles cost no more than £4 12s. 6d.

Lastly, the steward gave an order, not to a wine merchant but to some unknown person in France, for three of the pièces, or French casks, of Sillery, or still champagne, which was just beginning to appear in England.

1664. Sillery wine, 3 pièces bought in France at £12. 8s. 4d. the pièce.   £37 5s. 0d.
And for custom, freight and charges in England.   £7 1s. 0d.

£44 6s. 6d.

The bottles into which the wine was poured from the casks this year might still be of stone. A number of stone bottles were certainly ordered and twelve gross of corks. There is no mention, as it happens, at all of glass bottles. Nevertheless, something new in glass was acquired.

The Earl of Bedford had already had some Venice glass upon his table. This had been bought in London four years earlier from the firm of John Greene at the King's Arms in The Poultry, who imported it. Now, fifteen dozen wine-glasses of various kinds and five dozen glasses especially for claret were ordered in Venice from the famous firm of Aloisio Morelli. They came to London in the ship *Supply*, whose commander was Captain Haddock, and, being landed on Thames-side at Ivy Bridge, were carried across the Strand to Bedford House, whence they were despatched to Woburn.

The purchase of the Sillery wine and the arrival of the wineglasses in 1664 were pleasant preliminaries to the great purchase of 1665.

In that year the usual supplies of claret and Burgundy were laid in, with some Rhenish wine and a quantity of the drier variety of sherry or Canary called sack. Then for the first time in the accounts came the entry:

1665.—'Shampaigne' wine. £1 14s. 8d.

This was three years before the date on which the cele-brated Dom Pérignon received his appointment as cellarer of the Benedictine abbey of Hautvillers. Unfortunately, as Monsieur André Simon has pointed out, the story that this worthy priest was the man who learnt how to 'put the bubble in the wine' is not substantiated by the facts. Dom Pérignon neither discovered, nor invented, nor created sparkling champagne. Far less was he, as he has sometimes been claimed to be, the first to use corks. What he did was to introduce them to the somewhat belated notice of the monks at Hautvillers, who up to now were still using the wads of oiled hemp. This seems as if it were to wreck the dom's reputation. It is not so. His claim to fame rests on the solid basis of having shown his fellow monks how to im-

prove the growth of their vines and to make the best use of
their vineyards and of having also introduced the blending
of wines from different growths, with the consequent result
of bringing prosperity to the champagne trade.

In the meantime England had not waited for the quality
of the wine produced at Hautvillers to be improved by Dom
Pérignon before adopting with enthusiasm the new drink.
Not for the first time, an exile from France had brought
something new and delightful into the land which received
him. Saint-Evremond, soldier, philosopher and courtier,
having come under the displeasure of the French King, had
crossed to England in 1661. The exile soon found himself
the centre of that part of society which delighted in good
eating and drinking no less than in wit and gallantry.
Saint-Evremond introduced them to some champagne and
they took to the novelty very kindly.

Here, however, arose a difficulty. The wine merchants
showed a distinct disinclination to stock champagne. This
was partly on account of the heavy duty that was immediately
put upon the import, but partly also because they viewed
with alarm the growing taste for it and thought it would
supersede the other wines, of which they already had a large
stock and which they did not wish to have left upon their
hands. Those, therefore, who wanted the new wine on their
tables—and they were many—fell back on the plan of
obtaining it through the kind offices of friends in France, or
through one of the ambassadors. The latter method, when
it could be employed, was the more popular of the two since
thereby the heavy customs duties were avoided.

The steward, William Baker, does not say whence he
obtained the first champagne that he bought for the Earl's
cellar in 1665. His later accounts show very plainly that
the Earl of Bedford did what everyone else did—commissioned friends in France to buy him a good quantity and
then distributed his surplus among his friends.

It is not surprising to find that Lord Crofts, who had bought the French coach for the Earl of Bedford in 1660, was active in the wine trade also, for he was a regular *entrepreneur* between his French and English friends. The champagne in which he was interested was mainly the Sillery, for he was on terms of the closest acquaintance with the Marquis de Sillery and was, not unnaturally, anxious to dispose of the products of his friend's vineyards for him to good advantage whenever it was possible. It may have been he who had introduced the wine to the Earl of Bedford in 1664. He certainly bought Sillery for the Earl in 1668 and in several subsequent years.

Champagne, when it did appear at Woburn, was evidently appreciated. Hereafter there were few years indeed in which it did not appear regularly in the accounts. Sometimes it was bought by the hogshead. One such, in June 1669, cost thirteen pounds. Two hogsheads bought the following February were fifteen pounds apiece. On the other hand, the wine sometimes came already bottled. In February 1676, four dozen bottles cost six pounds.

The merchants and others who sold wine to the Earl of Bedford need not, however, have been alarmed lest the new should oust the old. The case was very much the contrary. The old favourites, Bordeaux and Burgundy, Rhenish wine and all the varieties of sherry sack, not only continued to appear every year, but, as the Earl's household increased in number, were purchased in far greater quantities as time went on.

In 1671 the Earl of Ailesbury bought two hogsheads of wine at the port of Bordeaux for his fellow Earl.

My lord Ailesbury's bill for 2 hogsheads of wine.
Paid March 23rd, 1671/2, £15. 2s. 0d. and 5s. 0d. to the butler.

	£	s.	d.
1671/2.—2 hogsheads of wine for the right honourable the Earl of Bedford.			
The wine at Bordeaux.	4	0	10
Customs at London.	7	9	2
Freight, primage and average.		19	0
Cooperage, bill money, prisage, waiters, wharfage and cranage.		7	0
For porterage and cartage.		7	0
For 10 gallons of wine to fill up the 2 hogsheads.	2	0	0
	£15	3	0

Small wonder that, in view of the much greater quantities bought and with the addition of champagne, the bills for the wine at Woburn rose steadily year after year. Every few years, too, something new would be brought into the cellar, not perhaps such a great novelty as the champagne, but still offering variety to a connoisseur of wine. In 1670 a hogshead of what the steward called 'Lybos' wine was bought for ten pounds. This probably refers to a sweet dessert wine more generally known as Lesbos. Another hogshead of this was bought the following year for twelve pounds.

In that same year of 1671 a new variety of wine came again from France. The steward bought a puncheon of Navarre wine, which cost eighteen pounds. Navarre wine was the heavy Jurançon wine drunk on both sides of the Pyrenees, which Antoine de Navarre, father of Henri de Navarre, Henry IV of France, had insisted on pouring down the throat of his infant son when he was only a couple of hours old, to which the Navarrois attributed his success in more directions than one in later life. This was not quite a novelty in England, for already three years earlier the Duke of York had told Pepys that he had a new kind of wine called Navarre that he wished the diarist to taste. Pepys admitted that the wine was well enough, but added that he himself was much more interested in a new sauce which the Duke had given him to taste at the same time. The Navarre wine was, nevertheless, appreciated at Woburn, for it was bought on several subsequent occasions.

Five years after this, in 1676, some wine was bought through the Earl of St. Albans which was called in the bill 'Provence claret.'

To my lord St. Albans for Provence wine. £6 7s. 6d.
To the butler. ——————— 5s. 0d.

April 1676.—Received then of the right honourable the Earl of Bedford, by the hands of Mr. Bingley, six pounds seven shillings and six pence for one quarter part of a pièce of Provence claret. I say re-ceived, DE CHAIR. £6 7s. 6d.

This red Provence wine may, said Monsieur André Simon cautiously on surveying the list, have been a Rhone wine, perhaps even Châteauneuf du Pape. The price gives encouragement to this view. It is, however, as he admitted, just possible that it may merely have been the far more ordinary Cassis wine from the sea coast.

Whatever the nature of this wine, it found sufficient favour for the Earl to take some more of it from Lord Bristol. This he bought from his brother-in-law already bottled—four dozen bottles at £3 2s. 0d.

For 4 dozen bottles of wine from my lord Bristol's.

May 1676.—Received then from the right honourable the Earl of Bedford the sum of three pounds two shillings, being for four dozen of Provence wine. I say re-ceived by me, GEORGE CURTIS. £3 2s. 0d.

The considerable sums of money spent every year since 1660 by the steward on replenishing his lord's wine-cellar led up to the great year of 1684, during which he paid out £254 in all for wine. This was the top figure for the Earl's lifetime, although two subsequent years, 1688, when the total only dropped a pound below the record year, and 1691, when the figure was £236, ran it very close.

By far the greater part of the £254 in 1684 went on the ordinary wines, which were bought in great quantities. Ten pounds, however, were again reserved for something in the nature of a new purchase. In this year, for the first time as far as can be seen, the name of port appeared in the accounts of the Earl of Bedford. There were two hogsheads of it; they cost five pounds apiece and they were bought through Mr. James Houblon.

March 1684.—To Mr. Houblon for two hogsheads of port wine. £10 0 0

Here was another great success. The Earl and his family had taken kindly to most new wines introduced and port was no exception to the rule. It would be pleasant, but not veracious, to add that its introduction coincided with the arrival of the Earl's attacks of gout and the necessity for his visits to Tunbridge Wells to drink the waters. Unfortunately, the gout and the drinking of the waters considerably preceded in date the tasting of the new drink.

Port may in general have been responsible for an increase of the gout, but that was no deterrent to drinking it. Presently it began to form a considerable item in the wine bills and from 1691 onwards the white variety was added to the red.

There is no further mention of getting wine through Mr. Houblon and in the nineties port for Woburn was, as a matter of fact, nearly always bought from a wine merchant called Chaplin.

Chaplin sold other wines than port. It is not without significance in the history of the wine trade that from this time onwards, that is from the beginning of the nineties, the Earl of Bedford's steward bought his wine more frequently from wine merchants and less frequently through friends of the Earl than hitherto. Also, previously, each wine had usually been bought from one particular salesman. Now a merchant such as Chaplin was selling all kinds of wine. In the month of April 1693, the Woburn steward had an account with him for over seventy-five pounds.

The right honourable the Earl of Bedford.
Debt to Joseph Chaplin.

		£	s.	d.
March 28, 1693.	For 2 quart of Canary for tastes at 7s. 0d. the gallon.		3	6
April 1.	For a hogshead of red port wine.	15	0	0
	For a hogshead of white port wine.	15	0	0
	For 68 gallons of Canary at 7s. 0d. the gallon.	23	16	0
	For a hogshead for the Canary.		10	0
	For 7½ gallons of Canary in bottles at 7s. 0d. gallon.	2	12	6
April 4.	For 34½ gallons of white port at 5s. 0d. gallon.	8	12	6
	For the half hogshead.		5	0
	Paid the carman to Bedford House.		2	6
	For 4 gallons of red port at 5s. 0d. the gallon.	1	0	0
	For 2 quart of Canary for tastes at 7s. 0d. gallon.		3	6
	For corks.			4

		£	s.	d.
April 19.	For 30 gallons one quart of red port at 5s. 0d. gallon.	7	11	3
	For the half hogshead.		5	0
	Paid the porter to Bedford House with the half hogshead.		2	6
	For one quart of sherry and one quart of Palm for tastes and 2 quart bottles.		4	0
		£75	8	7

But in spite of the growing intrusion of wine merchants, Lady Bristol, now an old lady approaching her eightieth year, had, three years earlier, again been active on her brother's behalf and in the year 1691 had sold him, for £5 8s. 0d., six dozen bottles of red port. Servants at least must have regretted the gradual dying out of this custom, for to bring over the bottles meant always a handsome gratuity.

Bill for port wine, with 10s. 0d. *which is my lord's gift to Lady Bristol's servant.*

	£	s.	d.
1691.—To the right honourable the Earl of Bedford.			
Paid for 6 dozen of red port at 1s. 6d. per quart.	5	8	0
For 5 dozen of quart bottles.		12	6
For 2 dozen of pints.		4	0
For the taste.			11
Paid porterage.		3	0
For corks.		1	0
Paid waiterage.			6
	£6	9	11

Port was the last, and some would say the greatest, of the new wines which the Earl tasted in his lifetime. The wine bills during the late eighties and the nineties show the noble wine making more and more frequent appearance in the cellar and later on, no doubt, upon the table.

Brandy is said to have been made in France as early as 1533, but it took some time to penetrate into England. Whether or no there were drunk at Woburn any of the home-made fiery spirits distilled from various sources which were extremely popular in England in the seventeenth century does not appear. Brandy from France certainly only came late into the bills, the first time in 1680.

John Newman's bill.

		£	s.	d.
March 1680.	A bottle of oil for Chelcroft.		1	6
	A bottle of brandy.		1	0
	The three horses coming up to London, charges at St. Albans and diet.		8	3
			10	9

Newman's bill, it should be noticed, includes oil as well as brandy. When six years later more brandy was bought, it came from the oilman, Daniel Doddridge, who had long supplied oil to the abbey.

The oilman's bill for brandy and oil.

Bought of Daniel Doddridge.

		£	s.	d.
June 1686.	For one runlet of best brandy containing 3 gallons and a pint at 3s. 8d. per gallon.		11	5½
	For 6 quarts less ½ pint Genoa oil at 1s. 4d. per quart.		7	8
			19	1½

THE WINE-CELLAR

The Earl was not deterred by the rising prices, which were the result of ever-increasing customs duties, from continuing to buy the spirit. In 1690 the price was four shillings and sixpence a gallon against the previous three shillings and eightpence. Two years later it had gone up to ten shillings and in 1693 the Earl's steward had to pay twelve shillings, although at the same time he procured an inferior kind of brandy for eight shillings.

CHAPTER XI

THE STABLES AND TRAVEL

MASTER ANTHONY SENHOUSE, gentleman, who rode in the coronation procession behind his master, was the first gentleman of the horse to be mentioned in the accounts. He remained at Woburn between 1660 and 1668 and then was promoted to be agent to the Earl for the estate of Thornhaugh.

His salary as gentleman of the horse was only twenty pounds a year, but he was provided with rooms; was given board and all his clothes.

Senhouse was succeeded in 1668 by William Bankes, gentleman, at the same salary.

On the whole, the gentleman of the horse changed more often than any of the other officials of the Earl, perhaps because it was a post from which promotion might be expected. Anthony Senhouse's successor only remained a few years and then was succeeded by Thomas Gregory, who, in his turn, quitted the stables for the household in 1689 in order to take the place of Dixy Taylor on his retirement.

Gregory, unlike his two predecessors, was a married man with a family and was given by the Earl for his residence a good house on the estate known as Whitnoe Grange, where he lived with his wife and sons, one of whom became a doctor.

As in 1641, so to the end of the Earl's life the arrangements for transport were divided between the land and the water. But the gentleman of the horse had nothing to do with the barge on the Thames. That remained in the charge of the steward of the household, who saw to its regilding and general repair. He also provided the liveries for the bargemen, made of broadcloth lined with orange baize to correspond with the gowns of the porters at Woburn Abbey and Bedford House. Besides using this barge when he was in London, the Earl continued on occasion to have a boat hired in which he would proceed to Westminster or elsewhere. But after 1660 this occurred much less frequently than it had done earlier. In any case, it was the business of the steward of the household to make the arrangements.

The gentleman of the horse was required to devote himself to the stables, the kennels and the mews, for the upkeep of which, and for certain other expenses, he received each month imprest money from the receiver-general.

Neither Anthony Senhouse nor his successors had any occasion to complain of niggardliness on their master's part for, after 1660, their department was kept up on an extremely liberal scale.

During the last forty years of the Earl's life the sum received by the gentleman of the horse for the general expenses was never less than one thousand pounds in a year and it was an exception when it sank as low as this; in most years it was half as much again or more. In 1661, the great year of the coronation, it was £1,708. In 1663 it was £1,300. Twenty-one years later, in 1684, it was £1,260. That is to say, after the return of the King and the blossoming forth of the Earl's household, the money spent upon the stables was never less than five times as much as it had been during the first year of the succession. Every year now, in fact, it was a considerable slice out of the Earl's income.

The money, however, covered a good deal. It provided for the upkeep of stables, mews and kennels, including everything new that was bought, whether horse, hawk or dog, coach or chair. Nearly all the provisions, too, in the shape of straw and foodstuffs had to be purchased, for the estate did not supply them or only in very small quantities. Liveries and all clothes provided for the men were also reckoned in with the stables money. So, too, were the greater part of the travelling expenses for the household. But in the matter of wages the gentleman of the horse had no responsibility, except for the men who were brought in to do odd jobs for an hour or so, or were engaged on the road for that purpose. The wage bill proper was the business of the steward of the household.

Throughout the whole period the gentleman of the horse had under him for stable work fourteen or fifteen men. These included the footmen, who divided their time between stables and house, as well as the coachman, or men, and the postillions. Besides these, a number of underlings were employed, nearly all of them casual helpers engaged by the day or by the hour.

The bills for the clothes that the gentleman of the horse had to provide for his men were always fairly high. Besides the regular liveries, all the men and boys were given, either of custom or by grace, a certain number of boots, shoes, shirts and so forth every year. The liveries, including the frieze capes for protection against cold and rain, came from a tailor. But the housekeeper, or one of the women servants, often made up the cravats, when these were worn, and some of the shirts.

1669.—Paid for necessaries for the page, viz.: for a cloak lined with serge—£1. 13s. 0d.; a pair of boots, several pairs of shoes and buckles—£2. 15s. 3d.; gloves—8s. 6d.; 2 cravats—3s. 0d.; a large comb and 32 yards of ribbon—12s. 0d.; and to Mistress Abigail in full of her bill for shirts for him and a footman—£1. 6s. 3d. In all, with 9s. 0d. to Mr. Taylor for a cap for him and 13s. 6d. paid for making his winter suit and coat.   £8   0s.   6d.

For 9 frieze coats at 15s. 0d. each for 4 footmen, the coachman, postillion and 3 grooms—£6. 15s. 0d.; a coat for Francis, the footman—£1. 0s. 4d.; and for 2 cloaks for his lordship's own footman—£3. 6s. 0d. In all, with £1. 3s. 6d. for a frock, a hat and 2 pair of stockings for the new footman.   £12   4s.   10d.

1671.—Paid for sundry necessaries, viz.: for his lordship's page for his coat, a pair of leather stockings, for gloves, boots, shoes, hats, combs, for 4 half-shirts and 3 laced and 3 plain cravats, with £1. 10s. 0d. given him at twice by his lordship's order—£9. 15s. 6d.; for 3 pair of shoes for her ladyship's page and mending others—10s. 6d.; for 3 frieze coats for 3 grooms, 2 for the coachman and postillion, and 5 coats for 5 footmen at 15s. 0d. each—£7. 10s. 0d.; for 4 falconers' hats lined with orange shalloon and bound about with orange galloon at 10s. 0d. each hat, with 11s. 0d. for a piece of ribbon for the falconers' clothes—£2. 11s. 0d.; for 2 shirts for Frank, the footboy, and for a pair of gloves for him—12s. 0d.; and for a frock and trousers for the postillion—12s. 0d. In all   £21   11s.   0d.

Every year there was much doing with the horses. Sometimes a horse would be bought from or sold to a dealer, but it was pre-eminently with his friends and neighbours that the Earl kept up a brisk interchange of animals, buying, selling and exchanging.

1661.—Given back to the Duke of Buckingham's servants of the £95. 0s. 0d. received for the 3 coach horses.   £3   12s.   0d.

1671.—Paid for several horses bought this year for the service of the said Earl, viz.: for a coach horse bought of Sir . . . Stroud, with 17s. 0d. given his man and for other charges—£29. 4s. 0d.; a bay gelding bought of Mr. Duncomb—£50. 0s. 0d.; a grey gelding bought of Mr. Dodsworth for Thomas Nun, the huntsman, with 13s. 6d. for a saddle and cloth for him—£13. 19s. 6d.; the strawberry stone horse—£38. 0s. 0d.; a grey stone horse bought of Mr. Watts, with 10s. to his groom—£43. 10s. 0d.; a black coach horse bought of Mr. Lacey belonging to the Earl of Suffolk—£27. 10s. 0d.; in exchange for the gelding bought for Captain Digby, with 5s. 0d. to the horse courser's servants—£10. 15s. 0d.; to Mr. Thursby in exchange between a chestnut gelding and a brown stone horse—£24. 0s. 0d.; and to Burrage for a mare given by his lordship to George Punter—£1.50.0d.; in all £237 18s. 6d.

The horses were constantly put out to grass, but not on the Earl's own land. Occasionally they were sent to Toddington, which was near at hand, but more often they went either to Hyde Park, which was the place most favoured, or to some fields in the Isle of Dogs.

Bill for the horses' grass at the Isle of Dogs.

	£	s.	d.
1687. April 25 the 2 bay geldings, one black gelding and a grey gelding came to grass.			
The black gelding went out May 16; being 3 weeks at 5s. 0d. per week comes to		15	0
For bleeding.		1	0

	£	s.	d.
The 2 bay geldings and the grey went out May 23, being 4 weeks at 5s. 0d. per week, comes to	3	0	0
More for bleeding.		3	0
April 26 the great black gelding came in and went out May 3, being 4 weeks at 5s. 0d. the week.	1	0	0
For bleeding.		1	0
Field keeper.		2	0
Grooms' drink at several times.		2	2
	5	4	2

Bill for the grass horses at Hyde Park.

	£	s.	d.
1688. For the white gelding grass from May 19 to July 25, which is 9 weeks and 4 nights, at 5s. 0d. a week.	2	7	10
For the black gelding grass from June 26 to July 25, which is 4 weeks and 1 night, at 5s. 0d. a week.	1	0	8
For the field keeper.		2	0
	3	10	6

The coaches bought about the time of the coronation, including the French coach that came too late, seem to have served their owners for many years to come by dint of being carefully and at frequent intervals repaired, relined and repainted. But the Earl and Countess were not now dependent on the heavy conveyance only, for another four-wheeled carriage, lighter and more elegant than the cumbersome coach, had come into fashion with the Restoration. The 1611 edition of the *Bible* had spoken of a 'charet'; later editions changed the word to 'chariot.' Charets, or light carts, had long been provided in the stables at Woburn

Abbey for carting goods or hay. In 1682 the Earl added to the stables at Woburn Abbey a light vehicle for his own conveyance called indifferently by his gentleman of the horse a 'charet' or a 'chariot.'

May 1682. To the mercer in full of his bill for velvet for the new 'charet.' £24 0s. 0d.

To the glassman in full of his bill for glasses for the new chariot. £10 14s. 0d.

To the coachmaker in full of his bill for the new 'charet.' £53 10s. 0d.

To the fringemaker in full of his bill for the new 'charet' and horse clothes. £14 10s. 0d.

This chariot was elegantly painted and japanned by 'Mr. Pink, the painter,' whose name goes far to justify the invention of the game of 'Happy Families.'

June 1682.—To Mr. Pink, the painter, in full of his bill; £25. 0. 0. for japanning and painting the new 'charet'; the other £5. 7. 0. for painting other coaches, etc. £30 7 0

Eleven years afterwards another chariot was bought and this time was even more elaborately decorated by Mr. Pink.

May 1693.—For a new chariot, that is, body, carriage, ironwork, wheels, carving, leather, brass, inside fringe and glasses. £43 0s. 0d.

Mr. Pink the painter's bill.

£ s. d.

March 1693. For colouring a ledge of a footboard red in oil. 6

		£	s.	d.
April.	For colouring a moulding of a bottom side olive colour and a ledge of a foot-board red in oil.		1	0
	For japanning a chariot liver colour and painting his lord-ship's arms and supporters and coronets and garters in com-partments and purple flowers and silvering and lacquering the antics and iron work and carving of the body and car-riage and colouring the under carriage and wheels.	13	0	0
May.	For gilding with fine gold the blaze on both sides of the major's ensign of the county regiment.		10	0
	For making up and socketing the ensign.		2	6
	For colouring a foot-board red and a plate olive colour in oil.		1	6
		13	15	6

Mr. Pink was also the painter who did up the old coaches with plenty of colour and gilt. Therein, as in the decoration of the new chariot, the Earl of Bedford was contravening a royal proclamation. So great a crowd of rich coaches, each rivalling one another in grandeur of painting and gilding, had appeared in Hyde Park after the Restoration that an edict had been issued in 1661 forbidding the excessive gilding of such vehicles as leading to waste of gold. The injunction was a dead letter from the first. Gilt coaches and chariots remained the fashion without let or hindrance. It was a fashion led by the King himself, who was one of the foremost in breaking his own proclamation.

The first mention of a sedan chair in the accounts had been in January 1642, when the Earl and Countess had gone for their ride and had borrowed the money to pay the men. Either of them may or may not have bought a chair during the Commonwealth. But the first entry of a purchase of the kind belongs to the coronation year, when a chair was bought for the especial use of the Countess.

1660.—Paid for a chair, or sedan, bought by Mrs. Betts for the service of the Countess of Bedford.   £6 0 6

The carriers for the Countess had a livery similar to those who attended the coach. Later, as each of the daughters grew up, she was given her own sedan chair, with her carriers.

The entire family, or, more truly speaking, that part of it which was at home, removed to London once every year. The migration generally took place in February or early March and the return in May or June. But sometimes the family would not go up until the summer months or even the early autumn. In that case they came back in December. This annual migration was perhaps the most important event of the year in the normal life of the stables. It was certainly so for Bedford House.

For some days before the one on which the family them-selves proposed to move, the gentleman of the horse and the steward of the household, with the assistance of the clerk of the kitchen, together supervised the dispatch from Woburn to London of all the pieces of furniture, plate and bedding needed to supplement the resources of Bedford House. They also sent up quantities of provisions for the use of the family while they were in town.

Some of these goods travelled to London in a wagon, or wagons, supplied from the stables, but for the greater part the services of the local carriers were requisitioned. The carriers also took up a number of clothes bags, containing some of the personal effects of the family and of the servants. The charges were divided between the stables accounts and those of the steward of the household, according to the nature of the goods sent up and the particular official who had made the arrangements.

1665.—A cloak bag bought for his lordship's use. 16s. 0d.

Another for Mr. William. 19s. 6d.

1666.—To Francis Barnes, £17. 14s. 6d., and to John Asby, £18. 19s. 0d., two carriers, for several carriages by them between London and Woburn, and Woburn and London this year. £36 13s. 6d.

1685.—The expenses of Mr. James Clendon, clerk of the kitchen, in December 1685, with the wagons, etc., at St. Albans and other places on the road, with 13s. 6d. to porters and others for loading, unloading and watching the wagons then. £4 9s. 6d.

1685.—Paid to Edward Cooke, carrier, in full of his four bills for the carriage of goods, etc., from Bedford House to Woburn Abbey and from thence to Bedford House from the 16th of March 1684/5, to the 30th of December 1685, as by the said bills and his acquittances given thereupon examined appeareth, the sum of £29 9s. 0d.

The family went up to town, as they had done in 1641, in one or more of their own coaches, generally stopping to bait and sometimes to sleep at St. Albans. Sometimes they stopped before this, at Dunstable. To get as far as that town from Woburn by coach was an exhausting process. The road ran through what is now Hockliffe, but was then, not without reason, called Hockley in the Hole. Foot passengers and riders had the use of a high causeway, but the road itself along which the coaches had to pass was indeed what it was often called, 'a sad road,' full of sloughs and muddy holes. Just before Dunstable bad became worse by reason of a hollow dip, followed by a steep ascent, now long done away with. This was the last straw as far as the coaches were concerned and it was very fine, dry weather indeed in which it was not necessary to employ the man who waited with a rope here to help drag the heavy load up the slope, for which he was always rewarded with sixpence.

Of the household, or that part of it which accompanied the family, Mr. Thornton, in common with the receiver-general and the gentleman of the horse, usually rode. The menservants rode also. The maidservants occasionally rode; were sometimes, especially the ladies' own maids, given a place in the coach, but very often travelled with the goods that were being sent up in wagon or carrier's cart.

1667.—Paid upon the removal of his lordship's family from London to Woburn and from Woburn to London again, viz.:
For the expenses of his lordship at Dunstable and St. Albans. £10 15s. 0d.

1685.—Paid by the accountant for the charges and expenses of the remove of his lordship's family from Woburn Abbey to Bedford House, and for carriages within the time of this account, viz.:
The expenses of his lordship, with the Lady Russell and their retinue, at the Bull at St. Albans upon the said remove, with £1. 6s. 6d. given to the music and to the servants and poor there and on the road. £12 11s. 6d.

1685.—Two housemaids coach hire and expenses on the road to London. 14s. 6d.

Such of the clothes and other personal possessions of the family as had not gone up beforehand in boxes or bundles in the carts, or hung on to the carriers' nags, were put into the now popular portmantle, or portmanteau, and stowed under the seat of the coach.

June 1681.—To the trunk-maker for the two
boxes to go under the seats of the coach.   15*s.* o*d.*
May 1694.—For a portmantle trunk by Mr.
Whale.   18*s.* o*d.*

The turmoil in the stables at Woburn Abbey prior to the departure of the family was equalled by that of the preparations in the London house. When the time for the removal was at hand one of the principal menservants was sent up, with two or three assistants, to help 'furnish the house' against my lord's coming. Sometimes, if a particularly big arrival were expected and there was a great deal to be done, Mrs. Dawson, the wife of the assistant to the receiver-general, also came up to help Mrs. Bruce, the housekeeper. The latter, in the meantime, had sent for a number of women to come in from outside to scour the pewter, wash the win-dows and floors, and help with the cleaning generally. The women who undertook this casual labour were not, like those who came to help in the garden or house at Woburn Abbey, dignified by their own names in the bills. They were just 'women who came in to clean,' not Widow Whitbread, or Goodwife Goffe, who lived on the Earl's estate and were well known to everybody in the establishment. The bills for their labour and for the cleaning materials they used were made out at Mrs. Bruce's dictation, but not by her herself, for she could not write.

	£	s.	d.
July 1675. For washing sheets and napkins before the great wash when the two masters was in town.		2	0
For four pounds of soap.		1	0

	£	s.	d.
For six pounds of candles.		2	6
For three women one day to wash.		4	6
A woman two days to help to dry up the linen.		3	0
For oil, ashes and sand to scour.		1	8
A woman to scour two days.		3	0
For washing of twelve pair of sheets at 4d. per pair.		4	0
For two pounds of soap to scour the great room.			6
For nine pounds of soap.		2	3
For four mops.		4	0
For Fuller's earth and sand to scour the rooms.		1	8
For removing of goods from Mr. Robert's chamber and other rooms.		2	0
For removing them again and setting up.		2	0
A woman six days to help to wash all the rooms after the workmen left the house.		6	0
A woman six days for scouring and washing the rooms and cleaning the irons against the family's coming to town.		6	0
A woman to help to air the bedding when the family came to town.		2	0

The return to Woburn was exactly similar to the coming up; the procession of carriers' carts first of all, then the coaches which contained the family, with the stop at St. Albans, while, left at Bedford House, Mrs. Bruce proceeded to clean again.

	£	s.	d.
July 1675. For soap for the great wash when the family left London.		4	6

	£	s.	d.
For two women to wash after his lordship's being in town.		3	0
A woman four days to help to make clean the house when the family went out of town.		4	0

Besides the big annual removal, there was always coming and going between Woburn and London, and, as the sons and daughters, and presently the grandchildren, grew up, it was often convenient for them to use Bedford House as a resting place for one or more nights. Every one of these visits is echoed in Mrs. Bruce's bills, with the mention of the two women for a day when Mr. William and Lady Verney came to town, another for a day in the house against his lordship's coming, and the three women who came in to wash when Mr. William left town.

The carriers by no means depended upon this one removal for profit from the Earl, by whom they were at all times given plenty of employment. Their long and detailed bills—nearly all the carriers could write their own names and, in some cases, make out their own bills well and clearly —show that every week and on two or three days during the week goods travelled between Woburn and Bedford House. Sometimes it was domestic traffic: a basket of fowls and three turkeys, with a basket of eggs went up to London; a box and a bundle of pots and glasses came down. At other times purchases for the Earl, barrels of oysters, young fruit trees, new plants for the garden, a stove from Holland, were delivered at Bedford House and then brought down to Woburn by the carrier.

In London hackney carriages were still hired, although not as often as previously. But the stage coach, if we can trust the accounts, was comparatively little used by the Earl or his family, or even his household. But as time went on some of the servants began to make use of the coaches which ran past Woburn to London. There was a quick coach called the Flying Coach, in which a place from Woburn to town cost eleven shillings, and, more frequently used, there was the Dunstable coach, which charged only six shillings for the same journey.

The Countess never, as far as is known, left England. The Earl was satisfied with such foreign experiences as he had gained during the two years he had spent out of England as a young man. Woburn was their home and in Woburn, for the most part, they remained. Anne quitted it seldom and her husband, as a rule, only for a few days at a time, although perforce his absences were more frequent than hers. He went very occasionally to his estates in the west, but more often to Thorney to survey what was being done in the fens. He paid formal visits to the Court and to friends, or sometimes to Cambridge, where he had special connections, both in business and friendship, with Trinity College.

A visit to Cambridge was always a great ceremony, with splendid dinners given at the Red Lion in that town. The journey was made by way of Royston, amid the sound of harps, trumpets and bells, for the Earl, whenever he rode in state, had music wherever he went. After 1675, when his daughter Diana was married to Lord Alington of Wymondley, the opportunity of a journey to Cambridge was often taken to pay her a visit on the way.

One such jaunt to Cambridge, in 1689, cost just under seventy-five pounds.

A bill at Royston.

Laid out in your lordship's journey to Cambridge.

	£	s.	d.
October 12, 1689. The bill at Royston for meat and drink.	1	5	0
And to the servants of the house and poor.		3	6

		£	s.	d.
October 13.	Coachman and groom's bill at Royston all night.	1	12	6
	Spent at Cambridge, horses, groom and self.		5	6
October 15.	To the ringers.		10	0
	To a harper.		5	0
October 16.	Music morning and dinner.	1	0	0
	At Trinity College.		11	0
	To Mr. Hering's servants.	1	0	0
	To the town clerk.	3	4	6
	To the sergeants.	1	5	0
	Crier, bellman, beadle, housekeeper.	1	0	0
	And to the poor's box and the prisoners' box.	2	3	0
	The ostler's bill.	3	3	10
	The bill for wine and glasses broke.	4	17	9
	To the poor at inn when your lordship took coach.		7	6
	The bill at inn for 2 dinners and supper.	35	9	6
	To porters that fetched the wine.		2	0
	For oil of bitter almonds by Mr. Collas.			6
October 17.	To the servants at my lady Alington's.	14	2	6
October 18.	Spent at Royston for diet and saddle horses.		15	6
	Coachman and the groom's charge all night.	1	11	4
	Shoeing a horse by the way and at Mr. Brown's.		1	0
	Given to a mad woman at Royston by Will.			6

The whole expense is £74 16 11

Nearly half of the amount of money spent went to the Red Lion for the noble dinners and suppers.

Bill at the Red Lion, Cambridge.

The right honourable the Earl of Bedford's bill.

		£	s.	d.
October 15, 1689.	For a large pike with all sorts of fish about it.	2	18	6
	For a surloin of beef.		13	0
	For making a pasty.		12	0
	For a shoulder, neck and a breast of mutton.		7	0
	For a couple of geese.		8	0
	For a dish of capons and sausages.		9	6
	For a ham and eight chickens and cauliflowers.	1	10	0
	For a dish of collared pig.		11	0
	For a 'frigize' of rabbits and chickens.		5	0
	For salading.		1	6
	For a dish of mince pies.		8	6

Second Course.

	£	s.	d.
For 2 dishes of all sorts of wild fowl.	1	15	6
For a brace of pheasants.		7	6
For a brace of curlews and partridge.		5	0
For a dish of fat chickens and pigeons.		8	6
For a stand of all sorts of pickle and collared eels.		17	0
For a large jowl of sturgeon with a rand about it.	1	15	0

	£	s.	d.
For a dish of all sorts of tarts with ladies' tarts about them.		11	6
For a dish of fruit.		3	6
For lemons and double re-fined sugar.		3	6
For oil and vinegar.		2	6

Supper.

For a shoulder of mutton.		3	6
For gherkins and capers.			6
For a dish of wild fowl.		6	0
	£15	3	6

Bill at the Red Lion, Cambridge.

The right honourable the Earl of Bedford's bill.

October 16, 1689.

For a brace of carp stewed with some perches ranged about them.	1	9	0
For a chine of mutton and a large chine of veal.	1	0	0
For making a pasty.		13	0
For a dish of tongues, udders and marrow-bones, with cauliflowers and spinach.		11	6
For a couple of geese.		8	0
For a hash of calf's head with sweetbreads.		11	6
For a dish of turkeys in a dish.		12	0
For a dish of collared pig.		0	0
For a dish of stewed oysters.		6	0
For a couple of pullets with oysters.		6	0
For a grand salad.		1	0

Second Course.	£	s.	d.
For 2 dishes of wild fowl.	1	4	0
For a jowl of sturgeon.	0	0	0
For a dish of fat chickens and rabbits.		8	0
For a stand of pickles with oysters, anchovies and tongue.		4	0
For a dish snipes and larks.		6	6
For a large Westphalia ham with tongues.	1	5	0
For recruiting a dish of tarts.		3	0
For a dish of partridges.		4	6
For a dish of whipped silla-bubs.		7	6
For a dish of artichokes.		3	6
For a 'solamagundy.'		2	0
For a dish of fruit.		3	6
For lemons and double re-fined sugar.		3	6
For oil and vinegar.		2	6
For my lord's table for butter.			4
For cheese for the servants.		1	0
For bread and beer.	6	19	8
For firing.		13	6
For porterage.		1	0
	18	11	0
first day	15	3	6
	33	14	6
For a rump of beef.		5	0
	33	19	6
Given to the house.	1	10	0
	£35	9	6

One journey away from Woburn was taken at intervals of every two or three years, not for pleasure, nor for business but for reasons of health. From 1665 onwards gout as well as rheumatism regrettably took the Earl out of his own home either to Bath or to Tunbridge Wells in order that he might drink the waters.

An earlier generation had favoured visits to 'the' Spa in Belgium. But that resort now had its rivals in England. The necessity and expense of obtaining a passport, the inconvenience of the journey, not to speak of the peculiar characteristics of the waters which divided England from the Continent—'by reason of the roughness of the sea we put back again,' wrote one of the Earl's sons—all combined to make the gentlemen of England and their wives look with a favourable eye upon the medicinal springs that had already been found, or were now being discovered, in their own country. The watering-places of England began to flourish greatly.

The Earl of Bedford went to Bath at least once—in 1675—but the spa he favoured most was Tunbridge Wells. The springs there closely resembled those in Belgium and had been discovered, or at least brought to the notice of the public, in 1606 by Lord North. They speedily became popular and, when patronized first by Henrietta Maria and then by Catherine of Braganza, the supremacy of the Wells as a health resort and a social centre was assured.

The Earl went to the Wells frequently, although not every year.

At the spa a house or rooms were hired for his use—those were profitable days for the residents at the Wells—either in the town or just outside. In 1665 he took a house at Southborough.

1665.—To Edward Herbert, by the hands of Oliver Bennett, in pursuance of his

lordship's order of the 3rd of July 1665, for
his lordship's use of his house and furniture
at Southborough, near Tunbridge, at
£41. 0s. 0d. the week, for one month ended
the 4th day of the same month, and for beer
that was spent there.   £24   0s.   0d.

On another visit nine years later, in 1674, the Earl and
Countess lodged for just over three weeks at the house of
some people called Downes at Bowers, not far from the
Wells. They took with them four attendants, two women
and two men, and eleven horses in all, seven for use in the
coach and for riding and four pack horses.

The arrangements were made not by the gentleman of
the stables, but by the gentleman of the privy purse. The
latter travelled to the Wells to choose the rooms and paid
the landlady ten shillings in advance to secure them. He
supervised the preparations for the journey and took places
in the coach for the attendants. Once his lord and lady were
established at the Wells, he went to and fro, paying the bills
and keeping a general eye upon all the arrangements, and
when the visit was over pinning his papers neatly together,
endorsing them :

1674.—The account of his lordship's expenses three
weeks odd days from the 18th of June to the 11th of
July . . . at Mrs. Downes at Bowers near Tunbridge.

The rooms were rented at six pounds a week. The bills
for catering, the stabling and provender for the horses and
all incidentals brought the whole up to something like
thirty-one pounds each week. The incidentals included the
apothecary's bill and the fees for the attendants at the Wells,
authorized and unauthorized. The expenses of the journey
to and fro were additional.

Bill for the last nine days at Tunbridge Wells.

An account of £40 I received at Tunbridge, viz. £30 the 4th of July 1674, and £10 I took up and charged on Mr. Collop the 6th of July, 1674.

	£	s.	d.
1674. The apothecary's bill.		7	11
To the doctor, a guinea.	1	1	6
To the dippers for water and necessary rooms.	2	0	0
To the poor at coming away.		10	0
To my lady for a charitable use.	1	0	0
To Mr. Downes his 3 maids.		7	6
To Mr. Downes his men at the coachman's desire.		2	0
To a poor old man that drew our water.		2	0
To 3 gate keepers, poor people—for my lady.		3	0
To my lady to dispose at the Wells.		2	0
For 3 rooms in the stage coach at 7s. apiece.	1	1	0
To Mrs. Pitts for herself and 2 maids on the road.		3	6

My own expenses.

	£	s.	d.
To the Earl of Leicester's groom.			6
Letters to and from London.		1	5
For looking to my horse at the Wells all the time.		2	0

Bills and charges homewards.

	£	s.	d.
2 bills of the farriers.	1	0	0
Coachman's bill.		7	8
Tom Coles' bill for kitchen and fire all the time.	4	12	0
Butcher's bill.	4	1	4

	£	s.	d.
Mr. Downes his bill for the stables 9 days.	7	13	0
His bill for 9 days' lodging.	8	0	0
To Sir Charles Cartar's coachman for my lady.		2	0
Robin Nelson's bill for bread, beer, candles, etc.	3	6	6
To the fiddlers.		5	0
Charges on the road home.	1	9	3
	£38	1	1

Remains out of the £40   £1 18 11

From the Wells the Countess went on to the other watering-place, as pre-eminently 'the' Bath as ever the Belgian resort was 'the' Spa. She considered that the waters there agreed with her better and were far more beneficial in the long run to her health than those at Tunbridge Wells, which her husband particularly favoured. She also had another reason for liking Bath, for a visit there gave her the company of her eldest son. Francis, Lord Russell, was now, in 1674, a complete invalid and his life had only a few years to run. He had long since exhausted the possibilities of the health resorts on the Continent and, in his melancholy fashion, was visiting those in England. Bath was among the watering-places especially prescribed for him and thither his mother often accompanied him, the only considerable journey she ever made apart from her lord.

These visits normally appeared in the accounts of the gentleman of the horse. That to Tunbridge Wells was an exception. The books of the gentleman of the horse were as beautifully kept as those of the receiver-general. As a rule, he confined himself strictly to his own province in what he paid out. But from 1680 onwards he often set down that he had given small sums of money to 'poor French people' who had come 'to the door.' Sometimes they had done a piece of work in return, sometimes the money was a gift pure and simple. The Revocation of the Edict of Nantes was casting its shadow before.

March 2, 1681/2.	Given to several poor French men and women.	£1	18s.	6d.
March 4.	To a poor French man.		5s.	0d.
March 6.	To poor French that had no bread nor meat.		1s.	8d.
March 13.	Given this week amongst the poor French Protestants.		5s.	2d.
March 15.	To a French school-master.		5s.	0d.
March 20.	Given in money to the poor French people that came for alms that had none of the meat nor bread.		5s.	0d.
March 23.	To the Frenchman in all that japanned the 'charet.'			6d.
March 23.	Given amongst the French people that had no bread nor meat.		3s.	4d.
March 27.	Given among the French people that had no bread nor meat.		2s.	6d.

CHAPTER XII

SPORT AND GAMES

THE fifth Earl's grandfather, William, Lord Russell of Thornhaugh, as well as his father, the fourth Earl of Bedford, had been keen followers of falconry in the days when it had been the most popular sport with the aristocracy and the squirearchy, superior in its attractions even to coursing.

The grandfather had, it was true, always been credited with having preferred an even more exciting form of the chase. One of the alleviations of his onerous task as Lord Deputy of Ireland had been hunting the wolf with a spear, and this sport, on the whole, he had judged superior to any other. In England, where it was denied him, he had been well content to ride out with his falcons and his hawks.

The wolf-hunter's son, afterwards the fourth Earl of Bedford, had as a little boy learned as a matter of course to practise falconry. Cornelius van Ceulen painted a charming portrait of him as a lad of fifteen or sixteen with his falcon— a peregrine—on his wrist and his leashed spaniels at his foot. The youth is dressed, in contrast to the sombre black of his later years, in soft yet gay hues of lilac and green. The young face is fresh and untroubled by any care. When later, the business of life, both public and private, became overwhelming, the part taken in sport by the man who was now fourth Earl of Bedford was chiefly confined to the reading of letters in which a friend, or one of his bailiffs, gave him details of some marvellous hunt that the writer had enjoyed, sympathizing with the regret that the Earl must feel in not having been present. The latter had, indeed, but

FRANCIS RUSSELL, AFTERWARDS FOURTH EARL OF BEDFORD

little time for such amusements. Nevertheless, he kept up his mews, although in a very modest way, and was faithful to his sporting dogs, one of whom, the most delightful of animals, Van Dyck has immortalized.

The mews and the kennels were taken over by the fifth Earl. It was impossible for him to spend much on either during the first year of his succession and whatever he might have done a little later was frustrated by the coming of civil war. He did, however, continue to buy hawks and falcons during those years and that was something, for many country gentlemen put down their mews during the years of the Civil War and the Commonwealth. Some of them never re-established them.

When Charles came back to England the heyday of hawking had passed. For amusement there was the rival attraction of horse-racing. Charles, for one, had no doubt that this was the sport of kings. He set upon it the seal of his royal approval and went to Newmarket to watch the horse-racing where his grandfather, James I, the last true falconer of the English monarchs, had watched his hawks swooping down on their quarry.

The Court and fashionable society flocked to Newmarket in their monarch's train. But horse-racing alone would never have completely satisfied the country gentleman while there was game in England to be hunted. Now, however, the rapid popularization of the shot-gun gave him an opportunity of satisfying his sporting instincts by another method than taking out his hawks. Slowly, though none the less surely, the shot-gun triumphed over the hunting bird.

The triumph became more rapid and more complete as agricultural improvements turned uncultivated marsh and fen land into cultivated land, with the consequence that many wild birds, particularly such as herons and water fowl, upon which the hawks were accustomed to prey, tended to diminish in numbers. Some varieties disappeared altogether.

The Earl of Bedford, following in the footsteps of his grandfather and father, was the individual primarily responsible for the changes that were making themselves felt in the fen country. But he was not in any way peculiar among his countrymen in managing to combine a keen interest in agriculture with an equally keen interest in sport. He differed only from some others, the more progressive sportsmen, in preferring the form of sport to which he had been accustomed from his youth. There were still many districts in England in which he might let his hawks fly with every prospect of finding good quarry and he was content to do so, even when some of his friends yielded to the attraction of the shot-gun.

As a consequence of this conservative instinct, the Earl's falconry, like other parts of his establishment, bloomed with renewed splendour after 1660 and, as the years went on, he tended to spend more rather than less upon it. He loved his birds as he loved the sport and, once he had money to spend, grudged the mews nothing.

Hawks of every kind were found in those mews. There were the short-winged hawks, or goshawks, and the long-winged birds who were the falcons proper. The names of these last, seen in the account books through the years, make a noble list. There were the brook hawks kept especially for hunting the duck and water fowl and others of every possible variety for pursuing other game, brought from Scotland and Ireland, from Nova Scotia and New England, while North Africa supplied the swift-flying desert hawks. Every year birds were purchased or exchanged. Sometimes the transaction was with a friend or neighbour, sometimes with a dealer, the latter often a Dutchman.

1660. Paid for a flying goshawk, with
    8s. 8d. for her trimming with
    cranes and bells.   £6   8s.   8d.

1662. Paid to a Dutchman for a falcon, £11. 5s. 0d.; for a lanneret and tercel gentle—£2. 2s. 6d.; and for a falcon bought of this accountant —£6. 0s. 0d.   £19 7s. 6d.

1663. Paid to Mr. Michell for a goshawk and lanner.   £15 0s. 0d.
Given to him that brought a cast of hawks from Scotland.   £5 0s. 0d.
To him that brought home the hawk called Tomson that was lost.   £1 10s. 0d.

1669. To Mr. William Poulton, one of his lordship's falconers . . . for mewing the Nova Scotia hawk.   £2 10s. 0d.
Given to a falconer that brought a cast of hawks from New England.   £2 0s. 0d.

1670. Given by my lord's order to two servants belonging to Sir Nicholas Armerer, bringing the present of an Irish falcon.   £1 10s. 0d.

1671. Paid to Mr. Michell for a lanner which was exchanged for a cast of lentners belonging to the Lord Brook—£15. 0s. 0d.; a goshawk bought of Mr. Squire—£8. 0s. 0d.; a cast of flying tercels—£5. 2s. 0d.; a gaggard hawk—£2. 0s. 0d.; a hawk bought of a Dutchman at Newmarket—£4. 5s. 0d.; and for a cast of brook hawks—£11. 2s. 6d.; in all, with £4. 0s. 0d. paid to Mr. Scarborow for mewing the cast of Scotch hawks, £2. 0s. 0d. for mewing a brook hawk, and 5s. 0d. given for taking up the Scotch hawks.   £51 14s. 6d.

This fifty-one pounds odd spent in 1671 was the high-water mark of money paid for hawks in any single year.

The food for the hawks, which included live pigeons, and the furniture and trimmings were comparatively inexpensive. The hoods cost, as a rule, five shillings apiece; very occasionally six shillings were paid for one. Hawking gloves, for the servants at any rate, were a shilling apiece. Besides these, jesses, swivels, leashes and bells had to be provided. On an average, between thirty and forty pounds a year met the expenses of the food and the furniture for the birds.

1663.—For pigeons and other meat bought for the hawks—£7. 14s. 2d.; for keeping a Barbary tercel eighteen days, for hoods of several sorts, silver-feathered bells, beaver and other gloves, lures, varnels, luring bells, jesses, canvas bags and flannel—£8. 9s. 0d.; 2 guns for the falconers and mending of others, for shot, powder and a pouch, 2 crossbows and arrows—£9. 19s. 6d.; charges of the falconers in the time of hawking, with some more provisions for the hawks—£17. 16s. 8d.   £43   19s.   4d.

The head falconer was attached to the stables, but was independent of, or at all events considered that he ought to be independent of, the gentleman of the horse.

The same man, Robert Squire by name, served the Earl as head falconer for at least thirty-five years. His wages were high—a hundred pounds a year. Later they were increased to as much as a hundred and twenty pounds. But, as against this, he was not given board, he may not have been given clothes and he almost certainly paid rent for his cottage on the estate. Squire had several men under him, including his own son, but when the Earl rode out on a big hawking party two or three of the footmen became falconers for the time being and accompanied their master in that capacity. The favourite, Clem Robinson, was in particular often indulged with a day's hawking, either by himself or as part of the Earl's cavalcade.

1685.—To Clem, the footman, at several times, going a-hawking and hunting.   12s.   6d.

The men wore the usual brown and orange livery with special falconer's hats, which were provided for them by the gentleman of the horse.

The hawks were constantly let fly in the neighbourhood of Woburn itself, especially in the direction of Dunstable. There the downs and the adjacent high-lying woods and heath of Whipsnade always afforded good sport. This was pleasing to the inhabitants of Dunstable, for the expedition usually included a great dinner either at the Crown or the White Hart Inn in that town before the company returned home, with the customary gratuities to the ringers who hastened to peal the bells on the announcement that the Earl was coming and to the poor who ran to the inn when the same news reached them. On such an expedition the gentleman of the horse had to expend anything between three and ten pounds.

August 1689.—The expenses of his lordship, with his retinue, in August 1689, at Dunstable, with 19s. 0d. given to servants, ringers and several poor there, and with £1. 10s. 0d. given to music and trumpeters, etc., at the abbey.   £8   8s.   0d.

The facilities, however, that the Earl's own neighbourhood afforded him did not entirely satisfy him. In the neighbouring county of Hertfordshire particularly good hawking was to be obtained in and around Baldock. The

Earl frequently rode over in that direction, but it was a long ride if it were to be combined with a day's hawking. A house in the neighbourhood, Quixwood, belonging to the Dowager Countess of Salisbury, was standing empty, and shortly after the Restoration it was taken on a long lease, at sixty pounds a year, to be used as a centre for the hawking parties.

When the Earl went to visit any of his married children his hawks usually went with him. 'I shall not bring my beagles,' he wrote to his son William in September 1672, when he was proposing to visit the latter at Stratton in Hampshire, 'only my hawks. Send me word whether harvest be in with you; if it be not, I will leave my hawks behind.'

Another visit on which the hawks always accompanied their master was to Hampton Court. Every few years, after the Restoration, the Earl went thither for a hawking and hunting party. He was there in the summer of 1662, when both Charles and Catherine—for once, it is to be hoped, enjoying each other's company—were in residence for several weeks. This was an unusually lengthy stay at Hampton Court for the King and was never repeated. He continued to pay short visits there, but they tended to become few and far between. The game, however, was carefully preserved and the arrangements for sport carried out. Sometimes, instead of going to Newmarket, the King would come over for a day's stag-hunting. More frequently, the Earl of Bedford and his fellow peers were bidden to go there for a few days to take their enjoyment in hunting and hawking.

On those occasions the gentleman of the horse as well as the head falconer nearly always accompanied the Earl, as well as a number of servants, together with the birds, dogs and horses. The Earl himself was the guest of the King, but he paid for the board of all his retinue and provided for both his birds and his beasts.

January 1669/70. At Putney, saddle horses passing over and beer for the servants.	1*s.*	6*d.*
Your Honour's coach passing over.	2*s.*	6*d.*
Two grooms' board wages at Hampton Court for five days.	15*s.*	0*d.*
Horses' hay and corn for five nights.	£2 0*s.*	0*d.*
For my diet five days at Hampton Court, with other expenses.	£1 0*s.*	0*d.*
For the falconers and their two horses for seven days.	£2 2*s.*	0*d.*
For carriage of pigeons from London to Hampton for the hawks.		8*d.*
For hogs' hearts for the hawks.		8*d.*

These visits were not even checked by the accession of James II, who might have been expected to have refrained from showing hospitality to the father of William, Lord Russell. But the Earl was hunting at Hampton Court in 1688 and, judging by his servants' table bills, did himself very well there.

The last recorded date on which the Earl went to Hampton Court was in 1693 and as he was then over eighty years of age it may have been one of his last hunting parties. On the other hand, his vigour is attested to have been such that he may very well have continued his sport after this time. The cook's bill for the supper eaten on the way does not suggest any diminution in his appetite, if he took his fair share of the meal. This he probably did, no doubt to the dismay of his doctor and of his daughter Diana, if either of them ever got to hear about it. Both at this time wasted a good deal of energy in protesting against the heavy meals which he so much enjoyed, especially in the evening.

Provision for the board and lodging of the hawks at Hampton Court was made as carefully as for the Earl's servants. With the hawks went the spaniels. 'How necessary a thing a spaniel is to falconry!' exclaimed the author of *The Gentleman's Recreation*, and many a dog appeared with his master or mistress in the portraits on the walls of the gallery at Woburn. Chiefly, these were spaniels, but one painting at least of the Earl himself, not at Woburn but at Chatsworth, shows a beautiful coursing greyhound standing by his master's side. But to be put into a picture was the only tribute paid to the dogs. No dog in the accounts, whether a spaniel or a coursing hound, is ever mentioned by name, or assumes the individuality of Tomson, the hawk. The entries are always on purely general lines—so many dogs to be fed and looked after.

1664.—Paid for biscuit, broken bread and chippings, for barley, graves and other provisions bought for the beagles and spaniels— £29. 7s. 1d.; to the huntsmen upon their bills and for some other necessary expenses about the dogs, with £2. 3s. 8d. for 30 pair of dog couples—£6. 5s. 10d.; in all (besides the straw bought for their litter accounted for under the title of provisions for the stables).   £35 12s. 11d.

The most interesting event in the history of the kennels was when three greyhounds, which were used for coursing both hares and deer, were dispatched to Amsterdam at the cost of a pound a head.

1664.—For the transportation of three greyhounds to Amsterdam.   £3 0 0

The cost of keeping all the dogs came to anything between twenty-five and thirty pounds a year, including the
straw and so forth supplied for them, which was made a
separate entry in the stable accounts.

Besides hunting at Hampton Court the Earl also hunted
in Hampshire on those occasions when he went to visit his
son William, when the latter was in residence there. Sometimes he hunted round Woburn. Here was a good supply
of deer. That was well, for, even when the Earl himself
did not go to the hunt, venison had to be secured, for
general use in the house, to send up to the London house
and to have ready to dispatch as presents. Gifts of venison
went regularly to the Earl's friends and each year a brace
of bucks was sent to Trinity College, Cambridge, in recognition of business relations.

July 1676.—Received then of the right honourable the
Earl of Bedford a brace of bucks and forty shillings in
monies for the use of the Master, Fellows and scholars of
Trinity College. I say received by me, JOHN STAGG, *Manciple*.

The arrangements for hunting were entirely under the
control of the gentleman of the horse. There was, indeed, a
head huntsman. He, however, was a far less important and
far meeker figure than ever was the head falconer. The
latter, as far as possible, asserted his independence of the
head of the stables department. The head huntsman did
nothing of the kind. In the social hierarchy of the stables
he was in every way of a lower status. His wages were only
sixteen pounds a year as compared with the falconer's
hundred pounds. He was, however, allowed board wages.
The falconer made out all his own bills and memoranda of
expenses in a good, clear hand. The man who filled the
office of huntsman in the stables at Woburn for many years
could, judging by the signature, only just write his name
with extreme difficulty.

This man, Thomas Nun, entered the Earl's service about 1660 and continued in it until his own death thirty years later. But in spite of being always overshadowed by the magnificence and busy importance of the head falconer, not to speak of some of the footmen, he is in his own way a curiously significant figure. He is always there in the background carrying out his unobtrusive work. Then at last he comes into the limelight in the accounts of an illness which proved fatal.

December 1690. To Mr. Charles Ferrer, chirurgeon, by his lordship's order the 23rd of December 1690, in full of his bill for physic, etc., for Thomas Nun.   £16   0s.   0d.

To Batt the porter's wife for looking after him while sick 29 weeks at 3s. the week, with 11s. to James the street porter's wife for watching with him 11 nights.   4   18   0

Paid for a coffin and shroud, etc., for him, with 2s. to the searchers and 6s. for a certificate.   1   5   0

To Mr. Beech for wine at his funeral.   1   4   0

And paid the parish fees, etc., for burying him.   1   7   8

In all so paid as by several bills and acquittances and the accountant's book of particulars cast and examined appeareth the sum of   £24   14   8

All the bills for firearms, other than those purchased for military purposes, were entered in the stables accounts. But it is entirely characteristic that, as far as can be seen, neither the Earl nor any of his sons while they were at Woburn ever had a shot-gun bought for them. A good deal of gunpowder and small shot and occasionally a gun did, however, figure in the bills. They were purchased for the men and boys whose business was to deal with the birds 'that come to the garden to eat the cherries.'

As for horse-racing, that attraction said nothing to the Earl whatsoever. During his own lifetime meetings were instituted with great success on Wandon Heath, close by Woburn, to the great delectation of the neighbourhood, who attended in their crowds. But there is no sign that the Earl of Bedford ever went to these races, even though they were, so to speak, held at his own door. Much less did he go to Newmarket.

Games were another matter. The Earl had been accustomed from his youth up to bowls, tennis and billiards as forms of recreation apart from the play at dice or cards in which he also indulged. The bowling green in the northeast corner of the garden at Woburn was at all times carefully kept up. A tennis court may possibly have been built during the Earl's lifetime. Even if it were not so, neither the lord of the house nor his family were deprived of the game, for the gentleman of the chamber constantly entered in the privy purse accounts that he had paid out money for his lordship's expenses at the tennis court and for rackets.

1661.—Several times at the tennis court. £4 18*s.* 0*d.*

1664.—Extraordinary payments, viz.: for a little trunk for your lordship's writings, for a French book, for rackets and at tennis court, and for oil of myrrh. £3 16*s.* 8*d.*

Such entries read as if the Earl went out of his own house when he wanted his game of tennis. Possibly they refer to days when he was at Bedford House in the Strand. There were a good number of courts in London to which men of position frequently repaired.

Indoors, billiards were extremely popular. Probably the game was already played in the house in the time of the fourth Earl. In 1664 at any rate his grandson, William Russell, a young man of twenty-five, newly returned from his sojourn abroad, arranged for the introduction of a really good table with all else needed.

1664.—To the joiner for a billiard table— £15; for his pains in going down to Woburn Abbey from London to fit it, by the appointment of Mr. William Russell—£3; for 6¼ yards of fine green cloth to cover it—£3. 8. 9.; and for the billiards, the port and balls and other appurtenances to the table—£3. 14. 6.   £25 3s. 3d.

CHAPTER XIII

THE GARDENS

THE Earl of Bedford had two gardens to consider, one in London and the other at Woburn Abbey.

The London garden lay behind Bedford House and below the built-up terrace which was the favourite promenade of the family. It was laid out in an entirely formal style and was divided in two by a broad gravel path, running from the terrace right to the garden wall. On one side of this path was an arrangement of four square flower-beds. Narrow gravel paths ran between them with small fancy stone erections at points where they intersected. In the early summer the flower-beds were filled with tulips. Whenever—and it was very often—tulips were purchased for Woburn Abbey, a good supply went always to Bedford House. On the other side of the dividing path was what was known as a wilderness, one of the most popular devices in the gardens of the day. This was an arrangement closely akin to the even more popular maze and consisted of groups of trees and bushes cut into ovals, squares and angles by an elaborate series of narrow alleys. This wilderness in later years was the particular pride and pet of the Bedford House gardener and a good deal of money was spent on its upkeep. Young shrubs and trees were often bought to restock it, many of them being what the gardener described as of the thorny variety. There was also a small herb plot. Altogether the London garden must have been a pleasant enough place.

Who acted as gardener at Bedford House during the earlier years does not appear. Thomas Gilbank was there in

1660 and had probably held his post for a few years before this. He remained there until his death in 1684, when he was succeeded by one Thomas Todd. Gilbank's wages were forty pounds per annum for the whole time. He was a married man with a wife and family. He may have had quarters in Bedford House, or may have lived in one of the smaller houses belonging to the Earl near by. His successor, Thomas Todd, did live in one such, a house in Maiden Lane, not far from the mansion that had formerly been occupied by Sir Cornelius Vermuyden, but closer to the wall of Bedford House, whence he could easily reach his work.

Whoever was gardener at Bedford House was the person through whom, to a very great extent, plants and all kinds of gardening appurtenances wanted for Woburn Abbey were purchased. Nevertheless, although he was often required thus to undertake the stocking of the garden at Woburn Abbey, he had nothing whatsoever to do with the management of the gardens there. They had their own head gardener.

The first known gardener at Woburn was a man called John Comines, who was certainly there in the late sixteen-forties. His extremely uninteresting bills merely mention brooms, nails and other garden tools.

Some time during the fifties Comines was succeeded by a man called George Bradford. Bradford left behind him only one bill for the purchase of plants.

A bill of what charges hath been disbursed by me, George Bradford, in the gardens from Michaelmas, 1657 to Michaelmas, 1658.

	£	s.	d.
For repairs, garden implements, twine, etc.	2	12	7
For five Flemish cherry trees.		5	0
For one May cherry tree.		1	0
For new onion seed one pound.		3	0

	£	s.	d.
For one peck of Sandish pease.		2	0
For three ounces of carrot seed.			9
For 1 ounce of purslane seed.			4
For eight ounces of radish seed.			8
One ounce of sweet marjoram seed.			6
For half an ounce of endive seed.			2
	£3	6	0

This not very magnificent bill does not represent all that was spent on the gardens in that one year. Although they were still far from the importance to which they afterwards attained, yet even at this time they were a bigger affair than the bill implies. But the seeds and roots were by no means always bought at this time by the gardener. The mention of a box of plants is quite likely to occur in the accounts of the bailiff of Woburn, which is understandable, and likewise in those of the gentleman of the privy purse, which is stranger.

Signs, however, are evident that from this year of 1658, or thereabouts, the gardens, in common with most of the other departments, began to receive more attention and to have more money spent upon them than hitherto. Another gardener named Rowse succeeded Bradford and he clearly was allowed a freer hand than had been his predecessor. Rowse, however, did not last very long.

The important appointment was made in 1663 or perhaps a little earlier. John Field became gardener at Woburn Abbey.

The name of John Field has attained some celebrity in the history of gardening on account of his connection with the laying out of the famous nursery gardens at Brompton Park, which were founded by George London. London, who had had considerable experience as a gardener, was at that time gardener to Bishop Compton and when, in 1681, he decided to start business as a nursery gardener, he applied to two gardening acquaintances for assistance. One was Cook, head gardener to the Earl of Essex at Cassiobury, and the other was Field, gardener to the Earl of Bedford, not at Bedford House, as some books state, but at Woburn Abbey itself.

John Field's connection with the Brompton nursery, which John Evelyn pronounced the greatest work of the kind he had ever read of in books or seen in his travels, has given him more celebrity in the gardening world than the fine work he did in the gardens at Woburn. It could scarcely have given Field himself more pleasure.

A man who cared for his business of gardening could rarely have found a more congenial post than Field did when he came to Woburn. For once the time and the place and the man all met together. The Earl was eager to improve and develop his gardens; he now had the money wherewith to do so and methods of improvement were at hand, for rapid advances were being made in the introduction of new plants and the better growing of old ones. He was likely to give his new gardener every encouragement in his work.

But Field's good fortune went beyond this. He was a married man and it was presently discovered that his wife was an admirable sick nurse. The family promptly employed her in this capacity and her gratuities added substantially to Field's own wages of eighty pounds a year. Between them, they must have earned an extremely comfortable income.

It was not only a case of a comfortable income, but of a very happy home. Added to his gifts as a gardener, Field had another, perhaps one of the greatest gifts that can be bestowed upon any man—the capacity for exciting affection. The happy relationship between himself and his wife was the subject of frequent comment in letters written by the family of his employer. They themselves were not behindhand in feeling affection for him. The sons and daughters loved John as they loved Nurse Field. No one except Mr. Thornton, not even Dixy Taylor or Mr. Gregory, who served the family so faithfully, was ever spoken of in the terms of affection used towards the gardener. He was always and for ever 'dear,' or more often 'very dear,' John Field.

When Field first came to Woburn he found, according to the survey made by Sir Jonas Moore, flower gardens encircling the house on three sides, north, south and east. They were laid out in the same formal style as those behind the house in London. The parterre had beds of various geometrical shapes intersected by grass or gravel paths, with a fountain or a statue at the important points of intersection. Beyond these flower gardens was a small kitchen garden, two cherry orchards and a bowling green.

The first years of work in the gardens were devoted to improving what was there already. Far more lavish orders were given for plants for the flower-beds than had formerly been the case and for these the two gardeners, Field at Woburn and Gilbank at Bedford House, were directly responsible. The buying was no longer entrusted to anyone and everybody. Sometimes Field seems to have procured the plants, roots or seeds direct. More often an order was sent to Thomas Gilbank to buy them in London and send them down to Woburn Abbey. In the early summer the parterre was gay with tulips. Other purchases were nasturtiums, larkspurs and polyanthus. These, with their vivid colours, were bought for show. But sweet-scented flowers were always sought after and none were bought in such quantities as were those called gilly, or July, flowers, which might be either wallflowers, stocks, or clove-scented pinks. All of these flowers, distinguished by their warm aromatic scent, were called in the seventeenth century, as in the previous one, indifferently by the names which represented the English version of the French *giroflée*. Only very occasionally did either Field or Gilbank trouble to write anything more than that they had bought a hundred, or two hundred, or more, roots of gillyflowers, making no distinction of what kinds they were, much less mentioning the varieties. Sometimes, however, they did remark that they were stock gillies or clove gillies.

Not until 1671 did Gilbank set down the names of the 'six and thirty roots of July flowers of several sorts' sent to Woburn for which he had paid thirty-six shillings. The names included the Empress Court; the Count Mansfield; the Virgin of Middlesex, as well as the Virgin of England; the Bride of Canary; Bohemia's Crown; and Grave William.

That year of 1671 was an important one in every respect in the history of the Earl's garden, for it was then that he determined upon making some big alterations. In the spring the surveyor Philip Moore was sent for to come to Woburn. A survey was taken of the gardens and the orchards and as the result a scheme was drawn up embodying many improvements.

These included a thorough restocking of the flower gardens and the making of some new beds. Beyond the gardens the bowling green was remade and on it a stand was erected. This was a high seat approached by fifty steps. Whoever sat up there could command, as they were intended to do, a fine view of the park and could also see the hunting of the deer. No detail better pleased Miss Celia Fiennes when, in the course of her celebrated ride through England on a side-saddle in the early years of William and Mary, she came to Woburn to see the gardens there.

The improvements and alterations in the flower gardens and on the bowling green were, however, but side issues in the eyes of the Earl, his gardener and his surveyor. The important changes were to be made in the orchards and in the kitchen garden.

The kitchen garden, with the two cherry orchards, lay on

the west side of the house on either side of the avenue which led up to the main entrance. Before 1671 there had only been a modest collection of fruit trees other than cherries and a certain amount of wall fruit. The suggestions made by Philip Moore amounted to nothing less than putting kitchen garden and orchards 'into a new model according to the design agreed upon by his lordship' at a cost of just over a hundred and thirty-three pounds.

The work was commenced early in November of 1671 and occupied at least six months. John Field, like his predecessors, had no regularly paid under-gardeners. All the labour needed in the garden was supplied by casual workers, both men and women, who were paid by the day or by the hour. An extra number of these were now called upon.

This additional employment in the winter of 1671 must have been a boon and a blessing to the out-workers. They were paid at the usual rates for employment in the garden, which varied from tenpence to as much as eighteenpence a day, according to the nature of the work they were doing. This winter they had many more days' work than usual and they were especially fortunate in the perquisites they received in the shape of food and clothes. One week John Field spent £1 3s. 0d. on buying cloth and other things to make Francis Chandler, one of his labourers, a suit and coat and paid another four shillings for having it made up. He also bought lockram for shirts for several men and boys, paid for having it made up and also disbursed several sums for the doubtless very necessary work of washing the boys' shirts.

Other men and boys who came in during these strenuous months to carry loads or shift gravel were able to earn small sums from twopence to threepence or fourpence two or three times a week.

By the time the spring had come, a number of new

orchards had stretched out into the park beyond the two original cherry orchards, which were close to the house, and had been planted with apples, pears, plums and quinces.

Nor were the cherry orchards themselves neglected. English poets delighted in invoking the charms of the cherry tree and its fruit. Every garden of any pretensions at all had its cherry orchard, or orchards. Celia Fiennes, when she paid her visit, noted with approval how pleasant and well-kept were those at Woburn. The beauty of the orchards, whether at the time of the blossom or the fruit, was enhanced by grouping some of the trees around ponds. While the work of reconstruction was in process, the Earl added what the taste of the time considered an extremely decorative detail. He caused to be made a stone figure which represented an old woman who had formerly been employed at Woburn for weeding. This was placed amidst the cherry trees and was so lifelike that approaching visitors believed they had come upon a real person. A similar figure, another old woman, holding a cat in her lap, had been put into the courtyard at Bedford House. Such stone effigies were extremely popular. But mythology had its say also and yet a little later the Earl ordered four statues of Greek gods and goddesses for the Woburn flower gardens. These have been allowed to survive, while the two old women have disappeared.

The cherry might take pride of place as the truly English fruit, the 'cherry ripe' of fruit-sellers and poets. But choicer fruits were now being far better and more freely cultivated than heretofore. Philip Moore's scheme provided for extensive plantations at Woburn of apricots, peaches, nectarines and all kinds of plums, especially the newer varieties. Many of these were grown as wall plants; on the other hand, some were standards and were put into the new orchards.

The stocking of the new orchards and the restocking of

the gardens began at once. Here Gilbank, in London, gave a considerable amount of help.

All landowners procured new plants and trees from one another and most gardeners did a flourishing trade with their colleagues. While the new gardens were being made Thomas Gilbank, instructed from Woburn, paid visits to several important gardens for the purpose of making purchases. Among others, he went to the garden of Sir Henry Capel, afterwards Lord Capel of Tewkesbury, at Kew. This garden was celebrated for its fine fruit trees and Gilbank now bought young pear, cherry and plum trees from the head gardener. They were sent, or he brought them, to Bedford House by river, and then an unusual incident occurred, for the Earl ordered him to bring them himself to Woburn. This was quite out of the ordinary, for as a rule Thomas Gilbank, no doubt to the satisfaction and perhaps at the behest of the head gardener at Woburn, was always kept strictly to his own province, which was the garden at Bedford House. However, on this occasion he did come to the abbey.

After this Gilbank went to Brentford and bought from Mr. Francis Ball, gardener, a number more fruit trees— pears which had been grafted on quinces, dwarf cherry and apple trees, and plum and apricot trees. Finally, he visited the gardener called William Looker, or sometimes Lucre or Lukar, who had supervised the gardens at Somerset House for Queen Henrietta Maria when she was Dowager Queen.

1671.... To him [Thomas Gilbank] more for 45 pear trees at 1s. 6d. each, and for 6 cherry trees and 3 plum trees, all sent to Woburn, and for a mat to pack them up from Kew and Barnes to Bedford House.   £4 1 0

And given him by his lordship's order
for going to Woburn.   £2   o   o
To Mr. Francis Ball, gardener at
Brentford, for 60 pear trees of
several sorts grafted on quince stocks,
100 dwarf cherry trees of several
kinds, 20 dwarf apple trees of sundry
sorts, 10 plum trees and 10 apricots,
with 18s. od. for packing them up
in mats, and carrying of them to
Bedford House.   £15 18   o
And to William Looker, gardener,
for sundry sorts of fruit trees sent
likewise to Woburn, with charge of
making them up and sending them
to Bedford House.   £2   5   o

All these establishments continued to supply trees and
plants for the Woburn Abbey gardens, but neither Gilbank
nor Field placed their entire dependence upon them. An
increased number of nursery gardens were now springing
up in the neighbourhood of London and these were well
patronized by the Earl. To one of them in particular Thomas
Gilbank went very frequently on behalf of his master. This
was the garden in Whitechapel of which the proprietor was
Leonard Gurl, sometimes called Captain Gurl, whose name
was also written Gerle and Quarle.

Gurl's garden was pre-eminently one for fruit trees of the
finer and rarer sorts. Gilbank went there on several occasions
and made a fine collection of young trees to send down to
Woburn. They included Persian peaches, Roman nectarines,
Orleans plums, Bergamot pears and cherries of all kinds.
Besides these, he chose a number of wall fruit plants,
chiefly cherries.

Then in 1674, when the new orchards must have been in
good trim, he gave Gurl a really noble order for all sorts

of the choicer fruit plants, including four of the famous
Elruge nectarine trees whose name perpetuated that of their
grower in an anagram, and many unidentifiable varieties.

Mr. Gurle his bill for trees sent to Woburn Abbey. £10 11 6
*Bought of Leonard Gurle at the nursery near Whitechapel,
London.*

		£	s.	d.
November 1674.	2 peach Admirable.		10	0
	4 Elruge nectarines.	1	12	0
	1 Provence peach.		2	6
	1 Venetian peach.		5	0
	1 Verona peach.		5	0
	1 Red Magdalen.		5	0
	2 Florence peach.		10	0
	1 Katherine peach.		5	0
	1 Morello peach.		4	0
	1 Steven's nectarine.		6	0
	1 Modena peach.		5	0
	1 Purpurrey peach.		5	0
	1 Amber peach.		3	0
	1 Orleans peach.		5	0
	1 Bona Magna plum.		1	0
	4 Matchless plums.		4	0
	2 White Prunella plums.		2	0
	2 Mussell plums.		2	0
	2 Vedosh plums.		2	0
	2 Violet plums.		2	0
	2 Morocco plums.		2	0
	1 White Pardrigone plum.		1	0

French pears.

		£	s.	d.
	2 Mulbe bush.		5	0
	2 Nonsuch.		5	0
	2 Booneritons.		5	0
	2 Gross Rowslettes.		5	0
	2 Saint Lazenge (?)		5	0
	2 Primordine Magna.		5	0

Cherry Standards.	£	s.	d.
1 Duke cherry ⎫			
1 Orleans ⎭		2	0
1 Nonsuch cherry.		2	6
1 Roman apricot.		1	6
1 Masculine apricot.		2	6
1 Virgirtue pear French.		2	6
1 French Berry pear.		2	6
2 Golden Pippins.		2	0
1 Pearemaine.		1	0
1 Golden Russet.		1	0
4 Portugal quinces.		6	0

The order further included a number of specimens of what were extraordinarily popular at this time, namely, the dwarf fruit trees, chiefly plum and cherry, which had been brought to great perfection by the royal gardener Rose, who had grown them with much success at Hampton Court and elsewhere. His were much admired and George London, writing of them in a book which he called *The Retired Gardener*, challenged all Europe to equal them. Even Monsieur Quintinnie, director-general of the fruit and kitchen gardens of Louis xiv, did not feel able to accept the challenge. In England every landowner who had any pretensions to having really good orchards tried to establish these dwarf fruit trees in them.

Woburn had boasted of such dwarf trees in the cherry orchards even before the years of expansion. In 1668 and 1669 Gilbank had sent down a number of red, black and Bleeding Heart cherry dwarfs. Now, in 1674, a number of others were sent, with some plums.

	£	s.	d.
Cherry dwarfs.			
1674. 2 Dukes; 2 Carnations.		4	0
2 Cluster Flanders.		2	0

	£	s.	d.
1 Great Flanders.		1	0
2 Portugal quinces.		4	6

Dwarf plums.

1 Mussell.			
1 Primordine.			
1 Black Prunella.			
1 Pessod.		8	0
1 Red Primordine.			
1 Bona Magna.			
1 Orleans.			

A special place in the orchards was reserved for these dwarf trees, which stood round one of the ponds.

Finally, with the 1674 order Gurl supplied free of charge a number of young trees in order to 'make good those that died last year.' This was in strict accordance with the guarantee that he always gave with his fruit trees, 'all which he warrants to be the same as they are expressed in his bill and to supply with the best of every sort in case any fail or die.'

The orders given by the Earl this year must have been thoroughly satisfactory to his gardeners for, besides the consignment from Gurl, Gilbank was sent to Mr. Mordan, the nursery gardener, to get some special young peach trees and also once more to Sir Henry Capel's. This time he bought from the latter's gardener the special peach which was called after the master of the house and some nectarines and peaches which may possibly have been named after himself, together with a very precious young vine.

A bill for the right honourable the Earl of Bedford.

	£	s.	d.
1674. For a basket to put nine dozen of preserving apricots in I sent to Woburn Abbey and for boat hire when I brought them to Bedford House.			10

	s.	d.
For boat hire from Chelsea to the Old Swan three times since Michaelmas, when I went to Captain Gurl's to choose trees to send to Woburn Abbey.	2	o
For boat hire from Chelsea when I sent the Berry du Roi pears and the Rozelean pears to Woburn Abbey.		6
For boat hire when I went to Bromford and Chiselhurst and to Sir Henry Capel's.	1	6
For 4 peach trees I had of Mr. Lord Mordan, nursery man, one violet musk, one Magdalen, one peach.	10	o
For a box to put them in.	2	o
Sir Henry Capel's peach was put into that box and Gilbank's 2 nectarines and Gilbank's peach and a vine [of] which the juice is as red as ox blood.		

16s. 10d.

The purchase of fruit trees of all kinds from many different quarters went on steadily throughout the Earl's lifetime. The varieties already in the garden were often renewed and added to and, as a new kind was heard of, so a plant of it came down to Woburn. The arrival of French dwarf pears in 1676 marks an attempt on the part of the French gardeners to rival the English dwarfs.

Round about 1681 John Field was busy in helping his friend, George London, to found the new nursery gardens at Brompton Park. This he managed to combine with his work as gardener to the Earl of Bedford, for he never left that post. Once the Brompton gardens were fully established, it was only natural that plants should be ordered from them on behalf of the Earl. Whereas, however, Leonard

Gurl had chiefly supplied the finer named varieties of peaches, nectarines, cherries and pears, London usually sent to Woburn trees and bushes of the commoner garden fruits, although he did send some of the finer kinds as well. A big order in 1685 included some peaches and nectarines as well as mulberry trees, but the bulk of it was for apple and pear trees—over two hundred of the former and fifty of the latter—and currant and gooseberry bushes, a hundred of each. In subsequent years, on the whole, Gurl continued to supply the finer fruits while apples, pears and fruit bushes for the kitchen garden came from George London.

London, however, did very often sell the Earl fine flowering shrubs. In 1692 he sent six red honeysuckles, at a cost of two shillings, to Woburn. Indian jasmine came from another nursery gardener called James Rickets.

Rickets grew special peach trees, which were named after him, and several young trees of these Rickets' peaches were sent to Woburn. He also supplied the Earl with pots of the lily called the Lily of Constantinople. He did not say in his bills whether those sent were the red Martagon lily or the white lily, both of which were called 'of Constantinople.'

The kitchen gardens lay next to the house, between it and the orchards. The greater part of the stock required for these was bought by John Field himself, not ordered through Gilbank. Field very often went to a namesake of his own, George Field, who may have been his brother, for the young plants, roots and seeds that he required to fill the gardens with vegetables and herbs. While he was making his purchases he nearly always included a certain number of the commoner sort of flower seeds, such as Canterbury bells, candytuft and lupins. But in particular he bought marigold seeds and they, as well as clove gillyflowers, had their true place in the kitchen gardens as well as in the flower gardens, since the cooks often required both for preserving in vinegar and sugar for use in the winter as 'sallets.'

John Field the gardener's bill for seeds for Woburn Abbey.

		£	s.	d.
December 1675.	1 ounce of stock gilly flower seed.		1	6
	1 ounce of radish seed.		1	6
February 1676.	1 ounce of short cucumber seed.			6
	1 ounce of long cucumber seed.			6
	1 ounce of purslane seed.			3
	1 ounce of parsnip seed.			2
	1 ounce of red beet seed.			6
	2 ounces of cabbage lettuce seed.		1	0
	1 pound of the best orange carrot seed.		4	0
	1 ounce of leek seed.			6
	2 pounds of the best onion seed.		14	0
	$\frac{1}{2}$ an ounce of celery seed.			3
	For Canterbury bells seed and scarlet beans.		2	0
	$\frac{1}{2}$ a peck of peas.		2	0
		£1	8	8

A bill for seeds.

		£	s.	d.
January 1680.	For 2 pound of radish seed.		2	8
	For 1$\frac{1}{4}$ ounces of purslane.			5
	For $\frac{1}{4}$ of an ounce of cauliflower.		1	3
	For 1 pound of orange carrots seed.		2	8
March 1680.	For 2 pounds of Strasburg onions.		6	0
	For 2 pints of egg peas.		2	6
	For lupins.			3

	£	s.	d.
For several sorts of flower seeds.		1	0
For ¾ of an ounce of cardus seed.			3
For 1 ounce of leek seed.			2
For ½ ounce of bugloss seed.			2
For ½ ounce of salsify seed.			6
For ½ ounce of sweet basil.			6
For ½ ounce of summer savory.			$1\frac{1}{2}$
For 2 quarts of rouncival peas.		1	0
For 1 ounce of stock July flowers.			8
For 2 pruning knives.		3	0
For 2 dozen of baskets.		3	4
	£1	6	$5\frac{1}{2}$

Besides going to the dealer, who may have been his brother, Field also visited the gardeners of neighbouring landowners to obtain some especially choice plant or seeds. Sir Henry Anderson's gardener supplied artichoke plants and the same came also from a Mr. Spicer. Plants and seeds, too, were often exchanged between landowners or sent by one to another as a present, and there was many a man who, like Addison's Will Wimble of later days, was pleased to go from one side of the county to another carrying a couple of tulip roots in his pocket from one friend to another. When the messenger was an under-gardener, or one of the other servants, he was well and substantially rewarded for his trouble.

Other orders for the kitchen gardens were given to Gilbank, notably thirty dozen garden sticks that were imported from Holland.

Passing through the orchards and kitchen gardens

towards the house, an archway at the end of the cherry orchards led on to a terrace running immediately under the west front of the house, on to which the windows of the state rooms looked. Here, in the summer, were kept potted trees of oranges, lemons, myrtles and aloes, which, in the winter, were either removed into the house, or into the new orangery, especially arranged for their reception, where they might enjoy the warmth of a fire, or were placed into troughs and covered with boards for their better protection.

Parkinson declared that while orange trees could be—as indeed they were—grown with great success in England by means of thoroughly protecting them in the winter and giving them all the sun available in the summer, the same methods availed nothing for lemon or citron trees, which, in this climate, never lived for any length of time. The Earl of Bedford certainly had citron and lemon trees below his dining-room window in the summer as well as the oranges, but Celia Fiennes, who saw them there, had no interest in inquiring whether or not there had been any true success in growing them.

Mr. Kemp for orange pots.

	£	s.	d.
June 1681. For 40 troughs for the orange trees at 6*d*. and 3*d*. putting on.	1	10	0
Given him for his journey.	1	0	0
	£2	10	0

As far as glass frames were concerned, nearly all Field's energies were devoted to the growing of melons, which had now become a comparatively common delicacy. Usually the frames were made locally, and mended locally as well, for the bill for breakages was a heavy one.

		£	s.	d.
April 1687.	For mending of 14 musk melon glasses comes to.		7	o
	For 3 quarries of new glass in the melon frames.			3
	Made 4 large melon glasses.		16	o
	Mending 4 melon glasses comes to		3	o
May.	Mended 3 melon glasses.		4	o
	In the melon frames repaired 3 lights and 60 quarries.		7	6
	For mending a watering pot for the garden.			6
February 1688.	In the melon frames repaired and banded 6 old lights.		6	o
	In the melon frames 87 quarries of new glass.		7	1
	For 6 squares in the melon frames.		5	o
	For 2 lights repaired and banded and 45 quarries in the melon frames.		5	o
	To the fisher man 20 pounds of plummets.		5	o
	To John Newman 5 pound of small bullets.		1	8
March.	Spent to fasten the pipes to the new coolers in the brewhouse, 10 pounds of solder.		8	4
	For a piece of large pipe.		1	o
	For 2 days' work of my self and man.		7	o

In 1685 there was another burst of particular activity on the part of the Earl and John Field. They created, at a cost of over three hundred pounds, a new plantation within the park at Woburn, walling it round with bricks made within the park. At the same time, they planned another new orchard. Finally, John Field was empowered by his master to procure from Holland a number of stoves for the purpose of warming the orange house. This was one of the occasions when the two were not in perfect agreement. The buyer of the stoves was John Field's friend, George London, of the Brompton market gardens, who often undertook commissions of the kind and sometimes came down to Woburn to advise on planting. Here there was some trouble over the cost of the stoves and the proper ratio of exchange between the Dutch guilder and the English pound.

John Field to George London.

From Woburn, *October* 19, 1685.

MR. LONDON,

I did not receive yours till Sunday night late, so I did not show it to my lord till this morning, and I could not persuade his lordship that the stoves came to above ten pounds for all you wrote that they cost 160 guilders and 110 came to near ten pounds, so he has ordered Mr. Petty at Bedford House to pay you ten pounds and no more. To be sure you will be paid the rest when you come down when you show him your charge. It vexes me to think that he ordered you but ten pounds. I told him they cost near fourteen pounds. I prayed my wife to write to you to let you know I would write to you to-day. She went to London to-day morning and is at the Charterhouse. My lord says I shall not plant the trees till you come. Therefore, I and his lordship expect you here so soon as the stoves come. In the meanwhile, I remain, with my kind love and service presented to you,

Your loving partner,

JOHN FIELD

Field was carrying out his last services for the Earl. He had been at the abbey for over twenty-two years when in the winter following that in which he wrote to Mr. London he fell sick. The apothecary prescribed cordials and blistering plasters and a dose of sweet almonds with rhubarb. The illness was not, however, of a kind that could be cured. Within a few weeks the patient was seen to be worse and a doctor named Waller was called in by the Earl. He, too, prescribed cordials, plasters and emetics, and again they were useless. On 22nd March 1687 John Field was buried in the Woburn churchyard, a man greatly beloved, of whom Lady Diana wrote: 'Mr. Field is dead. I beseech God to comfort the poor widow, for I do really pity her. A better and happier couple never was, but it shows the uncertainty of the content of this world's good, which ought to put us in mind of making a provision for hereafter. All my servants are in tears for poor Mr. Field and I believe all that know him are so.'

After Field's death no one took his place as far as the hearts of the family were concerned. There was indeed a gardener, who was quite well paid, but he was just the gardener, no longer 'dear John Field.' No alterations on a big scale were again carried out in either park or garden. Some of the glamour seems to have disappeared. Not that either park or garden were neglected. As before, the orders went to London and to Gurl and to others quite regularly, and to them was added a new purveyor of supplies. This was Mr. Edward Fuller, who had a flower and seed shop near the Strand bridge. John Field had never patronized him, but after the latter's death Fuller sent flower and vegetable seeds quite regularly to Woburn Abbey.

Bought of Edward Fuller at Strand bridge.

January 1690. Seeds:

	£	s.	d.
1 bushel of beans.		5	0
1 peck of Barnes peas.		4	0

	£	s.	d.
1 peck of short hotspurs.		3	0
1 peck of egg peas.		6	0
1 peck of long hotspur.		3	0
1 peck of redding.		2	6
1 peck of sandwich.		2	0
2 pecks of maple rouncivals.		6	0
3 pounds of onions.		12	0
½ pound of Spanish onions.		2	0
1 pound of cabbage lettuce.		4	0
2 pound of radish.		3	0
1 pound of spinach.		1	4
1 ounce of cauliflower.		5	0
1 ounce of savoy.		1	0
6 ounces of purslane.		3	0
4 ounces of red beets.		1	4
3 ounces of curled endive.		3	0
1 ounce of celery.		1	0
4 ounces of cardus.		1	4
2 ounces of leeks.			8
½ pound of parsley.			8
4 ounces of parsnips.			4
5 ounces of nasturtium.		5	0
2 ounces of stock gillyflower.		1	0
3 ounces of sweet marjoram.		3	0
Amaranthus tricolour.⎤ of		2	0
Marvel of Peru. ⎪these		2	0
Humble plant. ⎧ a		2	0
Collatra. ⎦little.		2	6
for a sack, 3s.; for 7 bags, 4s.		7	0
for 2 baskets, 2s.; paid to send to the carrier, 2s.		4	0
2 dozen of double mats to cover my melons.		18	0
1 dozen of melon glasses.		14	0
6 spades.	1	1	0
2 watering pots.		10	0

		£	s.	d.
	25 tuberous roots.		blank.	
April 1690.	Egg peas 8 quarts.		8	0
	Candytuft seeds 4 ounces.		4	0
	For a bag.			6
	For 2 large tuberous roots.	1	5	0
	Total £10	10	0	2

Besides flower and vegetable seeds, Fuller also supplied gardening tools af all descriptions.

Bought of Edward Fuller.

		£	s.	d.
January 1687/8.	For 12 double bass mats.		10	0
	For 4 garden spades.		14	0
	For 2 double tin watering-pots.		9	0
	for 2 pair of garden shears.		7	0
	For a garden line.		2	0
		£2	2	0

CHAPTER XIV

THE LIBRARY

THE library at Woburn Abbey—a noble apartment at the south end of the west front—was, like the picture gallery, partly preserved at the instance of the fourth Duke when the house was later rebuilt. The situation was delightful: the southern windows opened on to a flower garden; the west windows looked across the bowling green and orchards to the panorama of the park.

In 1700 the room contained one hundred and fifty-two books, including manuscript volumes. The Earl and Duke, however, had not kept all his books at the abbey, or even the greater part of them. Bedford House in the Strand held two hundred and forty-seven volumes more.

On the death of the owner a reckoning was taken of the books in both houses, not merely the number of books in the two libraries, but a list of their titles also.

Two men set to work to make the catalogue. It is easy to picture the one laboriously writing down the names of the books at the dictation of the other as he moved along the shelves. Unfortunately this second man, in order to get the work over and to save as much trouble as possible, often dictated only a shortened title, which he got from the back of the book. Had he opened the volume to see what was on the title-page he would have found a more detailed wording. As for his companion, who was writing at his dictation, he did not ask—was hardly likely to have asked—how to spell the names read out, nor did he always hear correctly what was said. Hence the misspellings and curious slips arising from his attempts to render what he heard, or thought he had heard, phonetically.

Some fifty of these books whose names were so taken down have survived. Most of them have probably rested more or less continuously on the shelves. A few of them, having wandered into other collections, subsequently sold, were at different times bought back. Of the fate of the other three hundred odd discarded as taste in literature changed and room was needed on the shelves for other books, who shall say? The dustbin and the fire were always available.

The process of discarding had not unnaturally been continuous from the beginning. Certain of the books in the library of the fifth Earl were inherited, but their numbers by no means corresponded with those which some of his predecessors had been known to possess.

Francis, second Earl of Bedford, great-grandfather of the fifth Earl, had had a library of two hundred and twenty-one books and four manuscripts. These he had kept in two cases. One was a long trunk and the other a great chest bound with iron. Some years before his death in 1585 the Earl had had a list of the volumes made—for what purpose it is not known. The man who made this inventory did his job very thoroughly. In any event he had to handle each book and open it in order to get at the title, for prior to 1660 few, if any, books had their titles lettered on the back. He wrote out all the titles from the title-page in full and for many of the books he added an elaborate description of the style of the binding, even to the gilt on the edges and the hues of the covers and the ribbon ties. Altogether he left a very pretty description of the outward appearance of a great nobleman's library, with much blue, red and green relieving the more monotonous brown and black.

The gaiety of the bindings somewhat belied the contents of the books, in which the influence of Calvin and his school was predominant. No one reading the titles could fail to remember that the owner had been one of the little group of English residents in Zurich during the reign of Mary and later had kept up a close connection with the Swiss reformers.

That theological books outnumbered all others was not surprising. That would have been the case everywhere. After all, very few books of literary interest were published before 1584. But it is not without significance, in view of the contents of the library in subsequent generations, that two memorable books, *Euphues* and *The Shepheard's Calendar*, both of which appeared in the Earl's lifetime and both of which represented something new in literature, are missing.

Neither the charm of the bindings nor the worthy contents of the volumes stood in the way of the library being broken up. Less than twenty can be said with any certainty to have escaped the dangers consequent on the rough and tumble of a book's existence and have survived to the present day. Most of their former companions had probably disappeared within a comparatively short time of the owner's death.

In the next generation Lucy, third Countess of Bedford, had had many books dedicated to her, but comparatively few of the volumes she had possessed survived even to get as far as Woburn and be placed in the library there.

Of all the rooms in the house which he had built, the library was the one peculiarly identified with Francis, fourth Earl of Bedford. There he had sat, surrounded by his books, writing and meditating, meditating and writing. The ten great folio volumes which were the work of his own pen are carefully preserved, as he himself in his will expressed a desire that they might be, although perhaps he would hardly have dared to hope that they would still be in existence after an interval of three hundred years.

Thirty other manuscript volumes which the Earl had collected, well-known political and theological treatises, have been kept also. Among them the discourse of *Mr. Prinne against Vanity of Hairs and Locks, etc.* is covered with scribbling and comments in the Earl's own handwriting. It is not the only one. The fourth Earl could seldom keep his pen off any book that he was reading, as these thirty surviving volumes which once had belonged to him show well and clearly. But it was the custom of his age. Scribbling on a book was then by no means the heinous crime which a later generation judged it to be.

How many printed books the fourth Earl possessed in all is doubtful, but forty at least of such that were in the library in 1700, all published in his lifetime—that is, before 1640—almost certainly belonged either to him or to his father.

The subjects of those printed books ranged over religious writings, always with an anti-Roman bias; history, chiefly constitutional treatises and works on the history of France and Rome; economics; a little on foreign travel; and some classics.

Such was the nature of the library taken over by the fifth Earl of Bedford on his succession in 1641. During the next sixty years many books were discarded; many other books were bought. Yet could the Earl's predecessors have visited his library, even in 1700, as stocked by the chaplain and librarian Mr. Thornton, they would have surveyed the collection with eyes that saw nothing particularly strange or obnoxious in the subjects of which the books treated. In his choice of reading matter the fifth Earl was consistent to inherited tastes and inherited traditions.

The long list of works on dogma and doctrine, as well as the collections of sermons and homilies, whether the author was one of the prominent evangelicals or a nonconformist —the influence of this school of theological thought was still and was for long to be predominant at Woburn—reflect the profound conviction felt by men of the type of the Earls of

Bedford that learning, like the conduct of life, must be based upon religious teaching centred upon the Bible.

At the same time, their essentially practical type of mind looked for variety, when they wished for variety, in their reading, in such books as dealt with geography, travel and history and, in particular, with agriculture. They were good classical scholars, but the amount of classical literature in the library was surprisingly small.

As far as is known no copy of the works of any dramatist was on the library shelves in 1641. Certainly nothing of the kind was there in 1700.

The non-appearance of the dramatists is matched by that of the poets. The absence of the works of Herrick, Suckling and Richard Lovelace is less surprising than that of their brother poets who wrote on sacred themes. No one loved flowers better than did the Earl of Bedford, but to read Herrick's invocation *To the Daffodils* was unnecessary when he could see them growing in his own garden. That neither he nor his chaplain and librarian, John Thornton, cared for the poems of men who represented the High Anglican school of thought, even those of such a sweet singer as George Herbert, is not astonishing. At first sight it does seem to be so that they should also have excluded those poets whose themes were based upon religious ideas akin to their own. All that Milton expressed in *Paradise Lost* on God and man corresponded with the convictions of the Earl of Bedford. Neither that work nor any other of those of the greatest poet of the period were put into the library at Woburn. The expression of religion through the vehicle of poetry, whether in the form of allegory, lyric or epic, was alien to the Earl's turn of thought. He took his theology, as he took his politics, dry.

No book among all those that were being published at the time on architecture, pure philosophy or mathematics appears either in the inventory or on Mr. Thornton's book

JOHN THORNTON

bills. This is the more extraordinary because John Thornton had a considerable reputation in Cambridge as a mathematician. Any books on mathematics he bought must have been placed in his own room, not in the library.

In the list of books, such as it is, bought for Woburn during the period of the Commonwealth, the name of Richard Baxter is predominant. For that matter it continued to be so throughout. The link between Richard Baxter and Woburn was a personal one. The preacher and writer was the intimate friend and constant correspondent of Mr. Thornton. He was also the protégé of the Earl, who helped him by personal gifts as well as by the purchase of his books. Baxter was among the many who, as he wrote to Mr. Thornton, had every reason to 'thank my lord for his great liberality.'

Incomparably the most popular of Richard Baxter's works with the authorities at Woburn was *The Sincere Convert*. Besides the copies in the library, almost every member of the family, certainly every one of the younger generation, possessed his or her individual copy.

Not the Earl himself, nor even Mr. Thornton, could be expected to buy all the books of such a prolific writer as Baxter, but it is curious that among the bills and in the inventory there should be no mention of *The Saints' Everlasting Rest*, which for generations to come was to be counted an English classic. Possibly, however, this volume was one of those called in the lists simply 'a book of Baxter' without any specific title.

Most of Baxter's writings, like those of many others, were bought for the library in sheets, unbound. The normal wholesale handling of books was then in sheets and continued to be so for at least a century. The retailer either bound them for sale in his shop, or supplied them in sheets to those of his patrons—especially his wealthy patrons—who employed a binder of their own.

The Earl of Bedford sometimes bought his books already bound up and sometimes sent them to his own binder. The latter practice had its advantages since the purchaser need not have the book bound unless, after perusal, he judged it worth while. If he did so judge it, he could and did choose a binding suitable to his own library. A bill for November 1658 shows that three books by Mr. Baxter—the titles not stated—were bought in quires. Two of them were thought worth binding.

November 1658. Three books of Mr. Baxter's in
               quires.   4*s.* 6*d.*
               Binding two of them.   1*s.* 0*d.*

Two other works by Mr. Baxter, purchased earlier, went to the binder at the same time as the newly bought books. The one was a copy of *The Sincere Convert* and the other was a book set down as *The Call*, which probably refers to *The Call to the Unconverted*, which had been published the previous year. *The Call* was to be bound in murrey-coloured leather. This colour was always a favourite one for the leather in which the books for the Earl's library were to be bound, but on the whole the more sober hues of brown and black predominated. The later library was by no means such a gay affair as had been that collected by the great-grand-father.

The printing of books, theological and otherwise, was often made possible by means of gratuities from patrons or by a subscription list. No one was more frequently called upon than the Earl of Bedford for this kind of assistance towards the cost of printing a volume and he almost always responded. Such assistance was usually given through Mr. Thornton. The tutor was in close touch with many of the nonconformist and evangelical divines besides Mr. Baxter, more particularly with those at Cambridge, so that he was the natural channel through which the Earl was approached for subscriptions and benevolences. They were given throughout the period of the Commonwealth and again after the Restoration, even to the end of the Earl's life.

July 1675.—To Mr. Hugh Davis, minister, the 7th of July 1675, by his lordship's order, sent by Mr. Thornton, towards printing a commentary on the Scripture, his lordship to have one of the books when printed.   £5   0   0

Besides sermons and homilies, the Earl also subscribed to the printing of Bibles.

July 1689.—Received then the sum of five pounds from the Right Honourable William, Earl of Bedford, being part of what he was pleased to subscribe towards the printing of the Welsh Bible in octavo, who is to have the full value of his money in Bibles, according to the proposals in that behalf. I say received as above for my master, Sir Thomas Lane, by me, PETER SERGEANT   £5   0   0

1689.—To Dr. Horneck, his lordship's gift towards printing of Irish Bibles.   £5   0   0

When regular 'Proposals for a Subscription' were drawn up, the book in question was often issued in separate volumes whose publication not infrequently stretched over many years. The payment was then generally called for in instalments: so much on subscribing; so much when the book was put to press; so much on the delivery of the first volume; and so forth.

Among others, the works of Dr. Manton, one of the most popular of the Presbyterian writers, were published in this way. He was another intimate friend of Mr. Thornton and also of the Earl, who had given him the living of St. Paul's, Covent Garden, in 1656. He was a prolific preacher and writer and put forth a series of volumes which began in the sixteen-fifties and continued to appear for many years after his own death in 1677. The Earl of Bedford was a subscriber to many of the works and was still paying instalments for some volumes as late as 1689, twelve years after the author's death.

Another subscription was to a work of a different nature.

1685.—His lordship's subscription to Mr. Ellis, his book to teach to spell and read. £2 0 0

It is not clear whether Mr. Ellis's book appeared in volumes or no.

Throughout the Commonwealth the chief variety in Mr. Thornton's purchases was supplied by the school books which he selected for the boys and girls in addition to their religious primers.

The tutor and chaplain did not supply the Earl with the news-books. That was left either to the steward of the household, or to the gentleman of the privy purse. Unfortunately, only a few scattered accounts of these officials remain for the years of the Commonwealth, and such mention of news-books as occurs in them is quite insufficient to throw any light upon the history of those publications. In 1653 at least, however, the steward managed to procure a news-book for his master fairly frequently. Sometimes the book came from London; sometimes one could be and was purchased either in Leighton Buzzard market or in the market at Woburn itself.

June 1653.	For a news-book from Leighton.	2*d.*
August 1653.	For a news-book from London for my lord.	2*d.*
	For a news-book at our market.	2*d.*

The years after the Restoration saw no slackening in the stream of theological works which was for ever flowing into the library. Now, however, far more than formerly, other accessions marked the successive changes in the political and social life in England.

Ceremony, regal and otherwise, re-emerged with the return of the King, and its re-emergence contributed to literature. The first great royal rite of the Restoration was marked by the arrival in the Woburn Abbey library of Thomas Ogilby's volume, called in full the *Relation of the Entertainment of His Majesty Charles II in his Passage through the City of London to his Coronation*. The price was two pounds and the Earl of Bedford bought a copy shortly after the ceremony.

Twelve years later the *Book of the Coronation* was joined by other books of ceremony. On the 3rd of June 1672, the Earl of Bedford was installed a Knight of the Garter at Windsor. On his installation he received the customary gift of the finely bound book of the *Statutes of the Garter*. Another copy of this was already at Woburn. Two Earls of Bedford before him, both the first and the second, had been received into the same order. The *Book of the Statutes* given to the second Earl, in its original covering, had and has survived. On its margins are some scribbled notes made in the handwriting of its former owner. His comment on various paragraphs was that they were 'popery.' The fifth Earl made no notes in his book; but there is no reason to suppose he would have objected to the notes in that of his predecessor.

With these *Statutes of the Order of the Garter* another book also arrived. Mr. Elias Ashmole, who had been Windsor Herald at the College of Arms since 1660, had written the history of the Order. With great acumen, he seized the opportunity of the Earl of Bedford having been installed a Knight to present him with a copy. The antiquary received the gratuity for which he had no doubt hoped.

1673.—To Mr. Ashmole, upon his presenting his lordship with a book entitled *The Order
of the Garter.*   £10   0   0

As was not unnatural, these books detailing ceremonies in
which the Earl of Bedford had himself played a conspicuous
part are among those which were never parted with, but
remain in the library, in their original bindings, to this day.
The works on the Order of the Garter were not the only
books which at this time emerged from the College of Arms.
The Heralds, having once more come into their own with the
Restoration, were busily writing up other subjects which
appertained to their office. Among them, Francis Sanford,
then Lancaster Herald, brought out by subscription *The
Genealogical History of the Kings and Queens of England.* The
work was a tolerably expensive one, the scheme for it being
seven volumes at five pounds a volume. The Earl of Bedford was one of the subscribers.

1678.—To Mr. Sanford, Herald, for the
History of the Kings of England (besides £5
formerly paid him).   £5   0   0

To books on ceremony were added many of the works on
history and geography that were being published, particularly after 1670, in some numbers.
As far as political history was concerned, the books which
appeared at Woburn did not run counter in the character of
their contents to those on theology. The history supplied
was the history of Protestantism in England and on the
Continent. The story of the reformation in Sweden and
France went alongside that of England. But a few standard
works, such as Fuller's *History of the Worthies of England,*
purchased on its first appearance in 1662, and the *Antiquities
of Ancient Britain*—books of antiquarian interest were becoming popular at Woburn as elsewhere—were bought.

The Earl of Bedford was himself no traveller and his sons had for the most part confined their journeys to Europe. Nevertheless, the geographical section of the library testified to the interest felt in the seventeenth century in the story of the uttermost parts of the earth, to which the Elizabethans had pointed the way. Many books were bought. One was the volume with the attractive title of *The History of Muscovy and Other Less Known Countries Lying Eastward of Russia as far as Cathay*, published in 1682. Among others were Speed's *Prospects of the Most Famous Parts of the Earth* and the English translation, published in 1680, of Tavernier's *Voyage to Tonkin and Japan*.

Yet another book in the library of a different nature than these spoke also of interest in foreign parts. This was the first published European dictionary of the Ethiopian language, which had appeared in 1661. Learning, especially theological learning, was progressing from Greek to Hebrew and from Hebrew to a study of the languages and antiquities of the Orient. In particular, a profound interest was awakened in the history of Ethiopia. The story of that country, with its ancient traditions of Christianity, appealed as much to the Bible student as it did to the antiquary pure and simple. The dictionary was the work of Jacob Ludolf, a native of Erfurt, who had lived much in Abyssinia and, with his *Grammar* and *History of Ethiopia*, held the field for nearly two hundred years. The dictionary itself—the copy is still at Woburn—is most admirably bound and printed.

In an age in which both the pamphlet and the ballad were being sold cheaply in the streets for the delectation of the populace as well as by booksellers, it was only natural that some—not all—should reach Woburn. Street ballads were apparently excluded, not so much probably because they were catchpenny as because poetry in that form no more than in any other appealed to the Earl of Bedford. At all events there is no mention of anything in the shape of a broadside being bought. Indeed the only time when the Earl, or one of his officials for him, seems to have condescended to buy a little poetry was in the month of September 1678, when a boy came to the house 'with verses.' What the verses were there is no indication, nor whether they were worth the two shillings and sixpence gratuity that was kindly bestowed upon the bearer.

If broadsides were not bought, pamphlets were; sometimes by Mr. Thornton and sometimes by Mr. Dixy Taylor as gentleman of the privy purse. Many of them were the usual political treatises and lampoons. But they also included a certain amount of more stimulating literature than was usually supplied for the library. Stories of 'horrible' murders'—not invented, but taken from real life—were extremely popular and sold freely in pamphlet form. Mr. Thornton did not buy these for the Earl, but the gentleman of the privy purse did.

May 1673.—A book of *The Murder of Mr. Baxter in New England.*   6*d.*

November 1673.—A book of *Murder in Gloucestershire.*   2*d.*

April 1674.—For two books of *The Murder in Essex.*   2*d.*

February 1674/5.—For two books of *The Prentice that Murdered his Mistress.*   2*d.*

Yet another class of pamphlet was that connected with the increasing interest felt in demonology and witchcraft, partly on religious, partly on historical grounds and partly no doubt because demonology and witchcraft made exciting reading. This was not, any more than were the stories of the murders, expensive reading.

February 1674/5.—For two books of *The Demon of Marlborough.*   2*d.*

Under all this—the relation of great ceremonies; the story of Kings; and the interest taken in murders and witchcraft —there was yet an undercurrent of seriousness which did not lighten but rather deepened as time went on. Within twenty years of the coronation signs began to appear that once more a crisis, religious and political, was at hand.

The stream of literature which put the history of Protestantism in the most favourable and that of the Church of Rome in the least favourable light had never really ceased. In the sixteen-sixties lives of Coligny, of Henry of Navarre and Gustavus Adolphus as well as Sully's *Memoirs* were already on the shelves at Woburn. Then, as the attitude towards the Church of Rome of Charles and of his brother and heir, the Duke of York, became more evident, the literature grew more alarmist and more bitter. Old histories such as *The Book of the Gunpowder Plot*, which was bought for Woburn in 1679 at a cost of three shillings, were revived. More significant was the fact that in 1684, when many were asking anxiously what would follow on the accession of James, Duke of York, to the throne, a new edition of Fox's *Book of Martyrs* was brought out in three volumes. A copy was purchased for the Earl of Bedford early in 1685 at a cost of four pounds. It was not the first or even the second appearance of the book in his library. All his predecessors back to his great-grandfather had had copies before him.

A variation of the same note was struck in the collection a little later. The year of 1685 was an ominous one for all who dreaded the domination of the Church of Rome. In that same year in which James II ascended the throne of England, his brother king Louis XIV signed the Revocation of the Edict of Nantes. The result was a great impetus given to the stream of Huguenot refugees which had already for some time past been entering England, and many of whom had already been shown charity in various forms by the Earl.

Literature, as both earlier and later in history, was enriched as a consequence of the sufferings of a people. Books written by refugees and others dealing with the history of the Huguenot movement both in France and after the exodus poured forth. There was every reason why many should be bought for the library at Woburn. The personal link of the Earl with the movement was an important one. The mother of his daughter-in-law, Rachel, Lady Russell, had herself been the child of a noted Huguenot nobleman, Daniel de Massue, Seigneur de Ruvigny. But quite apart from the personal connection, the Earl was sure to order and Mr. Thornton bound to buy French Protestant literature on both religious and political grounds. Many of the books chosen were among the most violent and the most controversial. The opening note was fitly struck by the purchase of J. A. de Thou's *History of the Bloody Massacres of the Protestants in France in the year* 1572. After that came many others, among which Peter Berault's *The Church of Rome Proved Heretic* was typical, to rest on the shelves alongside English writers whose themes were represented by Johnson's *Second Five Years' Struggle against Popery and Tyranny*.

Such books, both French and English, must in their day have formed a considerable group. The events of 1688 and 1689 brought yet another group into being.

In December 1688, when Parliament invited William, Prince of Orange, to undertake the administration of the country, the Earl of Bedford was at Woburn and Mr. Thornton was at Bedford House. It was very right and proper that the Earl should immediately desire his chaplain and librarian to send him a copy of the *Life of the Prince of Orange*, which was bought at a cost of two shillings. At the same time, or just after, Mr. Thornton bought the *Remembrances of the Proceedings of the House of Lords*, which related the debates by which the country changed its sovereign, and, finally, a useful volume called *The Memorial of the Last Twenty-Nine Years in England.*

The constitutional revolution had taken place. How long the result would endure no man could say. A flood of books and pamphlets bearing heavily against the late wearer of the crown and proving the righteousness of the revolution was being published. Among them Mr. Thornton bought two pamphlets: *Reflections on King James's Declaration* and another of the same kind, giving fourpence for the pair of them.

The purchase of a map of Londonderry at the price of sixpence commemorated the siege of that town by James the following July. This was presently followed up by a large coloured map of Ireland and by the book called *Bishop King's Account of the State of Ireland under King James,* which was published at the price of six shillings.

Then came the books and pamphlets which extolled King William as the others had abused King James and with them a quantity of literature bearing on and describing the political and military events which were now jostling on each other's heels.

Mr. Thornton's bill.

Laid out for his lordship from December 10, 1690, to November 10, 1691.

	£	s.	d.
Life of the Duke of Lorraine.		3	0
Reflections upon the Cities' Petition.			6
Magpie and three other pamphlets.			7
Sir William Temple's Essays (second part).		3	
A Letter to those that Rejoiced at the Taking of Mons.			6
Description of the Netherlands, with King William Entertained at The Hague.		1	6
Congress at The Hague.		1	2
State of Savoy.			8
		10	11

The campaign in Flanders had its maps as well as its literature. A map of Flanders cost a shilling and a map of the coast sixpence.

| 1691-1693. | A map of Flanders. | 1s. | 0d. |
| | A map of the coast. | | 6d. |

The material among the bills for the history of journalism is scanty indeed. Only scattered allusions to news-books occur before 1685. But in that year at least and henceforth the Earl of Bedford began to subscribe regularly for a news-book or letter which was called, as was so often the case, an *Intelligence*.

May 1685.—Received this 19th day of May, of Mr. Randolph Bingley, by the hands of Mr. Richard Petty, the sum of thirty-five shillings in full for one quarterly *Intelligence* due the 16th instant. I say received by me, WILLIAM MASON   £1   5   0

An *Intelligence* was supplied by several agents at different times. In 1692 the agent found himself in difficulties.

Thomas Minors to Richard Petty at Bedford House.

November 23, 1692.

HONOURED SIR,

Having received your favours hitherto, hope you will be pleased to continue them. Having had great disappointments from the country obliges me to presume troubling you, requesting that the sum of six pounds due next February might be paid now, being to complete the purchase of my shop, which must be this week; and in consideration of that, will send my lord a Letter every night. For your better accommodation, the bearer, my servant's receipt shall be your discharge.

I hope this may meet with success, which will render great service to, Sir,

Your ever most obliging and humble servant,

THOMAS MINORS

The first mention of the most famous of all the seventeenth-century journalists, Muddiman, is a late one. It is not until 1689 that a receipt incorporating that celebrated man's name occurs.

November 1689.—To Mr. Muddiman the 15th of November 1689, for news-letters sent to Woburn Abbey.   £2   2   0

That year other papers than English publications were being taken. In 1689 the Earl began to subscribe regularly to the paper called the *Amsterdam Gazette*.

1689-1690.—Paid to Mr. Bently the 6th of September [1689] and 1st of March 1689/90, in full of his two bills for *Amsterdam Gazettes*.   £3   18   0

October 1690.—To Mr. Bently the 6th of October 1690, for *Amsterdam Gazettes* for twenty-six weeks.   £1   19   0

Finally, news from France was also welcomed.

March 1694.—Pour la somme de trois livres sterlings que j'ai reçu de Monsieur Gregory pour les lettres de nouvelles que j'ai fourni à my lord Bedford jusques au jour de la Notre Dame de mars prochaine à Londres le 21 mars 1694.   £3   0   0

J. S. BOBIN

March 1694.—To Mr. Bobin, by his lordship's order, for the French news-letters to Lady Day, 1694.   £4   10   0

CHAPTER XV

THE PORTRAIT GALLERY

In 1700, the year in which William, fifth Earl and first
Duke of Bedford, died, one hundred and three portraits
hung in the Long Gallery at Woburn Abbey. The man who
drew up the inventory on the Earl's death thought it quite
unnecessary to mention either the persons represented or
the names of the painters. They were merely pictures, with,
for the purpose of the inventory, no value in figures attached
to them.

Thirty-two years later a sightseer who never at any time
showed the slightest objection to speaking her mind was in
the gallery. In the month of July 1732, Sarah, Duchess of
Marlborough, then in her seventy-third year, had arrived
at the abbey to visit her granddaughter, who had married
the reigning Duke, the third of his name. The young man
—he was twenty-four—escorted the old lady, carried in what
she herself described as a chair with short poles, round the
house, which she had never seen before. The rooms and the
corridors were thoroughly examined and much of what she
saw, she told another granddaughter in one of her characteristic letters, met with her approval. Then at last the
pair reached the gallery, the long room running at the back
of the salons the entire length of the west front, with windows
looking into the courtyard. There her young host—obviously
he was tired out after having paced beside his grandmother-
in-law's chair round the house—annoyed her considerably by
dropping into a convenient seat each time they made a halt.
The old lady's irritation may have accounted for her verdict

that she thought less than nothing of the portraits. The gallery contained indeed, she wrote to another grand-daughter, a great many pictures, but their only value, as far as she herself could discern, was that 'they belong to the family and [the persons are] in antique dresses.' One picture, and one only, she allowed to have some merit.

'But there is one picture of a Countess of Bedford that was charming. I mean her that the father forbid his son upon his death to marry. I really fear, if I had been a man, I should have disobeyed my father in such a case, for she was both beautiful and good.'

The Duchess had not got the story quite correctly since, after all, William Russell, afterwards fifth Earl of Bedford, had not been forced to choose between obedience to his father or marriage to Anne Carr. The fourth Earl had consented to the match and Van Dyck had, on the marriage, painted the portrait which the old lady now admired.

That was all that Sarah, Duchess of Marlborough, had to say about the pictures. It would have been useful indeed had she seen fit to add a few remarks, even had they been derogatory remarks, as to whose portraits in antique dress she had seen there.

Many portraits formerly in the possession of the family had doubtless never been brought to Woburn at all. Certainly and most unhappily, some of those which the Duchess saw and despised are no longer there, nor even in existence. Inventories and other papers indicate only too clearly the manner in which great pictures were taken down from the walls of the gallery as useless lumber and, if not put into an outhouse, were at the best relegated to the nursery or an attic, whence they often eventually reached an auction-room, supposing they had not been destroyed.

Later generations bitterly bemoaned the light-hearted and highly reprehensible manner in which their ancestors had rid themselves of something they did not want. They themselves tried to make amends. Some sixty years after the Duchess of Marlborough paid her visit to Woburn, the Dukes of Bedford, in common with many other heads of great houses, began to buy pictures. Sometimes it was a portrait which had been formerly in the possession of their family and, having been cast away, had seen many a vicissitude before it was purchased at an auction, to be restored to the ancestral walls. Other pictures were bought too, often because their subject had some connection with the past history of the family. Admirable collections of pictures were thereby created. They were, however, collections which concealed quite a promising number of false clues for their history, especially when, as is so often the case, the details for the story of the later buying are incomplete.

Hence the history of the portraits in the gallery at Woburn, like those in many another, can only be pieced together with difficulty. The difficulty is the greater because, before the day when the fourth Earl settled the family in the abbey, the family pictures were scattered among many houses, although no doubt the most important had been at Chenies.

Looking back at his family, the fifth Earl of Bedford could have traced their features no further than those of his great-great-grandfather, John, the first Earl, minister of Henry VIII, Edward VI and Mary. A painting indeed would hardly have existed of any of the predecessors of this nobleman, but there might have been a figure on a tomb, or a brass, which represented a member of an earlier generation. In this the house of Russell was unfortunate. At one time there may have been a recumbent figure on the armorial tomb of Henry Russell, the merchant squire of Dorset, great-grandfather of the first Earl. Henry Russell had died in 1438 and had been buried in the church of Holy Trinity, Dorchester. But in 1613 one of the terrible fires which only too often swept through a town had destroyed a great part of Dorchester and had devoured in its progress two churches, of which Holy Trinity was one. News of the destruction had been brought to Francis, Lord Russell, who had sent a messenger post-haste to Dorchester to make inquiries. In his own precise way, he had written out a list of questions that were to be asked and details that were to be looked for. He got little satisfaction in the replies. The messenger had stood in the burnt-out church, in which no vestige of any tomb was to be seen, much less a figure. But lying forlornly on the ground was a shield of arms. It proved to be the arms of Henry Russell, the well-known Russell arms, impaled with those of his second wife.

Henry Russell's son and grandson, grandfather and father respectively of the first Earl, had been buried not at Dorchester, but in the church of Swyre in the same county. Brasses mark their resting-places, but those brasses show no figures.

John, first Earl of Bedford, belonged to an age which saw the beginning of portrait painting in England. He was born in 1485, when Henry Tudor won the crown from Richard III, and died in 1555, when Mary Tudor had been two years on the throne. At least three portraits of this nobleman must always have been among the family possessions. The earliest shows Lord Russell, as he then was, grasping the long black rod which marked the office, which he held between 1537 and 1540, of Lord Comptroller of the King's Household. When the two later portraits were painted he was Lord Privy Seal and a Knight of the Garter. All three portraits were probably painted by one of the many followers and imitators of Holbein whose work so often bears his name, but was not executed by him.

Holbein himself, of very truth, did, however, make not a painting but a drawing of the first Earl of Bedford. This, the greatest portrait ever made of the Earl, is not nor ever was in any house belonging to the Russells. Under the title of 'The Lord Privy Seal with one eye'—Bedford had lost an eye in battle—it is in the royal collection at Windsor.

Another representation of the Earl as he was in life is in no picture gallery. His figure, made in marble, lies with folded hands upon his great tomb at Chenies. The face, with its long beard, is calm and resolute and the empty socket of one eye, with the lid drooping over it, is clearly shown. This was the man who successfully weathered the storms which beat about the ministers in the Court of Henry VIII.

The figure of his Countess, lying by his side, matches in its grandeur of conception that of her husband. Her face is as resolute and as dignified as his and gives the same impression of being a true likeness. This is the more fortunate since no portrait is known to exist of Anne, first Countess of Bedford.

The three paintings of the first Earl, with those of his son, the second Earl, the Elizabethan statesman, and the latter's children, form and must always have formed the nucleus of the family portrait gallery. The pictures of the second Earl, in his befurred clothes, show his face as heavy and plain as it undoubtedly was. 'The Earl of Bedford . . . is a monstrosity,' wrote De Spes, the Spanish ambassador. That was going a little far. But the concluding words, that he was also a heretic, explain the tendency to exaggeration. Nor do the portraits themselves do justice to the Earl's known sweetness of character. His sons had all the good looks that were denied their father. The handsome, thoughtful young faces, with just a hint of the pride of race that was so characteristic of the day, look down from the walls of the gallery, a perpetual reminder that 'golden lads and girls all must, as chimney sweepers, come to dust,' for three of these gallant youths never declined into old age, for death, by disease or on the battlefield, overtook them in their young prime. Of the second Earl's sons only the youngest,

William, afterwards Lord Russell of Thornhaugh, survived his father.

Around these family portraits at Woburn to-day are a series of pictures of the Tudor sovereigns whom the first and second Earls served. There, too, are portraits of their contemporaries and friends. The Cecil family, the Earls of Courtenay and Essex and many others are in their places.

Many of these pictures were undoubtedly given at different times to one or the other of the first two Earls in recognition of services rendered and friendship enjoyed. Among others, Holbein's Jane Seymour almost certainly once belonged to the first Earl of Bedford. He was closely associated with the Queen who gave Henry his 'most dearest son.' He held office under the boy King and during the last years of his life he served Mary Tudor as faithfully as he had served her father. The fine picture of that Queen by Il Moro which hangs on the walls at Woburn to-day, close by Hans Eworth's picture of her sitting with Philip in the state room at Whitehall, recalls that it was John Russell, first Earl of Bedford, in his old age, whom Mary sent to escort Philip to England.

But even though many and perhaps most of the portraits in the gallery at Woburn, as elsewhere, represented and do represent a close connection between the owner of the gallery and the subjects of the paintings, yet even in the sixteenth and seventeenth centuries other pictures were sometimes added to the collection on their own merits.

In the generation of the Russells succeeding that of the second Earl a lady who was far before her time in her appreciation of pictorial art married into the family. Lucy, sometime Lucy Harington, the wife of Edward, third Earl of Bedford, was a collector of pictures, not because they were family portraits, but because she recognised the skill of the painters. In 1617 the Countess described herself as 'a very diligent gatherer of all I can get of Holbein's or any other excellent master's hand.' Some such pictures, said Lucy, she had already found in obscure places. There was no doubt, added she, that there were other fine unknown pieces in the houses of noblemen and gentry who, because the pictures were old, made no reckoning of them.

How many such pictures Lucy succeeded in getting together and how many of them came to Woburn is unknown. But the gallery may well have a good deal for which to thank her. It is possible, even probable, that it was she who secured one unique possession. This is a picture representing Elizabeth, daughter of Sir Francis Cherry, who married Sir William Russell of Chippenham—no relation, as far as is known, to the Bedford Russells. The charm of the picture, a fine piece of painting, is great. The historical value lies in the fact that it is one of the only three known paintings which are signed in full by Gheerhaedts himself.

So also the collection may have to thank Lucy for the portrait of Queen Elizabeth, which is a Gheerhaedts studio piece. This picture can never have been the property of the second Earl of Bedford who served Elizabeth, for it belongs to a later day than his. He died three years before the great Armada came. But the picture has as its background two scenes from the story of that great fleet. The one shows it lying in the Calais roads with Drake's fire-ships advancing upon it. The other portrays the final destruction —the rocks, the great waves, the sinking vessels and hands uplifted in despair. This picture may be, probably is, identical with the 'portrait of Queen Elizabeth at length' which was at Woburn in the time of the fifth Earl. If so, it fared better than another painting which also hung then in the gallery and which had probably belonged to Lucy. This was a portrait of 'James I with his Queen and his son.' By whom it was painted, whether it was a good or a bad picture, will never be known, for no evidence can be offered for what may have happened to it after the moment when it was relegated to an upper room—an extremely poorly furnished upper room—not even at Woburn Abbey, but in one of the smaller houses.

A great number then, but probably not all, of the portraits which had been made of the earlier generations of the Russells who had not lived at Woburn, and some of those of their sovereigns and of their friends, were brought from various places to be hung on the walls of the Long Gallery in the new house when it was ready for occupation. With them came a few at least of the pictures which Lucy had, in her own words, so diligently gathered from other people's houses and at the same time the gallery was greatly enriched by yet another collection of sixteenth-century portraits, which was brought into the possession of the family by the fourth Earl's wife, Katherine, sometime Katherine Brydges, who had inherited them from her father and her grandfather.

Katherine's father, the third Baron Chandos, had been the patron of Jerome Custodis of Antwerp, a painter whose work except for a solitary specimen at Hampton Court is otherwise almost unknown. Two portraits by him, that of Baron Chandos himself and another of Elizabeth, afterwards Lady Kennedy, sister of the Countess of Bedford, came to Woburn. So also did others from an earlier collection of family portraits once in the possession of the grandfather of the Countess, Edward Fiennes, first Earl of Lincoln. Not the least among these was the painting by an unknown French artist of Lady Edward Fitzgerald, Countess of Lincoln, better known to posterity as the 'fair Geraldine' immortalized by the muse of the Earl of Surrey.

Between the original collection, the pictures added by Lucy and those provided by her successor, Katherine, the fourth Countess, the gallery began well. During the next seventy years more and yet more family portraits were painted for the Russell family, as for every other who had a house of any considerable size, in town or country, in which to hang the pictures. This fortunate demand for portraits was not so much due, perhaps was hardly due at all, to appreciation of great painting as consequent upon a wish to have likenesses of members of the family to put into the galleries. Connoisseurs of art, among whom King Charles the First was himself conspicuous, were still few and far between. But since the seventeenth century wanted portraits, it got them, and the result was that galleries were filled with many works which a later generation recognized as master-pieces and others which, if not worthy quite of the name of masterpiece, were at least examples of very fine painting.

The first portraits added to the Woburn gallery in the time of the fourth Earl were those made by Priwitzer, the almost unknown Hungarian artist, of the children of the house.

Alongside these pictures were two of the children's mother. Katherine, Countess of Bedford, was painted once in Gheerhaedts' studio and once, in 1634, by Cornelius van Ceulen.

Even amidst the opulence of the Elizabethan portraits, these, of a later generation whose taste both in clothes and jewels was at once more austere and more delicate than that of their predecessors, are still full of colour and gaiety.

In 1636 Van Dyck made his portrait of the Earl himself in his severe black, with the plain broad white collar. Looking at this picture it seems as if this great painting of a great nobleman must have dominated the other portraits around him then as it does to-day. Still more it seems that its merits as a painting must surely have always stood out. It is perhaps as well to remember, as an example of varying judgments in different generations, that the noble Duchess of Marlborough classed this picture with the others as of no interest except for the old-fashioned style of dress. The severity of that particular dress may, indeed, have alienated her.

Van Dyck made three other Russell portraits. Only one, that of Anne Carr in her white satin dress with the blue bows, painted on her marriage to the eldest son of the house, is at Woburn.

Some years before Van Dyck painted Anne, he had made a portrait of the young man who was to become her husband. William Russell was then about seventeen years old and his meeting with Anne as a marriageable girl and the plighting of their troth was still in the future. He was painted in company with another young man, his friend George, Lord Digby, who, as Earl of Bristol, became his brother-in-law. This portrait of two young men, scions of distinguished houses, in the heyday of their youth and beauty, never came to Woburn. It was painted for the Bristol family. Nearly half a century later, on 15th January 1679, John Evelyn dined with the Countess of Bristol in her Chelsea house and noticed the portrait among others on the walls. It is now at Althorp and an eighteenth-century copy made by Knapton is at Woburn.

The third Van Dyck portrait was yet another of Anne Carr. In this she is wearing a blue dress. For whom the picture was made and whether it was ever at Woburn are moot points. Known as one of 'Van Dyck's Countesses,' it is now and has long been at Petworth. Probably it came thither among the great collection of other paintings by Van Dyck which had once been the property of Jocelyn, eleventh Earl of Northumberland. On his death in 1669 his pictures passed to his daughter and heiress Elizabeth. This lady was grandmother to the Earl of Egremont, who was living at Petworth and exhibited the portrait of Anne, Countess of Bedford, in 1820.

The portrait may in the previous century have come into the hands of the Earl of Northumberland as a gift from the

Russells. The friendly connection between the two families was close and became closer when William Russell the younger, son of the fifth Earl of Bedford, married Rachel, sometime Rachel Wriothesley, who was sister to the Countess of Northumberland.

What is certain is that in 1661 William, Earl of Bedford, was in a position to have this picture copied. The work was done by a man known as Symon Stone, the 'picture drawer,' possibly one of the family of that name who were copyists of some celebrity. The copy, which can be identified, has remained at Woburn.

Mr. Stone, picture drawer—£10.

December 1661.—Received this 4th December 1661, of Mr. George Collop, by the hands of John Dawson, the sum of ten pounds for the copy of the Countess of Bedford's picture after Van Dyck. I say received, SYMON STONE   £10   0   0

The Earl of Bedford may have had this copy of his wife's portrait made because the original was not in his possession, or because it was about to pass out of his hands into those of the Earl of Northumberland.

After the Earl of Bedford, then William Russell, had sat to Van Dyck as a lad of seventeen, he was not apparently painted again until middle life, but two more pictures were made of the Countess, one by Theodore Russell and one by an unknown painter, both representing her as a young woman. Otherwise during the period of the Commonwealth and that of the early years of the Restoration, the two were, as parents are, more interested in having pictures made of their growing children than of themselves.

Peter Lely had come to England in 1641, the year in which Van Dyck died, and in the sixteen-fifties he was enjoying considerable favour under the Protector, whom he had

ANNE, COUNTESS OF BEDFORD

painted. About the year 1655 or 1656 Lely was called in to make a picture of the two elder Russell girls, Anne, who was then five or six years old, and her sister Diana, who was three or four. Lely showed the two sisters in a garden, with Anne helping herself to the red cherries which her sister held in her skirt. A little negro servant stood by their side holding a basket of roses. The parents must have been glad a year or two later to have possessed this picture, when, in October 1657, little Lady Anne was taken to her last resting-place in the chapel at Chenies, after eating the poisonous berries. They would perhaps have been even more pleased to have had another picture which showed the child as a single figure and had been painted for them by Verelst. The plump little figure, with the bare foot, is hugging her pet cockatoo.

This latter picture has another interest—a curious one. The cockatoo is well and clearly painted and all ornithologists agree there is no doubt that it represents a greater sulphur-crested cockatoo, which is found only in Australia. Lady Anne, or her parents for her, had acquired a specimen of the Australian cockatoo some two hundred years before that continent was known to Europeans. The explanation is, it has been suggested, a simple one. The birds are known to have been found as vagrants on islands and at sea far distant from Australia. One such must have so wandered and perhaps been captured by a sailor and brought back to England, to be bought by the Earl of Bedford. In the seventeenth century men who sailed in trading vessels were no whit behind their successors in bringing home curiosities, whether living creatures or otherwise and the Earl's officials were often at the Port of London.

After the little girls: the boys. As each was dispatched abroad with a tutor his portrait was painted for his parents.

In 1656, just before they left for France, the two elder

boys, William and Francis, were painted by Claud Lefèvre and the two were painted again on their return home from that first tour, in 1660. This time the painter Abraham Staphorst was employed. Having made the two portraits, he also made copies of them, and at the same time painted the two younger brothers, Edward and Robert, before they, in their turn, left England. Staphorst's charges were low, for he asked but three pounds apiece for the portraits with as much for the copies.

Mr. Staphorst's bill for pictures, £18 paid.

For the right honourable the Earl of Bedford.

February 1660/61.—My lord Russell's picture; Mr. William's; Mr. Edward's; Mr. Robert's; and two copies: one of my lord Russell's; another of Mr. William's; at £3 apiece.   £18   o   o

Perhaps the copies were made for Mr. Thornton, who now had to give over some of his pupils into other hands, although he retained his right of admonition and writing many letters. He was certainly given portraits of his pupils, for he mentioned them in his will. But the fate of these portraits by Staphorst is an excellent instance of how pictures can disappear. Nothing whatsoever is known of what became of them save one only, that of Robert, which survives at Woburn.

Another picture painted of yet a younger brother at this time has also survived. The Earl, sending his two little sons, James and George, to Westminster, desired to have portraits of them also. The picture of George—by whom painted it is not known—shows the little boy, primly dressed in a sort of grey baize or drugget costume, in his tenth year, just about to enter on his school career, the earliest portrait of a Westminster school boy that is known to exist.

During the sixteen-sixties and seventies Lely's reputation as a family portrait painter was growing daily. He was now living in one of the houses belonging to the Earl of Bedford in the Piazza in Covent Garden and he made a number of paintings of various members of the family for the Earl. He painted Lady Diana in 1667, as a girl of fifteen, and her brother Robert in 1671. He charged £29 10s. 0d. for the picture of Lady Diana and twenty-five pounds for that of Robert. The first price, however, included a frame, which was not the case with the second.

£29. 10. 0. Mr. Lely for Lady Diana's picture.

August 1667.—Received of the honourable the Earl of Bedford, by Mr. Dawson, for my lady Diana Russell's picture and frame, the sum of twenty-nine pounds ten shillings. I say received by me, JOHN WILKINSON   £29   10   0

February 1670/71.—Received this 14th of February 1670/71, of George Collop, Esquire, by the hands of Mr. John Dawson, the sum of twenty-five pounds for the picture of Mr. Robert Russell. I say received, P. LELY   £25   0   0

In the signature, as written, the 'P' and the 'L' are formed into a twisted monogram.

Besides Diana and Robert, Lely also painted, at some date unknown, their elder brother, William. This, of the three pictures, is the only one that has a continuous history, for it has always remained at Woburn. The portrait of Lady Diana disappeared for many years and only returned to Woburn late in the nineteenth century. The portrait of Robert has gone, perhaps for ever.

Finally, Lely painted the master of the house also. The Earl, after an interval of nearly forty-five years, began to sit for his portrait again. The reasons were fairly obvious. He was now a great man, in very flourishing circumstances, and had attained to the dignity of a Knight of the Garter. A commemorative portrait or portraits of him were desirable in the interests of the family. He also needed portraits to give away to his children and grandchildren and to institutions with which he was connected.

Two portraits were made by Lely, one in 1675 and one the following year.

The painting of 1675 was made as a present for William Russell. It is a three-quarter length and shows the Earl seated, dressed in one of his Indian gowns, which was a loose flowing robe of figured silk, a form of attire of which he was fond.

June 1675. To Mr. Lely, by his lordship's order, the 7th of June 1675, for his lordship's picture for Mr. William Russell.   £31   o   o
And to Mr. John Smith for a frame for it.   £3   o   o

William, now for some years a married man, presumably had the picture, with its frame, in one of his residences. His wife, Rachel, parted with little or nothing that had belonged to her husband after his execution and we must suppose that the picture remained with her until her death in 1723. Then for two hundred years it vanished into obscurity, to be found again in an auction room in the present century and placed among the Woburn collection.

The second and last picture made of the Earl by Lely is by far the greater of the two. This at least has never wandered from Woburn. The painter's charge on this occasion was double what it had been previously, namely, sixty pounds.

From the account of Mr. Collop, receiver-general.

May 1676.   Paid to Mr. Lely the 16th of
May 1676, for his lordship's
picture at length.   £60   o   o
To Mr. John Smith for a frame
for it, by his lordship's order.   £9   o   o
And for a case to send it in to
Woburn.   £1   5   o

Sir Peter Lely's receipt.

May 1676.   Received then of the Right Honourable the Earl of Bedford, by
payment of Mr. George Collop,
the sum of sixty pounds in full
for his lordship's picture at
length. I say received, P. LELY   £60   o   o

The picture was well worth the additional cost. It shows
the Earl, a man of sixty-three, still in the full plenitude
of his power, standing full length in all the glory of his
robes as Knight of the Garter. In his left hand is the hat
with the white ostrich feather in the midst of which stands
out clear and distinct the special black heron's plume, or, as
the receiver-general called it in the bill which he presented
to his master for its purchase, 'heron's top.'

Sir Peter Lely died in 1680 and was buried in the church
of St. Paul, Covent Garden. Within the next ten years,
certainly before 1690, another painter, Godfrey Kneller,
moved into a house in the Piazza.

Kneller made at least five or six portraits of the Earl and
may have made others. Four different receipts by the painter
for these pictures remain, which, incidentally, show his
rising scale of charges.

July 1682.—Received this 15th of July 1682,
of Mr. George Collop, by the hands of Mr.

Dawson, eight pounds for his lordship's picture
and thirty-five shillings for the picture's frame.
I say received, G. KNELLER   £9 15 0

June 1686.—My lord the Earl of Bedford's
picture.   £10 0 0

> [Signed by Bernhard Percy for
> Mr. Godfrey Kneller.]

January 1693.—Received from the right
honourable Earl of Bedford forty pounds due
in full for his lordship's picture in length by me,
G. KNELLER   £40 0 0

December 1694.—Received for His Grace
the Duke of Bedford's picture in whole length,
thirty pounds, by the hands of Mr. Petty, in
full, by me, G. KNELLER   £30 0 0

When the Earl commissioned a portrait of himself from
Kneller, he usually did so because he wanted one to give
away to a friend or relative. But two pictures of his grandchildren, the son and daughters of William, Lord Russell,
also painted by Sir Godfrey, have remained at Woburn and
were most probably made for the pleasure of the Earl
himself. In 1686 Sir Godfrey painted the boy as a single
figure and the two little girls in a group. The boy,
Wriothesley, afterwards second Duke of Bedford, was five
years of age and for his portrait was dressed in a Roman
costume. This cost the Earl twenty-five pounds for the
portrait, with two pounds ten shillings for the gold frame.
The charge for the little girls' group was comparatively high
at fifty-four pounds. This, however, included the frame.

	£	s.	d.
June 1686. For my lord's grandson.	25	0	0
For a gold frame to it.	2	10	0

> [Signed by Bernhard Percy
> for Mr. Godfrey Kneller.]

October 1686. Drawn for the Right Honourable the Earl of Bedford, the two daughters of my lady Russell, whole length, in one piece, in frame, in case for the same; comes in all to fifty-four pounds ten shillings.   *£54* 10 0

Received this 20th day of October 1686, of the Right Honourable the Earl of Bedford by the payment of Mr. Richard Petty, the sum of fifty-four pounds and ten shillings in full of the above-said pictures and frame. I say received by the appointment and to the use of Mr. Godfrey Kneller, by me,

BERNHARD PERCY   *£54* 10 0

Lastly, when Wriothesley, a boy of fifteen, was married to Elizabeth Howland, a girl of thirteen, the latter's mother had the portraits of the two painted to celebrate the occasion.

From Mrs. Howland's Account Book.

May 1696. Paid Sir Godfrey Kneller for Lord Tavistock's and my daughter's pictures in one piece.   *£50* 0 0

Paid Mr. Hugh, framemaker, for a frame for Lord Tavistock and his lady's picture in a piece.   *£5* 0 0

Two miniatures are mentioned in the Earl's accounts, one of which was made in 1679 of the Earl himself by a painter called Grossing. Nothing so far is known of the painter or of the miniature, which has disappeared. But in 1691 the Earl gave his granddaughter, Katherine, a miniature of her dead father, William, Lord Russell. This was painted either by Simon Dubois or his brother Edward. They were natives of Antwerp who had come to London about 1682 and had attained some reputation for painting.

		£	s.	d.
April 1691.	Paid by his lordship's order to Madame Dubois, the 3rd of April 1691, for the Lord Russell's picture in miniature for Mistress Katherine Russell, five guineas.	5	7	6
	For a crystal for it.		5	0
	For a shagreen case to put it in.		6	0
		£5	18	6

Pictures might be and were on occasion discarded from the gallery. But at least those kept there were well looked after. On one occasion a man called Peter Walton came down to the abbey for a fortnight in order to repair certain of the portraits. This is, thinks Mr. W. G. Constable, the earliest known account which records anything of the kind being done.

	£	s.	d.
November 1692. For repairing the picture of the Lady Elizabeth Bruges.	4	0	0
For repairing the picture of the Lord Chandos, Baron of Sudeley.	3	0	0
For repairing the picture of the Lady Frances Chandos.	2	0	0

	£	s.	d.
For repairing and lining the picture of the Earl of Southampton.	1	10	0
For repairing the picture of my lord Bacon.	1	0	0
For frames blacking and the panels glueing, and porters bringing the cases from the carriers and backwards.		15	0
As for my being at my lord's a fortnight, and coach hire.	7	0	0
	£19	5	0

Three of the pictures are those of the Chandos family. Two of them—those of Lady Elizabeth Bruges, afterwards Lady Kennedy, and the third Lord Chandos, father of the fourth Countess of Bedford, both painted by Jerome Custodis—are still at Woburn. The third picture, that of Lady Frances Chandos, has disappeared.

The portrait called the Earl of Southampton may represent either the first, third or fourth Earl of that name, all of whose portraits are in the picture gallery. Thomas Wriothesley, first Earl of Southampton, was the contemporary and friend of the first Earl of Bedford. The third and fourth Earls were respectively the grandfather and the father of Rachel, Lady Russell.

The portraits at Woburn under the fifth Earl were kept, for the most part, where they belonged—in the portrait gallery. Only a few were to be found in other parts of the house. Notably the Earl's own dressing-room held a full-length portrait of himself. The walls of the majority of the living-rooms had indeed no place for pictures. For Woburn, as for his London house, the Earl of Bedford continued faithful to tapestry hangings, which he seems to have preferred to the alternative mode of wood panelling. The fine tapestries at Bedford House which had been taken away by the Parliamentary commissioners in 1643 to pay the fine had been replaced and nearly all the rooms in the London house were still tapestry-hung on the Earl's death in 1700. Woburn Abbey had never lost its hangings and in 1664 they were supplemented by an important purchase when a set of five pieces depicting the Acts of the Apostles after the cartoons of Raphael was ordered from the royal factory at Mortlake.

> 1664.—To Mr. Francis Hullenberch, in full for the suite of hangings made at Mort-lake, with 10s. given his servant (besides £80 paid in part in the last account).   £229 14 0

These tapestries are still in existence, although no longer in the great drawing-room where Horace Walpole saw and admired them when he visited the abbey in 1751.

Some of these tapestry-hung rooms did, nevertheless, contain a picture, although not a portrait. Paintings of landscapes, then but lightly regarded, found a place, albeit a very modest place, at Woburn. One such was in one of the withdrawing-rooms, in the only spot on the walls where a picture might be put without interference with the hangings, that is over the fireplace. These pictures, called, as this one was in the inventory, 'chimney pictures,' were usually canvases let into recesses shaped to fit them.

The subject of this chimney picture is not stated in the inventory; nor is that of another landscape which the Earl bought as early as July 1660, from one of the few landscape painters of the day, Robert Streeter, or Streater. This last was not put into one of the sitting-rooms, but into the Earl's own bedroom, for which it had been especially purchased. The price was four pounds ten shillings. But the bill for yet another landscape picture does give some description of it.

January 1675/6.—To Mr. Dankers, by his lordship's order, the 26th of January 1675/6, as by his acquittance, for a landscape of Plymouth and the citadel there and parts adjacent.   £10   0   0

Of the family only the Earl apparently had a portrait in his bedroom, while such sitting-rooms as had a picture at all merely had one over the chimney-piece. Yet when the maker of the inventory went through the house in 1700 he noted certain paintings that were neither in the picture gallery nor yet in any of the best sitting-rooms or bedrooms. He found them, no less than eight in number, on the walls of some of the servants' chambers. There is only too much reason to fear that some, at least, of these may have been, in the words of that excellent judge of painting, Lucy, Countess of Bedford, fine pieces, relegated on account of age to obscure places.

CHAPTER XVI

IN SICKNESS AND IN DEATH

By far the most healthy and vigorous member of the family at Woburn Abbey in his own day was the Earl himself. He had, indeed, his ailments. His teeth were none too good and he frequently suffered from toothache, which necessitated the bringing to him of a tooth-drawer, who charged anything from five shillings to ten shillings for the operation. He had, too, a lighter, but yet irritating, affliction in his corns. A corn-cutter visited the abbey regularly to deal with them, sometimes once a fortnight, sometimes once a month, charging from half a crown to five shillings.

These two were minor troubles. He had a third more serious than either, for he suffered, at all events from middle life onwards, from bad eyesight. His oculist was the celebrated Daubeney Turberville, who had once been a royalist soldier and had then turned to the study of medicine and had become an eye specialist. He ordered the Earl to wear spectacles, which got broken or mislaid with remarkable regularity. There were few months indeed in which Mr. Dixy Taylor did not have to return to Mr. Collop an account either for purchasing new spectacles for his lordship, or for mending the old ones. Sometimes it was 'mending spectacles twice' in the course of a few weeks. Luckily the cost of neither purchase nor mending was high. The 'spectacle man,' Mr. Cox, charged five shillings for an entirely new pair of spectacles and anything from sixpence to half a crown for mending broken ones. Cox was one of the now numerous native spectacle-makers who were rapidly improving in their craft so as to outstrip their German rivals, from whom spectacles earlier in the century had been chiefly imported.

Cox was selling spectacles to the Earl, or mending the old ones, fairly frequently from the mid-sixties onwards. In May 1670 the Earl's eyes must have suddenly grown worse, or some sort of a crisis have occurred, for it was necessary for Mr. Dixy Taylor to send off his assistant, Lancelot Harwood, post-haste to Dr. Turberville, who was then at Salisbury.

To Mr. Harwood upon account of his journey to Dr. Turberville.

		£	s.	d.
May 1670.	For two post horses for myself and guide, the post boys' gratuities and my own expenses.	2	18	6
	My expenses there something extraordinary occasioned by some visits of the doctors and others and for horse hire twice to Bremer.	2	10	6
	Lost earnest when intended to come away with Monday's coach, but prevented by his lordship's letter, to his farther commands.		5	0
	Earnest for a coach for the doctor.	2	0	0
	My own coach hire home and expenses on the road.	1	13	0
	A pair of shoes, not thinking to stay.		3	6
		£9	10	6

One of the King's physicians, Sir John Baber, had per-fected a lotion for the eyes which he called 'Sir John Baber's eye water.' The cost was two shillings a bottle and one was frequently bought for the Earl, especially during the latter years of his life, as well as ophthalmic ointment. With the eye water was usually purchased a special feather with which to apply it.

March 3, 1681. Sir John Baber's eye water.	2*s.*	0*d.*
An ophthalmic ointment.	1*s.*	8*d.*
June 25, 1692. An eye water and feathers.	3*s.*	0*d.*

But for these weaknesses, the Earl enjoyed on the whole, from youth until extreme age, remarkable health. He took, indeed, the health precautions customary at the time—a regular letting of blood, a regular course of purging draughts and pills and, when necessary, sweating medicine—but these, like the visits to Tunbridge Wells and, later, Bath, were precautionary rather than curative measures.

Once only in his eighty-four or more years was he visited by a serious illness. In 1659 he went down with the dreaded smallpox. He recovered, and the anxiety felt over the attack turned to rejoicing that it had taken place, since it was known that anyone who had been smitten with smallpox and had recovered was likely to be immune from it for the rest of his life.

After this, the Earl's ailments were little more than matters of a few days' illness. He was subject all his life to attacks of colic, but they appear to have passed very quickly. In 1675 he had rheumatism in his legs and shoulders. This he took very ill and remarked he was sure he would be dead in a very few weeks. According to Mr. Thornton's correspondence, he could, in that gentleman's opinion and in that of the doctor, have been cured at once had he only yielded to their persuasions to take the medicine they recommended. In this matter, however, 'his lordship may not be prevailed upon.' The attack was ultimately cured by a visit to Bath.

Rheumatism, to a man who had not, it appears, hitherto suffered from it, seemed a terrible complaint. Actually the Earl's powers of recuperation were remarkable and hardly slackened even during the latter years of his life. When he was verging on his eightieth year the news that he had a very severe cold or an attack of colic, invariably brought letters from a son or a daughter, or both, written to Mr. Thornton or the gentleman of the chamber, advising remedies of all kinds. 'I have a medicine,' wrote one of them, when it appeared possible that a heavy cold would turn to pleurisy, 'that has cured the worst of pleurisies . . . and it is a powder made of three acorns and two peach stones, and take as much of it as will lie on a shilling in a proper vehicle.' Lady Diana almost invariably advocated abstinence from food, in which she firmly believed, and declared it would cure many ailments. Indeed her cry always was, in her letters to Mr. Thornton when any member of the family was ill, 'If he would come down to me, I should quickly cure him by fasting.' Her father had no particular belief in fasting either from food or from wine, nor did it appear to him very necessary, for it was seldom indeed that Mr. Thornton's letter announcing that the Earl was ill was not immediately followed by one telling of his complete recovery.

There is a payment of a pound to a 'gout doctor' in 1677 which was probably on his account, for attacks—mercifully they were only very slight—of gout afflicted him along with the rheumatism.

The health of the rest of the household, with one exception, was not as good as that of the master. The exception was Mr. Thornton. That gentleman was credited in the bills with considerably less medicine than anyone else, either because he had no faith for himself in that which he was fond of giving others, or because he had his own private store. In any case, there is no evidence that he was ever either sick or sorry.

The Countess of Bedford had many attacks of illness. Although, like many delicate people, she lived out her full span of years, for she was seventy when she died, she was a delicate woman for most of her life and during the last years of it an invalid. Except for the attack of smallpox after her father-in-law's death, no specific disease is ever mentioned in connection with her, but 'the time of her weakness' or 'the time of her sickness' is often spoken of quite apart from the births of her children, and from 1660 onwards nurses and doctors were constantly in attendance.

The principal medical men who were called in for the Countess and also for the rest of the household on serious occasions were Doctors Micklethwait and King, afterwards Sir John Micklethwait and Sir Edmund King.

Dr. Micklethwait had been assistant at St. Bartholomew's Hospital to the Dr. John Clarke who had come to Woburn when the Countess had had smallpox in 1641, and had married his daughter. He had been one of Dr. Clarke's successors as President of the College of Physicians and his portrait hangs to-day near that of Clarke. He was not a Court physician, but when Charles II had been taken seriously ill in 1681 he had been called in and had prescribed for the royal patient with great success.

Dr. King, well known as a great researcher and experimentalist, had had a more varied career. He had begun to practise as a surgeon, but he had shortly decided that he was better suited for a physician. Accordingly, he obtained his Degree from the Archbishop of Canterbury. As Court physician he had been summoned to Whitehall when Charles had shown symptoms of what proved to be his last illness. While he was in the room Charles fell down in a fit, whereupon King immediately bled him and the royal patient regained consciousness. The other physicians, coming in, exclaimed that King had undoubtedly saved His Majesty's life and the Privy Council, hearing of this, recommended a gratuity of a thousand pounds. It was never paid, for, before the warrant could be signed, Charles was dead. Dr. King was often brought to Woburn Abbey and it was he who attended the Countess in her last illness.

A third doctor who often came to Woburn, either for the Countess or for some other member of the family, was a Frenchman, Dr. Charlot.

The doctors did not always come to the Abbey to treat their patient. Sometimes it was done by correspondence. Mr. Thornton would write a letter describing the trouble and the doctor would reply in another telling Thornton how to deal with it.

Richard Lower to John Thornton at Woburn.

December 9, 1684.

HONOURED SIR,

I have received your letter concerning my lord's condition, which is his lordship's old distemper of the colic illness of his stomach, for which I would advise the taking of 'mirthall' water four days following, boiling three quarts to two in an earthen pipkin with either an ounce of manna in the first draught of it or else my lord may take of his stomach pills the night preceding the use of the water. After my lord hath taken the water, he may take six spoonfuls of the bitter wine which I have prescribed for twenty days following, which is the best thing I know to strengthen his stomach to procure a good appetite and digestion and to take off all those symptoms mentioned in your letters. Beside, I have sent a digestive powder to be taken before and after meals and some purging pills, to be taken four at a time in the morning once in a week or ten days, drinking some thin chicken broth on the working of them.

I doubt not but my lord will receive benefit by these things in a short time. I am, Sir,

Your most faithful humble servant,

RICHARD LOWER

At other times, if the symptoms were such that even Mr. Thornton's ready pen failed to describe them properly, the tutor would journey to town and see one of the doctors, generally Micklethwait. The latter would give instructions; Mr. Thornton would write them down and return to Woburn to superintend the carrying of them out.

Apart from Doctors Micklethwait, King and Charlot, who were well known and distinguished physicians, a number of men from the neighbouring towns, Bedford, St. Albans and Leighton Buzzard, came at all times to the abbey to minister to the lesser ailments of the household.

The tooth-drawer, whether a barber or a surgeon—both seem at different times to have fulfilled this office—was a frequent visitor, for the master of the house was not the only person who had difficulties with his teeth. The teeth of the household in general were constantly being drawn and the troubles, including what was known as 'scurvy in the gums,' caused by bad teeth, were common to all.

For the page.

October 1676.	Imprimis a purging aporem.	2s.	6d.
	Item a tooth drawn.	1s.	0d.
	Item a cordial powder.	1s.	0d.
	Item a lotion for his mouth.	1s.	0d.
		5s.	6d.

January 3, 1678.	Mary Bateson had her gums bled.	2s.	6d.
November 4, 1681.	Item Richard Berry curing the scurvies in the gums.	2s.	6d.

In any event, surgeons came to the house with great regularity, monthly or even twice in a month. Their arrival was not necessarily either to draw a tooth, which they may or may not have done, or to attend to a damaged bone, but often implied that the time had come round for a certain number of the family and of the household to undergo the process which was called in the bills alternatively bleeding, opening a vein or breathing a vein. Every one inside and outside the abbey, beginning with the Earl and including the women as well as the men, was bled several times in the year. The lists of names as put into the surgeons' bills suggest that each was taken in his or her regular turn, with an additional bleeding if the subject was so unfortunate as to be taken ill in between the treatments.

For the servants of the Right Honourable the Earl of Bedford.

		£	s.	d.
March 1, 1675.	Ann Johnson a vein opened.		2	6
March 3.	William Huckle a vein opened.		2	6
	Mr. Kirk breathing a vein.		2	6
	Mr. Nelson breathing a vein.		2	6
	And emplasters to his contusion.		3	0
	Christopher Peach breathing a vein.		2	6
	Richard Berry breathing a vein.		2	6
April 4.	Matthew Robinson open a vein.		2	6
April 5.	Ann Johnson open a vein.		2	6
	Mr. Kirk open a vein.		2	6
	Cataplasms for his contusion.		4	0
June 21.	Thomas Bell a vein opened.		2	6
		£1	12	0

To the right honourable the Earl of Bedford his servants.

		£	s.	d.
January 12, 1689.	Mr. Dodderidge bled.		2	6
January 22.	George Atkins bled.		1	6
February 13.	John Bradnock for the cure of a wound in his hand.	1	0	0
February 19.	George Atkins bled.		1	6
March 9.	Mr. Whale bled.		2	6
March 20.	Clement Robinson bled.		1	6
	James Evans bled.		1	6
March 26.	Mrs. Stacy bled.		2	6
March 31.	John Buttery bled.		1	6
	Thomas Tod bled.		1	6
April 18.	Richard Berry bled.		1	6
	Thomas Gresham bled.		1	6
April 23.	Thomas Evans bled.		1	6
April 26.	Robert Clark bled.		1	6
April 29.	Mr. Bingley bled.		5	0
July 1.	For a strengthening plaster for Robert Clark's shoulder.		2	6
July 10.	For another of the same.		2	6
July 14.	Richard Berry bled.		1	6
July 19.	Another strengthening plaster for Robert Clark.		2	6
		£2	16	6

When a woman was bled, or had a vein opened, it was often set down that it was done because of hysteria, or, in some instances, because she was 'distracted.'

November 21, 1678.—Item letting blood a distracted woman.   1*s.* 0*d.*

Cases of what was generally called hysteria were extremely common among the women and only to a degree less so among the men. Among the contributions of Thomas Sydenham, the eminent doctor and scientist of the day, to medical science was his study of the nervous complaints then grouped together either under this name or under the alternative title of hypochondria. These two ailments were, he held, responsible at that time for at least one sixth of all human maladies and in so far as men were less subject to them than women it was, he thought, on account of their more hardy and robust lives. Men who led sedentary or studious lives, particularly those at the universities, were, in his opinion, constantly afflicted with hypochondria, which was 'as like hysteria as one egg was like another.' As for women, they were, he went on, rarely quite free from one or the other afflictions which made up hysteria and the few who were so were such as lived a vigorous outdoor life.

The case of Francis, Lord Russell, always set down as melancholy, was only an extreme case of a common ailment combined, in him, with real physical disability.

Sydenham departed at the time from general medical practice in advocating for these nervous cases tonics either in the form of chalybeate or of bark. The latter he was perhaps the first to use for that purpose, although its efficacy in cases of ague was already well known. Minor remedies were given in the form of 'hysterical water' or preparations of hartshorn, which were often bought, in particular for the female section of the household.

Sydenham might use tonics as new, or almost new, remedies, but he no more than any other doctor went so far as to dispense with bleeding as a specific for hysteria as well as for keeping men and women in health generally. Nor did he abandon the other two great traditional remedies of purging and sweating.

In the case of almost every form of sickness pills and potions were ordered by the doctors to bring about purging and sweating and so to 'drive the poison out.' Even when

no doctor was called in, large quantities of such preparations
were purchased weekly from the apothecaries for the use of
all at Woburn Abbey, from the Earl down to the least of the
kitchen boys. 'The purging lotion again,' with the name of
the member of the family for whom it was required alongside it, was a regular entry and the household generally was
dosed with the same frequency and regularity as it was bled.

		£	s.	d.
1674.	*For Robin, the keeper.*			
	Imprimis a cordial for three doses.		2	6
	Item a purging potion.		1	6
	Item a cordial spirit.		1	0
	Item a journey		5	0
	For John Bradnock [the porter].			
	Imprimis an electuary by Doctor Stubbs			
	his directions.		2	0
	Betty Buskin, the laundry maid, a vomit.		1	0
	The housemaid, Judith, a vomit.		1	0
	For the coachman, two doses of pills.		2	0
			16	0

Besides the purging and sweating remedies, a big place
was filled in the bills by all kinds of pectoral juleps, lotions,
liniments, ointments and plasters for the treatment of the
chills and colds which constantly pervaded the household.
Not that anyone afflicted with either escaped the purging
and sweating. The other remedies were additional.

Among other items supplied for general use were quantities of antiscorbutics. Many forms of scurvy, not only
scurvy in the gums, constantly occurred. Francis, Lord
Russell, with whom, as usual, in this as in other things, life
dealt hardly, suffered more from this form of complaint
than any other member of his family. But he was by no

means the only victim. A particularly bad attack overtook the Countess in the year of the Restoration and even the Earl himself did not escape entirely, for draughts of anti-scorbutic tincture were prescribed for him in 1692. After being treated for scurvy, the patient was often ordered chalybeate water, which was also given as a stimulant after the bleeding process. The Countess, in particular, took tonics with great regularity. In her case the dose supplied was mainly what was called the pearl cordial.

In all these things the apothecaries in the neighbouring towns—two at least lived at Aylesbury—to whom the Earl gave his custom doubtless often encroached on the doctors' prerogatives, as they were very fond of doing, and pre-scribed for the patient as well as supplied the remedy.

A bill for medicines provided for the servants during March and April 1675 is similar to many another.

The right honourable the Earl of Bedford's servants.

March 27, 1675.		£	s.	d.
Mr. Wood's child.	Eight papers of powder with pearl.		4	0
	A cordial julep.		3	0
Mrs. Abigail.	A glass of antiscorbutic juices.		2	6
March 28.				
Mr. Burroughs.	Three doses of cordial pills.		3	0
	A lambative.		2	6
March 30.				
Mrs. Pitts.	A glass of antiscorbutic juices.		2	6
March 31.				
Mrs. Abigail.	The juices again.		2	6
Ann Johnson.	A plaster for her foot.		1	0
	A cordial bolus.		1	6
	A cordial draught.		2	0

313

		£	s.	d.
April 1.				
Mr. Robert's footman.	A plaster and oil of St. John's wort.			7
Coachman.	A box of pills.		1	6
Judith.	A gargle.		2	0
April 4.				
Mrs. Abigail.	The juices again.		2	6
April 6.				
Mrs. Magdalen.	Civet.			8
	A dose of pills.		1	6
April 9.				
Mrs. Abigail.	The juices again.		2	6
Lidia Long.	A pot of pills.		2	0
Mr. Wood.	A box of purging pills.		2	0
Mrs. Abigail.	Three doses of pills.		1	6
April 13.				
Mr. Robert's footman.	The plaster again.			6
April 15.				
	A gargle.		2	6
April 18.				
Mr. Bellingham.	A box of pills.		2	6
Mr. Cole's child.	A lambative.		2	0
	A glass of pectoral syrups.		2	6
	A pot of ointment for the stomach.		1	6
April 31.				
Lidia Long.	A box of stomach pills.		3	0
John Bradnock.	A lambative.		3	0
	Three doses of cordial pills.		3	0

In February 1679 a bill of nearly five pounds for medicines supplied to Lady Margaret refers chiefly to hartshorn, cordial pearl juleps, pearl powders and the inevitable pills and draughts.

Accidents of all kinds, especially in the stables, necessitating minor surgical treatment, were inevitable. The men were constantly damaging their limbs. There was always the apprehension of gangrene, and the sequence of rheumatism after a sprained ankle or a broken limb was but too well known. In the stables and kennels the men were bitten by the dogs and horses and kicked by the latter into the bargain.

		£	s.	d.
July 1653.	Paid to Mr. Gregory, the surgeon, for and about Erland's boy, his fall.		2	6
December 26, 1670.	Then received of Mr. Bingley, the sum of forty shillings for the cure of Frank, the footman, of a gunshot wound in his toe, for the use of my master, James Mollins.	2	o	o
	By me THOMAS HOBBS			
October 1678.	*A bill of my charges when I was at Berkhamsted.*			
	For dressing me for my bite and bleeding and for drink that I had home with me.		10	o
	Paid to the doctor for the time of my fever.	2	9	o
	For my lodging, nurse and diet.	2	1	o
		£5	o	o
November 21, 1678.	Item Richard Berry plasters for the bite of a horse.		1	o

The fees to the surgeons, doctors, tooth-drawers, corn-cutters and barbers were paid on a regular basis. The apothecaries, too, probably had their fixed charges and the amounts paid for each of the various medicines differ, like the fees paid to the surgeons and others, remarkably little over the whole period of forty years. Occasionally, however, the question of a fee was left to the generosity of the Earl, perhaps when the cure was performed by someone who could not be dignified by the title of doctor proper, or even apothecary.

	£	s.	d.
October 1676. Item the curing a boy that belongs to the stables thrust through the hand with a fork, my lord's pleasure.			
For the helper.			
Imprimis letting blood.		1	0
Item a purging aporem.		2	6
Item for other necessaries and dressings, my lord's pleasure.			

Bilious and liver attacks, colds and coughs, lesser accidents and hysterics, even rheumatism, were, when all was said and done, minor ailments. Others were far more serious.

Every year saw a certain amount of fever in the country, chiefly of the typhus type. At intervals of every few years came one or the other of those epidemics, fever in all its various forms, which swept the country and took a heavy toll of the lives of the inhabitants. Two of these fevers, the plague and the smallpox, have been given the most prominence and perhaps attained the greatest prominence in men's minds in the seventeenth century. Symptoms of illness which might prove to be one of these diseases caused terrified apprehension, which was only too often justified.

As a boy of ten or eleven the Earl had arrived at the abbey with his parents and his brothers and sisters in flight from the plague of 1625. As far as is known, none of the household had then gone down with it, although they heard of only too many of their friends elsewhere being smitten. There is nothing to indicate that the pestilence in any of the successive years when it was rife touched any of the household, either at Woburn or at Bedford House, until the outbreak of 1665, when the town of Woburn had forty deaths in two months. Among them were three, if not more, footmen from the abbey, where a number of the menservants, though apparently none of the women, were laid low.

1665.—To nurses for their attendance on sundry of his lordship's servants in the time of their sickness and for the burials of some of them, viz. of Thomas Bell, sickness, £5. 17. 6.; of John Harris and for his burial, 19. 4.; and of Robert Scarborow and for his burial, 16s. 10d. In all, with 7s. 6d. for looking to John Keeper and Thomas Cole in their weakness.   £8   1   2

Two years later another epidemic of some kind broke out among the servants at the abbey. It may either have been a slight recrudescence of the plague, or one or other of the indeterminate fevers which were rife at the time. There were two deaths among the footmen. Actually, although the sufferers at the time knew it not, the plague was about to disappear.

Other epidemic fevers did not so disappear. Some of them were so far from disappearing as to increase greatly in malignancy. 'Here abundance fall sick of the smallpox and other diseases, which will put us in mind of another world,' wrote Margaret Russell to Mr. Thornton. The more sober among the men and women of the seventeenth century felt with Thomas Fuller that thoughts of mortality were cordial to the soul. They heard only too often the beating of death's wings as a pestilence swept the country.

Among the infectious fevers smallpox had now for some time past been equalling, if not outstripping, the plague in the feelings of horror and dread which it excited. Yet one doctor, Thomas Sydenham, declared that the awful mortality from this infection need never be, were men but wise. He was referring to his medical colleagues. Smallpox, said Sydenham, was a natural process which almost every one had to go through once in his or her lifetime and arose from a proper desire of the blood to throw off impurities. It is true that towards the end of his life he somewhat modified this theory, but he continued to think of the disease as one which ought to run a very mild course. This, he was justified in pointing out, had actually been the case on its first appearance in England early in the sixteenth century, when it had seldom caused severe illness and had been confined chiefly to children. The later virulent epidemics were, in his opinion, the result of the folly of doctors who had encouraged the fever by over-nursing it. It is easy to criticize some of the obvious absurdities of Sydenham's theories to-day. Yet in many respects he was far ahead of his age. The cynical and those who distrusted doctors could see some foundation for his ideas in the conclusion, for which there is considerable evidence, that whereas the mortality of the plague had been far higher among the poorer than among the richer classes, the exact contrary was the case with the smallpox. The well-fed, well-housed, thoroughly doctored and nursed appear to have been seized by the fever and to have succumbed to it more easily than those of a more lowly condition who were less well provided for alike in health and in sickness.

The family of the Earl of Bedford at least had suffered sufficiently from smallpox. Margaret, the second Countess, had died of it in 1565. Lucy, the third Countess, had had her beauty ruined as a result of its ravages. The fifth Countess had been desperately ill with it after the death of her father-in-law from the same infection in 1641. Then the family had a temporary respite for some years. In 1659 the attacks began again with renewed virulence, commencing with the illness of the Earl himself early in the spring. His case was one of many during a notably bad year for the disease over the entire country, when the deaths in London alone rose to over fifteen hundred, nearly four times the number of the previous year. The epidemic slackened somewhat during the next year, that of the Restoration, although the return of the royal family was marked by two fatalities in the Palace of Whitehall, when first the King's brother, the Duke of Gloucester, died in September 1660, and next his sister, Mary of Orange, coming on a visit, caught the infection in the middle of December and was dead within a very few days. The following year, that of the coronation, things were worse, and William Russell fell a victim in July. He was so ill that it was thought for some time that he might not recover. Dr. Micklethwait was called in and several nurses were provided.

1661. Given to Doctor Micklethwait, the physician, at several times for his visits and advice in the time of the sickness of Mr. William Russell.   £45 0 0

Given by his lordship's order to the said Mr. Hinton for his extra-ordinary care about Mr. William in the time of his sickness—£10. 0. 0.; to Mrs. Fettiplace for her attend-ance upon him—£5. 0. 0.; and to a nursekeeper for her service about him by the space of six weeks at 8s. 0d. the week—£2. 8. 0. In all   £17 8 0

After this the smallpox was continually in and out of the Earl's bills and most of the members of the family had the complaint during the following years. They were fortunate in escaping fairly lightly. The next catastrophe was after the Earl's own lifetime, when first his young grandson and successor and then the latter's wife succumbed in turn to the disease.

Besides members of the family, few years passed without one of the household going down with smallpox. Some principles of isolation were certainly observed, although not on very definite lines. Nor did they extend very far. There is no good account of the Earl's own illness, but some of the entries referring to that of his son, who had two nurses, may mean that he was sent away from the house. Certainly in many cases a room was taken outside for the sufferer and his nurse.

1662.—For the charges of the sickness of Richard Petty, Mr. Collop's servant, when sick of the smallpox, viz. :

To the apothecary upon his bill—£2. 7. 0.; to the nurse for a month's looking to him and for what she laid out for him in that time, £5. 3. 0. and for chamber rent for the same time, £1. 8. 0. In all   £8 18   0

There is a detailed bill for the medicines supplied for this case of illness.

Mr. Collop's man.

		£	s.	d.
March 19, 1662.	Imprimis a glyster.		2	6
	Item an aporem.		3	6
	Item a cordial julep.		3	0
March 21.	Item the aporem again.		3	6
	Item the cordial julep again.		3	0

		£	s.	d.
March 22.	Item the aporem again.		3	6
	Item the cordial julep again.		3	0
	Item pectoral syrups.		2	0
	Item a gargle.		2	6
	Item a water for his eyes.		1	6
March 23.	Item a cordial bolus.		2	6
	Item a cordial julep.		5	0
March 24.	Item a pectoral.		3	0
	Item a cordial julep.		5	0
March 26.	Item oil of almonds.		1	0
April 3.	Item more oil of almonds.		1	0
April 10.	Item a purging potion.		2	6
April 12.	Item a purging potion.		2	6
		£2	10	6

Nothing is said about nursing outside in the bill for a footman who had smallpox in 1686, but another who had it one year afterwards was allowed board wages for himself and his nurse.

February 1686.—Received then from the Right Honourable the Earl of Bedford, by the hands of Mr. Bingley, in full for a fortnight's nursing James Evans of the smallpox the sum of forty shillings. I say received by me. £2 0 0
[The mark of Janet Willes.]

August 1687.—To Thomas Peake, one of his lordship's grooms, the 26th of August 1687, for board wages for himself and nurse when he had the smallpox, with £1. 3. 0. to the nurse for looking to him. £3 13 0

On one occasion, in 1670, two coaches were especially hired to carry the 'sick page and footman.' Their trouble may have been smallpox. On the other hand, it may very well have been one of the other numerous brood of fevers— 'the strange and fatal fevers' of Pepys. With the growth of scientific interest in medical as in other matters, these were the subject of earnest attention by such men as Sydenham, Morton and Willis, who, each in his own way, endeavoured to identify the different varieties of fever and in some cases to trace their incidence according to the age and condition of those afflicted. For the ordinary doctor and the apothecary the illness was simply, whether the patient were a royal princess or another, a 'fever.'

Doctors came to Woburn Abbey to attend a number of such cases of 'fever' during the forty years of the accounts, but an indication of its nature is very seldom given. In one instance, however, a name was supplied. In 1684 Mr. Bingley, the steward of the household, was attacked with the ague.

The sixteenth century had known the epidemic sickness called the ague in all its various forms but too well. The first Earl of Bedford himself had fallen a victim to it not once but several times. As distinct from malaria, this ague tended to be epidemic over the country for a definite period and then to disappear for some years. It had so disappeared in the early part of the seventeenth century, but had re-appeared in 1659 and then again about 1680. Mr. Bingley's may have been a late case of this last epidemic. One of the chief interests attaching to the ague at this particular period was the great controversy whether a patient should or should not be given Peruvian bark. Unhappily, there is no entry at all to say whether or no Mr. Bingley was treated in this way. He was certainly given a quantity of fruit, for there is a special bill for this.

March 1685.—Disbursed for fruit and other things then in my sickness. 15*s*. 0*d*.

Anyone in the household who had one of these infectious complaints, or who was otherwise dangerously ill, was provided with a nurse. The Countess had one with her permanently during the last years of her life.

Some at least of these nurses were the wives or daughters of men employed on the estate. Chief among them was the wife of John Field, the Woburn gardener, who, whether or no she was efficient as a nurse—she probably was—at least earned the affection and gratitude of the entire family. She came up to the abbey to do nursing and, besides this, was not infrequently sent for by one of the family if they happened to be taken ill while they were away. In particular, Lady Diana, when she had children of her own, often asked for Mrs. Field when they were ill; the latter had constantly to go up to town to nurse poor 'little Di,' who suffered from fits or convulsions. 'I have no thoughts to keep his [John Field's] wife,' wrote Lady Diana to Mr. Thornton, 'but bring her up with me to London, where I intend to fit myself with one [a nurse] as soon as possible, for I think it a very unreasonable thing to keep anyone's wife from them and had not done it so long but that my father did desire me to do it and said John would take it ill from me if I did part from her.'

Other women on the estate took their share of the nursing also. When the huntsman was seized with an unspecified illness which ultimately proved fatal, the wife of Batt, the porter, was paid three shillings a week for looking after him and the second porter's wife received a shilling a night for sitting up with him. Such nurses, like others who from time to time presented themselves, not being tenants on the estate, must have varied much in efficiency. Some, no doubt, were skilful enough, but at the other end of the scale were those who were quacks pure and simple, and often inefficient quacks at that.

When it was a case of infection and the nurse was sent to

live apart with the patient, she was put more or less in charge of all the arrangements, buying the provisions for herself and him, or her, for which purpose she was given board wages. In other instances, with damaged legs and so forth, the patient was not infrequently actually boarded out in the nurse's own house. In 1693 one of the men, with his wife, was boarded for nine weeks with Mrs. Elizabeth Knight, who charged twelve pounds for her services.

July 1693.—For nine weeks boarding of Hewin and his wife, medicines and the cure of his leg. £12 0 0

The same year Ann Gurney was paid seven weeks' board for lodging Miss Fox, the daughter of Mr. John Fox, who by then had become receiver-general, and an additional sum for dressing the young woman's leg.

August 7, 1693.—Received then from Mr. Bingley for seven weeks' board for Alice Fox and dressing her leg thirty-five shillings, being in full for the said Alice Fox. I say received by me. £1 15 0
[The mark of Ann Gurney.]

How the patient fared under this arrangement must have depended upon the kind of nurse whom he or she got. But there is frequent mention of great kindness and attention shown on the part of the attendant. To these women fell inevitably the lot, in a case of fatal illness, of being beside the patient when the end came.

The first of the adult members of the Earl's family to go was Francis, Lord Russell. He died in January 1678, and his brother William, long since the most prominent among the sons, became the heir.

Four years later came for the Earl two blows which might

well have overwhelmed a weaker man. The first did not concern death from illness, but death inflicted as a punishment by the State.

On 21st July 1683 William, Lord Russell, paid the penalty for his share in the Rye House Plot and died at the hands of the headsman on the scaffold which had been erected in Lincoln's Inn Fields. The Duke of York would have had it rather in front of Bedford House in the Strand, but on that the King placed his veto. William Russell's last letters, written in Newgate the night before his execution, lie at Woburn to-day, letters penned by a man who knew beyond any doubt that within twenty-four hours his life would have ended. On the 2nd of August his body was laid among those of his forebears at Chenies. Before a year had run from the day of his execution the vault was opened again to receive the body of his mother.

A later story in the family assigns the fatal illness of Anne, Countess of Bedford, to the sudden discovery of the circumstances of her own birth. If this really occurred, then Fate dealt hardly with the poor lady at this time; nevertheless it is difficult to believe that she had reached the age of seventy years without being aware of the history of her father and mother, nor could the behaviour of the former to herself and her husband during the early years of her marriage have left her with any illusions as to his real disposition. The misery and apprehension of those summer months of 1683 and the final consummation of the tragedy were amply sufficient, working upon her enfeebled state of body, to account for the weakness which ended in her death. Her health, never good after 1660, had become alarmingly worse in 1676, in which year, indeed, it had been freely said that she had not long to live. She did recover, chiefly, Mr. Thornton thought, owing to a consulting doctor whom he had himself specially recommended and who 'gave my lady much satisfaction in his discourse of the manner how her distemper began,' but she was never again anything approaching a strong woman. Her last illness was described, as all her others had been, simply as a 'great weakness,' and she faded out of life in the May following her son's execution, the gentle, lovable figure she had always been. Dr. King came from London to attend her and he was at her bedside when she died.

The elaborate arrangements for mourning and for funerals differed only in degree whether it was a member of the family who was dead or one of the household, at least among the upper branches of it. For one of the family the principal rooms were hung with black, the entire household—inside and out—were put into mourning and the funeral arrangements at Chenies were carried out with all the usual pomp and ceremony. There were no black hangings for a member of the household, but some of his or her colleagues were generally given mourning and the funeral, paid for by the Earl, was conducted with due solemnity.

Service with the Earl of Bedford seems to have made for longevity. The plague of 1665 and the indeterminate illness of 1667 accounted for the deaths of several of the younger men among the footmen. Otherwise the household as a whole seems to have survived bravely such illnesses and accidents as occurred, whether because of or in spite of the constant dosing by the apothecaries. Many of the officials and servants reached a good old age in the Earl's service and then were retired upon a pension. Such was the case with Dixy Taylor. But Dixy did not live to enjoy his pension long. At Michaelmas 1688 he made up his accounts for the last time and retired to live not in Woburn, but as one of the Earl's tenants in Covent Garden. He died on the 28th or 29th May of the following year and was buried in the church of St. Paul.

The bills for his last illness and the expenses of the funeral were paid by the Earl. Afterwards the papers were put together in a neat packet, the final record of a faithful servant. The accounts include all the customary charges, with a note of the fees paid to the bellringers of St. Paul's church and the money laid out for the black gowns, gloves, crape scarves and hatbands. Rosemary was provided to sprinkle on the coffin; and after all was over there were twenty-five gallons of claret and fourteen bottles of Canary for the mourners.

CHAPTER XVII

THE PRIVY PURSE: MAINLY APPAREL

M R. DIXY TAYLOR, in his personal attendance upon the Earl
and Countess was, at all events after the middle fifties,
indifferently known either as the gentleman of the chamber
or as the gentleman, or keeper, of the privy purse. So also
was Mr. Gregory, his successor in 1688, who came from the
mastership of the stables to undertake more intimate service
for the Earl in the house.

Dixy Taylor, and Gregory after him, made all the personal
purchases for the Earl and sometimes for other members of
the family that were not made either by Mr. Thornton or
the steward. If Mr. Thornton bought all the religious books
for the Earl's reading, the other official was at least entrusted
with buying the pleasant little twopenny stories of terrible
murders. Mr. Thornton supervised all medical treatment
whenever he was allowed to do so; the gentleman of the
privy purse paid the man who regularly came to cut his
lordship's corns, and provided such items for the toilet as
Bologna wash balls. One or the other even interfered
occasionally with the purchase of the apparel for the lord of
the house. But normally this was the particular duty of the
gentleman of the privy purse.

The word apparel had a wide meaning, for the items included besides all clothes such things as periwigs, ornaments
—gold, silver and jewelled—swords and sword-belts and
minor requirements for the toilet, as for the dressing-room.

The Earl could and did on such occasions as the return
of Charles to his kingdom and on the coronation day of the

23rd of April 1661 make himself into a very fine gentleman indeed. But the large sums of money spent on apparel in the latter year with particular reference to the coronation— over five hundred pounds—was the exception, not the rule. In other years the amount that was spent fluctuated between a hundred and twenty and two hundred and eighty pounds. This expenditure was not as uneven as it looked. Like others before and after him, the Earl of Bedford occasionally had an expensive year in which a great deal of his wardrobe had to be renewed, often preceded or followed by an econom- ical year when he had plenty of clothes and etceteras in hand.

No other great occasion ever called, in the Earl's opinion, for such preparations as had done St. George's Day of 1661. The same feast saw another coronation twenty-four years later. Charles II had died on the 6th of February 1685, and on the anniversary of his coronation, the 23rd of April following, his brother James was crowned. This ceremony the Earl of Bedford did not attend, for good and sufficient reasons. It was but two short years since the Rye House plot had sent William, Lord Russell, to the scaffold and that plot had been directed far more against the present occupant of the throne than against his predecessor. Under such circumstances, it is not surprising that the Earl of Bedford sought a letter to excuse him from coming to the Abbey.

1685.—Paid at the Secretary the Earl of Sunderland's office, the 7th of April 1685, to Mr. Bridgman and his clerk for the King's letter to excuse his lordship's attendance at the corona- tion. £3 0 0

The coronation four years later of William and Mary marked the triumph of the political party with which the Earl was identified. Then on 11th April 1689 he was present in the Abbey. But the additions to his wardrobe—

some extra yards of brocade, rather more gold and silver embroidery than usual, a new sword, some silver and gold buckles, and so forth—put little on to his ordinary bills. His garb, doubtless good and sufficient for the occasion, must yet have been subdued in comparison with the splendour in which he had shone forth twenty-eight years earlier, riding behind Charles II on the way to Whitehall. Now he did not even wear his own jewels. Much less did he buy any new ones for the occasion. A few were needed and these he borrowed—it was not unusual—from Mr. Child, the goldsmith. Child charged £5 7s. 6d. for whatever was lent and added another two shillings to the bill for the use of a pair of buckles.

It is only fair to add that in one respect the Earl did both himself and his new sovereigns honour. He still had the coronation robes which he had worn in 1661 and which had not been new even then, since they had belonged to his father, who had probably worn them at the coronation of Charles I. If they were to look as they should, it was necessary to have them thoroughly done up. The fur, the miniver of the cape and the edgings of the same round the flowing crimson velvet robe, must have gone to pieces, since the furrier to whom the gown was sent charged £74 0s. 6d. for replacements.

Two other events, personal to the Earl himself, did indeed make demands upon the privy purse, although less in the way of clothes than in other particulars. On the 3rd of June 1672 he was installed as Knight of the Garter. On the 11th of May 1694 he was created Marquess of Tavistock and Duke of Bedford.

For the Garter ceremony at Windsor recourse had first to be had to Mr. Arthur Blackmore, who was painter to the College of Arms. He provided the banner which would be put above the Earl's stall in St. George's chapel, together with the plate of arms to be fixed on the wall, where it still

remains. There were, and are, two earlier Russell plates
there, those of the first and second Earls of Bedford.
Blackmore also made the mantles, the wreath and the
cushion.

June 1672.—To Mr. Arthur Blackmore,
herald painter, in full of his bill for one great
banner painted and gilt with fine gold in oil with
his lordship's arms; for silk fringe and a staff
painted in oil for the same; for a helmet of steel
gilt, a crest carved and gilt, a sword with a cross
hilt, the pommel and chape gilt; graving,
enamelling and gilding the plate for the stall;
for six escutcheons gilt with fine gold, with his
lordship's arms, with Garter and titles; making
the mantles a wreath and cushion; for tassels of
silk and silver for the mantles and for silk and
gold fringe and silk and gold tassels for the
cushion.   £32   o   o

The material for the mantles or mantlings—all official
accounts use this word in the plural—fifteen yards at least
of blue velvet, with white taffeta for lining, and the crimson
velvet for the surcoat came from the Wardrobe. Sometimes
that department also supplied the crimson velvet to make
the cushion on which the robes, Collar and insignia were
placed to be carried before the Knight Elect, but on this
occasion it was bought separately.

The Earl of Bedford also bought his own feather—the
St. George's feather of white ostrich plume—sword, belt
and velvet cap, which altogether cost him another twenty-
nine pounds odd.

June 1672.—For a feather, a sword and belt,
and for a velvet cap, etc., provided for his
lordship's said installation.   £29   7   6

Besides these, and bought separately, was the very special black heron top to be placed in the heart of the white ostrich plume. The cost was twenty pounds, which appears to be high seeing that the herons were common enough birds to be fairly easily caught. Nevertheless, it was the regular price, for the same sum is mentioned in various accounts belonging to other Knights of the Garter.

The Collar of the Order, of red and white enamelled roses separated by gold knots, which, according to the statute of Henry VIII might not be 'sold, pledged or given away,' came from the royal Jewel House, with a commensurate fee to the official concerned. To the royal Jewel House it must return on the death of the Knight, while the Wardrobe awaited his robes. Sometimes both Jewel House and Wardrobe waited in vain and not all the energies of the Garter King at Arms and the Heralds, who were the officials responsible, could prevent both Collar and robes going as a legacy to the eldest son or a dear friend.

The Knight Elect also received from his sovereign a George and a Garter. But it was necessary to buy several more of both insignia. The fact that both the hanging ornament and the Garter itself were then and for long continued to be worn all day and every day meant a variety of each had always to be in the wardrobe, the greater for ceremonial occasions and the lesser for ordinary wear. Just before his installation the Earl bought two Georges. One, set with diamonds, came from Gomeldon, the jeweller, and cost a hundred and sixty-five pounds. The other, simpler in design, was of onyx set about with fifteen diamonds and was bought from Child for forty pounds. The Earl also treated himself to three Garters. Two of them were of diamonds and pearls and cost the one forty-four pounds and the other twenty-nine pounds. The third was a plain band in gold and white enamel, which came only to twelve pounds.

The actual fees for the installation were no light matter.

In this case either the Earl or his receiver-general for him
made a miscalculation as to how much ready money he would
actually require when he got to Windsor. In such a catastrophe a friend could usually be found ready to oblige with a
loan.

June 1672. To Sir Edward Walker, Knight, Garter Principal King of Arms, in full for all fees due unto him from his lordship, with £20 to the Dean of Windsor for plate for the altar there.	£242 10 0
To his lordship himself 6 guineas and a crown piece for the Lord Marquess of Worcester, the same having been borrowed of him to pay fees.	£6 14 0

These fees were heavy, but those payable on the creation
of the Dukedom in 1694 were a good deal heavier. Here,
too, the gifts, which were really compulsory gratuities, were
calculated on a far from modest scale. Every one concerned
with the creation, from the highest official down to the lowest
doorkeeper, had his hand stretched out.

The newly created Duke had to pay out £1,204 11*s*. 9*d*.
before he ever got to the House of Lords.

1694. *Mr. Attorney General.*
Paid to Mr. Attorney General for fees
for drawing the Bill for Their
Majesties' signature—£60.10.0.; to
Mr. Bernard at the Secretary's
office for fees for the said Bill pass-
ing there—£67. 10*s*. 0*d*.; to Mr.
Vernon, secretary to the Duke of
Shrewsbury, 50 guineas, and to Mr.
Attorney General 10 guineas, in all

60 guineas, being His Grace's free
gift to them for services done, the
said guineas coming, with the exchange, to—£66. 0. 0.; and to Mr.
Attorney General's clerks, His
Grace's free gift amongst them—
£2. 0. 0.   £196   0   0

Privy Seal Office.
To the officers at the Privy Seal
office for their fees—£105. 15. 0.;
to the clerks of the Treasury for
two dockets to the Lord Privy
Seal and to the Lord Keeper—
£2. 0. 0.; to the Lord Privy Seal's
secretary and other servants—
15s. 0d.; to Mr. Adney, secretary
to the Lord Keeper, for fees for the
receipt upon the docket 20
guineas, coming, with the exchange,
to—£22. 0. 0.   £130 10   0

Crown Office.
To Mr. Milton of the Crown office
for fees there and for the King's
servants, the Hanaper office, and
the great seal—£873. 1. 9.; to the
said Mr. Milton more as His
Grace's free gift to him presenting
His Grace with a gilt case to put
the patent in—£5. 0. 0.   £878   1   9

On the day of the introduction the receiver-general had
again to provide money.

Fees for His Grace's Introducing.

£   s.   d.

December 1694. To the Clerk of the Parlia-
ments.   10   0   0
To the Clerk's assistant.   1   10   0

	£	s.	d.
To the Gentlemen Ushers.	10	0	0
To the Yeoman Usher.	1	10	0
To the Garter King at Arms.	6	10	0
The eight doorkeepers.	2	0	0
And to Mr. Relfe.	2	0	0
	£33	10	0

And finally:

May 1694.—To a porter to bring home the Patent that created my lord Duke and Marquess. *6d.*

After this a certain economy was the order of the day. The Earl's Parliament robes, unlike his coronation robes which five years earlier had needed such extensive repairs, were in quite good condition. Only a slight alteration was necessary. An extra, a fourth, row of gold braid edged with ermine must be added to mark the new rank of the wearer.

1694.—To Mr. Pickney, the furrier, for altering His Grace's Parliament robes. £3 10 0

The only other immediate expense in connection with the new title was the alteration of the arms on three steel seal plates, which cost eleven pounds.

The clothes bill for this year was much as it had been in former years. The apparel bought for the Duke was neither greater in quantity nor yet better in quality than that which the Earl had required previously. Rather the contrary. In this particular year two hundred pounds were spent in all, an average amount divided over different items in the average way.

At all times the drain on the privy purse for apparel occurred in one particular direction. The clothes themselves cost far less than the trimmings and appurtenances which were necessary for a gentleman's costume. Any year in which these had to be provided lavishly was always an expensive one especially if, as was often the case, more heavy brocaded silk was used at the same time for the making up of the clothes than usual. The balance was redressed in a year when the renewals to the wardrobe merely took the shape of plainer garments—a cloth coat, or coats, a waistcoat and so forth.

The Earl's plainer suits were sometimes made up by a tailor in Woburn, who also supplied cloth for them. All his more important garments were made and the materials for them bought in London.

The London tailor—he was by no means always the same man—did not invariably or even as a rule provide the materials. Lengths of velvet, brocade and satin were bought separately from a mercer and sent to the tailor to be made up. So also the fine cloth from a draper. Occasionally, however, the material was entered by the tailor on his bill, chiefly when it was of a coarser or heavier kind, perhaps for a suit of a plainer sort, or for one of the ample cloaks, lined either with silk or with cloth, with which a man might protect himself from the weather.

The price for making up varied greatly. On the same bill, one dated June 1666, a tailor charged sixteen shillings for making one suit and coat of black cloth and only ten shillings for another of the same material. The latter, however, judging by the list of sundries, was of a less elaborate kind.

Every tailor's bill contained a goodly list of such sundries, for these at least he supplied. He found the figured silk, sarcenet, or fine cloth which was used for the linings, the wire and buckram for stiffening which was such an important part of the whole, and the flannel which was used, for the sake of warmth, as an interlining. He also furnished the ribbons which were used for binding and such small items as the hooks and eyes, often of silver, and so forth. Sometimes he provided the buttons and sometimes he did not. That depended upon the nature of the button. Anything of a less expensive kind was bought by the tailor and went down on his bill among the sundries. Buttons of gold or silver, or such as were jewelled, a fashion which came rapidly to the fore after about 1670, were sent to him for use. So also was the gold and silver lace which adorned the coats and waist-coats.

Herein lay the secret of the highest annual bills. The gold and silver which in different forms was used with such lavishness for the clothing of a gentleman in the seventeenth century involved the wearer in considerable expense. Besides the metal buttons and lace, the gold and silver thread which was used for embroidery and fringes, ornaments in gold and silver, loops, knots and hooks, often had to be bought.

In 1671 a bill for gold and silver lace and thread came to over eighty-seven pounds, although there was a reduction on this because a remnant of lace was returned.

Bought of William Gostlin.

	£	s.	d.
November 1671. 15½ yards of rich broad gold silver wire purl lace, cost £3. 13. 0. yard and 9s. yard to be allowed profit, which is 2s. 6d. per pound, which is £4. 2. 0. yard.	63	11	0
Per 75 ounces of rich gold silver purled foot, cost 5s. 10d. the ounce, which allowing 8d. the ounce profit at 2s. 6d. per pound, comes to 6s. 6d. per ounce and comes to £1. 11s. 6d. per yard.	24	7	6
	£87	18	6

Agreed to abate for a remnant of lace returned. £2 8 6

The sum then is £85 10 0

I do attest this to be a true note and do also warrant that it is as good gold and silver as any whatsoever and that it shall hold colour as long as any lace hath or can do, WILLIAM GOSTLIN

Whether the tailor put out the embroidery, or whether the work was done on the premises is doubtful. The bills look as if it was sometimes one way and sometimes the other. But in any case, the heavily embroidered and fringed belts and girdles came from a different establishment. For them the Earl went mainly to a woman called Elizabeth Gladwin, whose place of business was in the New Exchange.

Elizabeth Gladwin's Bill.

	£	s.	d.
April 1663. For a knotted fringe belt, black.	5	0	0
For 4 white tabby belts stitched.	4	0	0
For a girdle and frogged.		8	0
For a mourning belt.	1	5	0
For a coloured belt ribboned.		16	0
For a coloured fringe belt with buttons.	2	5	0
For a silver buckled belt stitched.	4	10	0
For a draw girdle and frogged.		16	0
For a silver embroidered belt.	5	10	0
For a silver embroidered belt with tufted fringe.	7	10	0
For a plain Cordivant belt coloured.		10	0

All bills did not, happily for the accounts, come to as much as this one, or that other for lace and thread bought in 1671. Gold and silver lace, like buttons of the same, could always be, and was, used again and again. Nor was it necessary to have so much embroidery done every year.

Nevertheless, the purveyors of metal materials, the fringemakers and the embroiderers received a good proportion of the amount that was spent annually on the clothes, even when no gala occasion was in question. Their share seldom came to less than thirty pounds, more often fluctuated round about forty-five pounds and in some years rose considerably beyond this.

Besides the trimmings, every costume demanded its accessories in the shape of ruffles, frills and cravats. Sometimes these were made at home; sometimes a sempstress was employed. In the latter event, the maker usually supplied the muslin and lace, that is if it were ordinary lace. On the other hand, the finer kinds were often bought especially from a London laceman or were brought from Paris or Venice.

Mary Kent, sempstress's bill.

	£	s.	d.
May 1689. 12 pair of fine holland socks, 1s. 3d. a pair.		15	0
1 fine large muslin cravat and large neck.		7	0
A fine muslin cravat to tie and a fine large neck.		6	6
2 pair of fine muslin cuffs, 2s. 2d.		4	4
	£1	12	10

The linen drapers provided holland, linen and cotton, both fine and coarse, for the underclothes, which, like the ruffles and cravats, were sometimes made up at home and sometimes by Mary Kent, sempstress, or another, although it is just possible that a few of them may have been bought

LIFE IN A NOBLE HOUSEHOLD

ready made. The home work was always undertaken by the housekeeper, who made up the handkerchiefs as well as other things. For this she was paid extra as she and the other maids were for the garments made for the stablemen. Regular bills were sent in for all the work done. Her small requirements, such as thread, tape, needles and so forth, she purchased as a rule from the pedlars.

1694.—To Mrs. Upton [housekeeper at Woburn] on her three bills for handkerchiefs and making them, for holland for socks and for making them and shirts, and for thread and needles, etc., with 3s. for altering socks and 2s. for tape points. £6 1 0

Mrs. Upton very often made the holland stockings or hose, as she did on the above occasion. They were also made by the sempstress. Others of leather, silk or worsted were bought from a hosier, chiefly from one Philip Hanbury who had a shop in the New Exchange.

For his boots and shoes the Earl very often went to a man living in Woburn. The Woburn shoemaker was quite a familiar figure.

Woburn also boasted a glover, and some gloves for the Earl and his family were certainly bought of him. Other gloves came from London. They were an important item in an outfit and a good many were bought in the course of a year. Sometimes they came from a regular glover, but hosiers and those who called themselves milliners also supplied them. They were made of all kinds of material—silk, velvet and leather, including, for the winter, doeskin 'with the hair inside.' Often they were richly trimmed with ribbons or embroidery. A pair of chamois leather gloves had fringes of gold and silver thread. Here, too, the fashion for scent, which was at one and the same time practical and

340

elegant, came into play. Many of the gloves were perfumed. The Earl of Bedford had at different times a number of pairs of 'jessemy' gloves, or gloves scented with jasmine, which were perhaps the most popular. He also bought others perfumed with frangipane—six pairs of these in 1665 alone —and at least one pair impregnated with ambrett, which was the hibiscus abelmoschus. Even if the gloves themselves were not scented, it was always possible to buy the sweet ointment called 'jessemy butter' to rub into the leather. This cost a shilling an ounce and, as a rule, half an ounce was bought at a time. It was sold both by hosiers and glovers, who also supplied the last refinement of scented powder for rubbing on to the hands before the gloves were drawn on.

The hosiers and the milliners also supplied the odds and ends of a toilet, ribbons and so forth, including gauze veils. A riding cap in silk or velvet would also sometimes come from a milliner. Other hats, castors and beavers, came from a regular hatter.

Three other tradespeople assisted in provision for the apparel. One was the armourer, whose accounts for a sword, or swords, supplied and repairs done to others might be anything from five to fifteen pounds during the year. The others were the periwig-maker and the Indian gown maker.

Periwigs cost a good deal of money and considerably augmented the accounts for apparel when they came into fashion after the Restoration. In 1672, when the wig-maker's bill reached the top figure of £54 10s. 0d., four periwigs were bought in all for the Earl, costing respectively twenty, eighteen, ten and six pounds. That for ten pounds was specifically called a periwig for riding. One old periwig was sent to be cleaned and repaired, for which the maker charged ten shillings. This year was one of unusual extravagance in wigs. In other years the account was round about twenty pounds, tending to sink in the latter years to something like fourteen or fifteen pounds. As time went on, either periwigs grew cheaper, or cheaper ones were bought, for the average cost appears to have worked out at ten pounds, or a little less, and certainly the Earl and Duke indulged in fewer, although it is satisfactory to know that he had the old ones more often cleaned.

Lastly, there was the Indian gown maker. The elaboration of the clothes worn, not to speak of their weight, although the seventeenth century endured that on their backs more easily than did later generations, must have made many a one, both man and woman, welcome the opportunity of wearing something really comfortable in leisure moments. The garments called Indian gowns supplied a felt want. They were loose, comfortable, silk négligé garments of the dressing-gown order and were divided into summer and winter gowns, presumably thin and thick. The Earl's gentleman of the chamber bought them for his master chiefly from Henry Kirk, Indian gown seller, whose establishment was in St. Clement Danes, although sometimes an odd gown appears to have been ordered from another well-known purveyor of them called West. The gowns were not expensive, running from thirty shillings to three pounds apiece. A gown costing the latter price was rather dear. They could also be relined. Henry Kirk undertook this work and every year some gowns went up to him from Woburn to be repaired and to have fresh linings put in.

The Countess favoured Indian gowns as much as did the Earl. No doubt as an invalid she found the easy-fitting, loose garment particularly comfortable wear. But, according to the more sarcastic of the French writers, all English people of the day were in love with this form of négligé, even to walking out in the gowns. 'She does want a gown indeed!' exclaimed Wycherley's dancing master in the play of that name. 'She is in her "Dishabiliee" . . . a great mode in England.'

A number of bills were always sent in for cleaning and

repairs, not only for the Indian gowns, Parliament robes and periwigs, but for every other kind of garment. The tailors undertook a great deal of this work, which often included relining and refacing. At other times a woman would be brought in specifically to clean clothes and to mend them.

These particular bills increased greatly during the last ten or fifteen years of the Earl's life. From his middle age onwards, indeed, he had always preferred a slightly old-fashioned style in dress, even when new clothes had to be bought. Later he clung to the clothes which he had been wearing with great affection and the bills for repairing and cleaning these rose at the expense of those for new garments, which sensibly diminished.

Apart from what the Earl actually wore, certain extras came under the heading of apparel.

In October 1687 an umbrella arrived at Woburn. The use of umbrellas was then just beginning to be appreciated, although they were still associated—a legacy of their Eastern origin—with protection from the sun rather than from rain. Usually they were carried by the servants—another reminder of the East.

October 1687.—To John Kemp the 21st of October 1687, for an umbrella sent to Woburn Abbey for the Earl of Bedford.   16s. 6d.

Two years later a couple of umbrellas were especially manufactured for use at Woburn.

		Jonathan Hibbert's bill.	£	s.	d.
August 1689.	For wood and iron work to two umbrellas to rule.		1	7	0
	For 17¾ yards of ticking to make the umbrellas at 1s. 3d. per yard.		1	5	0
	For 16¾ ounces of worsted fringe to the umbrellas at 5d. per ounce.			6	8

343

	£	s.	d.
For making the umbrellas.		6	o
For a piece of tape and tacks.		2	o
For a sacking bottom and nails.		12	o
For 2 long screws and nuts.		2	6
For a plain mat to pack them in.		1	o

This man who made the umbrellas was one who both made covers for furniture and sold a little furniture as well.

Some toilet necessities were entered under apparel and were bought every month. They included the utilitarian powder with which his lordship cleaned his teeth, as well as powder for the hair—in spite of the periwigs—and the powder for his hands, which, when it did not come from the glover or the hosier, was bought at the apothecary's shop. Orange-flower water and the Queen of Hungary's water were mainly for use after shaving. But the Earl, in common with every one else of his station, used many essences and other scented waters.

1689. Paid for powder for linen, hair and hands, for the Queen of Hungary's water and orange flower water, and for essence and balls, etc.	£2	4	o
For powder for his lordship's teeth.		10	o

The Earl's dressing-room also had to be properly supplied with scented powder. There it was either sprinkled loose on the dressing-table and among the linen, or put into little bags, which were called 'sweet bags,' for the same purposes. Usually the bags were of sarcenet and were sometimes made up by the invaluable housekeeper, or they could be bought ready made. The dressing-table itself always had its toilet cover—the Earl of Bedford favoured pale blue silk—with a pincushion and bags for the combs to match. A toilet cover 'sky coloured, with all its furniture,' cost in 1670 forty-five shillings.

How much the Countess of Bedford spent on her clothes

never appears. She must have bought them out of her three hundred pounds a year pin-money. During the latter years of her life she could have wanted very little since she is known to have been an invalid almost permanently on the couch or in bed.

In so far as the Earl of Bedford had a pet extravagance, it was smoking. A quantity of tobacco was bought each year earmarked for his own private use—the tobacco for his sons, when they were at home, was bought and entered separately. In some years as much as thirty pounds would be provided for the master of the house. In other years the amount would sink to twenty pounds. Very occasionally it was as little as eighteen pounds. Even granted that the Earl treated his friends from his own particular store, it still made him in the ordinary way a smoker of anything from half an ounce to an ounce of tobacco a day.

He smoked two kinds of tobacco, Spanish and Virginia. The latter was a much more economical smoke than the former. Unfortunately, most of the early accounts merely give the number of pounds bought, with the total cost, and do not specify in what proportions the sorts were mixed. In 1668, however, Spanish tobacco was ten shillings a pound, exactly the same price which on the same day bought three pounds of Virginia tobacco. In 1693 Virginia tobacco was selling for half a crown, while Spanish tobacco cost nine shillings and twelve shillings a pound. With the tobacco came pipes bought by the gross.

Hugh Gauntlett to Mr. Dixy Taylor at Bedford House in the Strand, London.

At the Swan in Amesbury.
1 *March* 1651.

MR. TAYLOR,

I have according to your desire sent you a gross of pipes according to your pattern. The pipes and the box come to

18*s*. 6*d*., which pray pay to the bearer that shall deliver the pipes. You may send to me every Thursday or Friday by the wain-men that lie at the King's Arms in Holborn. Thus, with my service remembered to you unknown, and my service to Mr. Massey, I remain

Your servant to serve you,

HUGH GAUNTLETT

One gross was a very modest number of pipes to be sent to Woburn in any one year. Usually the order was for twelve gross. As time went on they could be bought much more cheaply. In 1665 twelve gross, again with a box, cost only £1 2*s*. 6*d*. against the 18*s*. 6*d*. of 1651 for a single gross with a box. By 1695 they were cheaper yet. The most expensive kind of pipes then were only £1 16*s*. 0*d*. for twelve gross and a cheaper kind also sometimes bought for the Earl were £1 4*s*. 0*d*. for twelve gross.

With the tobacco came touchwood for lighting the pipes, which cost sixpence an ounce, and boxes for holding the leaf. In 1686 a box of tortoiseshell cost four shillings and one of the same material in 1698 cost five shillings.

The smoking materials represent the only money set down in the privy purse accounts that was spent on behalf of the Earl strictly for his own pleasure. How he disposed of the spending, or pocket-money that was handed him on demand by his receiver-general remains his own secret.

'Sundry other small disbursements' was a blessed term to the gentleman of the privy purse. But he sometimes went so far as to signify some of the items which were included therein. Such were payments for letters sent from or received at the abbey; all appurtenances for writing—paper, ink, quills, sand, wax and wafers; little boxes and cases that were required for some unknown purpose. Many odd items, too, that really belonged to other accounts were often included, probably because the gentleman of the privy purse was the only official on hand at the time—the hire of a coach or chair, which really belonged to the stables; the buying of a book, which should have been entered up by Mr. Thornton; and such little matters as a mysterious half a crown required by 'James-in-the-kitchen,' which should certainly have been paid by the steward of the household.

All this yet omits the final and, apart from the clothes, most substantial expenditure from the privy purse—the money paid out in presents, gratuities and charity.

CHAPTER XVIII

THE PRIVY PURSE :
GIFTS, GRATUITIES AND CHARITY

THE gentleman of the privy purse shared with the receiver-general and on occasion Mr. Thornton the purveyance of gifts, gratuities and charitable offerings. The task that was divided between them was no light one. Seeing that everything that was given, from the smallest coin to the present offered each year to the King, was meticulously set down, together with a note of the person who had received it, often with qualifying adjectives, the entries fill up no small space in the accounts.

The present that each year headed all the rest as long as the usage endured was the gift to the King.

This custom was one of great antiquity. But even during the reign of Elizabeth it had tended to become stereotyped. Those courtiers and subjects most closely in touch with Her Majesty still gave intimate gifts—a fan of feathers, such as that which she one year received from the Earl of Leicester; a jewel; a great salt. The wives of the peers, too, might present a piece of embroidery—in 1578 the second Countess of Bedford gave a doublet of murrey satin embroidered with gold and silver. Even so, many who had the obligation to give confined themselves to an offering of money, the amount of which was strictly regulated by custom and based on the status of the giver. An Earl was expected to give twenty pounds in gold. According to a letter sent to the Earl of Rutland, this covered the obligations of both the Earl and his wife. Anything given by them over and above this was an act of superabundance, graciously received by Her Majesty. So also the elegant purse in which the gold was usually placed was a courtier-like tribute.

The present was not exactly a free-will offering, however much the excess amount spent on the exquisite pieces of jewellery which some presented might be so. But if the money gift was to all intents and purposes compulsory, the donor got a substantial return. All courtiers and officials who were on the list of those entitled to do so received from their monarch a piece of plate of the correct weight, unless they were so far favoured as to be given a piece of jewellery or the like. The plate or jewel might be and usually was—at least from the time of Elizabeth onwards, if not earlier—selected from among the presents received by the sovereign.

It is permissible to picture Leicester or Raleigh ushered into the presence of Elizabeth to present her personally with the piece of jewellery or elegantly embroidered article of attire which had been especially designed for the purpose. Those who confined themselves to the twenty pounds in gold had very probably sent the gift through a regulation official channel, which is even more likely to have been the case in the next two reigns. But when the Earl of Bedford sent up his twenty pounds to Charles I on New Year's Day, 1641/2, by Mr. Dixy Taylor, it is not at all clear how the money was delivered. In 1660, when the accounts of the receiver-general of the Earl of Bedford were resumed, the manner of presenting the money was as strictly official as the amount of the gift itself. So also was the method by which the King made his present in return. Both the giving and the getting on either side went through the Lord Chamberlain's office.

The negotiations required were sometimes more elaborate and delicate than might be supposed, for certain difficulties of adjustment not infrequently arose.

349

The customary gift from the King to a nobleman of the standing of the Earl of Bedford was a piece of gold plate of the weight of thirty ounces. As in the days of Elizabeth, so in those of Charles II this plate was seldom manufactured for the purpose. On occasion it might be so; more often it came out of the store of such things in the Jewel House. Even granting the careful regulation of the weight of gifts, it was highly improbable that a piece, much less pieces, all weighing thirty ounces could be selected for each recipient to whom it was due. Therefore, when, as often happened, the plate weighed more than thirty ounces, the Earl of Bedford, or another, had to hand the difference in value over to the Lord Chamberlain. There is no instance in these particular accounts of the difference being the other way and the Lord Chamberlain having to make up the balance in money to the recipient.

On January 1st, 1660/61, therefore, the receiver-general sent twenty pounds in gold to the office of the Lord Chamberlain on behalf of his master. The money was put into a purse of embroidered silk and silver, which on this occasion and on every subsequent one cost nine shillings. Then, as the piece of plate sent for the Earl was slightly overweight, the receiver further paid into the Lord Chamberlain's office two shillings in respect of this. Finally, he handed or had handed to His Majesty's officials the handsome fees required for carrying through the transaction.

January 1660/61.—Presented the 1st of January 1660/61, to the Lord Chamberlain in gold for the King—£20; for an embroidered silk and silver purse wherein the gold was put, with 2*s*. paid for .the overweight of the plate given by the King—11*s*.; and to His Majesty's officers, which was by them demanded ,as a fee upon their delivery of the said plate then given to his lordship—£2. 5*s*. 0*d*. In all   £22 16 0

The next year the money demanded for the overweight was ten shillings as against which in 1663 a piece of the exact thirty ounces was delivered.

A further complication with which the Lord Chamberlain's office had to grapple and which again cost the Earl money was the rise in the price of gold. The twenty gold pieces still had to be given, but they could only be procured at a premium. Already in 1661 the receiver-general had to enter in his accounts that he had not only had to pay the ten shillings for the overweight of the plate, but also that it had cost him £21 6s. 8d. to procure the twenty pieces. Two years later, in 1663, the premium was as much as two shillings and twopence for each piece.

In that year the coin called a guinea was first struck. But it was not until 1667 that the receiver-general for the first time called the money sent to the King not 'twenty pounds in gold,' but 'twenty pieces of guinea gold.' Another fourteen years elapsed before, on January the 1st, 1670/71, he entered in his book that he had delivered to the Lord Chamberlain's office for His Majesty's New Year's gift 'twenty guineas.' The value of these, he said, was in all £21 10s. 0d.

The price of gold was not allowed to affect the return gifts. An earl got his piece of plate representing thirty ounces whether the metal of which it was composed was valued at five shillings and ninepence, six shillings, or six and sixpence an ounce, which were the normal fluctuations, without any readjustment.

When the Earl of Bedford received his New Year's gift, it might or might not be added to his collection of plate. Usually it was not. The virtue of the gift lay in the fact that it could be, and generally was, exchanged by arrangement with a goldsmith for something that the recipient really wanted.

351

Viner's bill, February 5, 1663.
£11.6.8. besides plate.

		oz. dwt. gr.	£	s.	d.
	Plate delivered for the use of the right honourable Earl of Bedford.				
February 1663.	A candlestick weight 33: 7 : 0 at 6s. 4d. is		10	11	3
	A candlestick weight 32 : 12 : 0 at 6s. 4d. is		10	6	5
			20	17	8
	For engraving the arms with palms and coronets.			4	0
			21	1	8
	Received per his New Year's gift from His Majesty 30 ounces of gilt plate at 6s. 6d. per ounce.		9	15	0
			£11	6	8

This process was repeated in most years and was always carried out by arrangement with Viner. No other goldsmith is ever mentioned and it is notable that the procedure went through Viner even after the bankruptcy of his business, which was brought about by the closing of the Exchequer in 1672. In fact it is just about the latter date that the part played by the goldsmith, according to the Earl of Bedford's accounts, as an intermediary, was brought into closer connection with officialdom.

In January of 1670/71 the Earl's receiver-general for the first time not only set down in his account of the New Year's gift that he had sent up his twenty guineas in a purse to the Lord Chamberlain's office, but added that besides paying the customary fees or gratuities he had also paid sixpence for a ticket 'to His Majesty's officers upon an assignment on Sir Robert Viner to deliver thirty ounces of gilt plate to his lordship.' Hereafter that entry, including the ticket money, was a regular one.

The Earl, or his receiver-general for him, clearly then told Sir Robert Viner what kind of plate the Earl required. Sir Robert Viner supplied it and sent in his bill, allowing for the assignment which he had received from the Chamberlain's Office, or on occasion from the Jewel House, for the thirty ounces due.

£6—*Sir Robert Viner, goldsmith.*
20*th March,* 1671/2.

	oz. dwt. gr.	£	s.	d.
March 1671/2. A deep basin weight	52 : 5 : 0			
at 5s. 9d. per ounce.		15	0	4
For engraving the coat of arms.			1	6
		15	1	10
Due to the Earl of Bedford for 30 ounces of gilt plate at 6s. 0d. per ounce.		9	0	0
Rest due		£6	1	10

Five years later a sillabub pot was chosen.

Right Honourable the Earl of Bedford.
Debtor to Sir Robert Viner.

	oz. dwt. gr.	£	s.	d.
May 1677. For a sillabub pot weight	50 : 05 : 00			
at 6s. per ounce.		15	1	4
For engraving one coat of arms.			2	6
		15	3	10

£ s. d.

Received of his lordship an assignment from the Jewel House for
thirty ounces of gilt plate at 6s.
per ounce.   9 0 0

Due to Sir Robert Viner £6 3 10

This sillabub pot was almost the last piece of silver
that the Earl ever paid for, or rather partly paid for, with
his present of gilt plate. From 1680 onwards all entries
regarding his present to the King and the King's to him
cease abruptly. There is no sign that the custom was ever
renewed during the twenty years that were to elapse before
his own death.

Another set of presents given as of custom also amounted
to an official obligation, one which endured longer than the
exchange of presents with the King. From at least 1660
onwards—almost certainly also during the reign of Charles I
—the Earl was expected every Christmas and New Year to
make a distribution among certain of the royal servants and
those attached to the Houses of Parliament.

The list of recipients was invariably headed by the King's
trumpeters. Then followed, as a rule, the King's footmen
and a series of doorkeepers, sweepers and so forth at the
Chapel Royal, at Whitehall and at the House of Lords.
Something like a regular tariff obtained and, happily for the
donor, it does not seem that more was expected of him when
he had a step up in the peerage. A very complete list of
what he paid out as Duke of Bedford in 1698 does not
differ greatly, either in the names of the recipients or in
the amounts which they were given, from earlier lists,
except for the addition of the regimental drummers and
marshals.

354

The account of the Xmas boxes and the New Year's gifts given by your Grace this year.

	£	s.	d.
1698. To the King's trumpeters.		10	o
To the drummers of the Guards.		10	o
To the doorkeepers of the House of Lords.	1	o	o
To the porters at Whitehall gate.	1	o	o
To the under-porter at Whitehall gate.		5	o
To the sweepers at Whitehall gate and the Parliament stairs.		5	o
To the marshal's men.		10	o
To the King's messengers.	1	o	o
To the yeomen of the Guards.	1	o	o
To the firemakers.		7	6
To the chapel keeper.		10	o
To the 20 drummers and marshals of Colonel Howard's regiment.	2	o	o
To the 20 drummers and marshals of Colonel Bond's regiment.	2	o	o
To the drummers and marshals of Colonel Shoreditch's regiment.	1	o	o
To the keepers of the Council Chamber and the under-clerks.	2	o	o

After the royal servants, and again by custom, came the gifts to the tradesmen's men who served Woburn Abbey and Bedford House and last, but not least, the man who carried the post letters. The latter usually got five shillings. Every head of a department had his list ready and presented it to the receiver-general, who handed over the necessary ready money.

To the Xmas boxes of the several tradesmen's servants belonging to the stables.

	£	s.	d.
1682. Saddler's men.		5	o
Farrier's men.		5	o

	£	s.	d.
Coachmaker's men.		5	0
Harnessmaker's men.		5	0
Tailor's men.		5	0
Corn-chandler's men.		4	0
Bitmaker's men.		2	6
Painter's men.		2	6
Fringemaker's men.		2	6
	£1	16	6

The other departments were no whit behind the stables and, taking all in all, Christmas and the New Year were expensive times. Every servant attached in whatsoever capacity to the household, either inside or out, at Woburn Abbey or at Bedford House, received, too, his or her Christmas box. But these were not put down among the gratuities; they were reckoned in with the ordinary wage list.

On the other hand, neither relatives nor friends apparently expected much in the way of presents at Christmas. If the Earl gave any, he met the cost out of some of the money which was handed to him for his private use by his receiver-general. But seeing that anything he gave on other occasions was always carefully set down, it is most probable that his benevolence to his friends and relatives, which was very great, was not especially shown at Christmas.

One celebration at least invariably implied a present. A christening called for either an order given to the goldsmiths for a richly chased piece of plate, or for a present in money. Usually when he gave money to or for the child, the Earl fixed the gift at nine guineas. The exception was the christening of William, Lord Russell's son, Wriothesley, who was afterwards the second Duke. Then sixteen guineas were given, although the Earl's other grandchildren had only received the regulation nine guineas which were also bestowed upon the children of friends.

1680.—To the Lord Russell, being paid by
him in standing for his lordship at Captain
Cheek's child's christening 9 guineas at 1*s*. 6*d*.
each—£9.13.6.; to his lordship himself at the
Lady Alington's child's christening 9 guineas
also at 1*s*. 6*d*. each—£9. 13. 6.; and to his lordship
more at the Lord Russell's son's christening
16 guineas at 1*s*. 7*d*. each—£17. 5. 4. In all   £36   12   4

Other presents to relatives and friends were spread over
the year. They very frequently took the form of plate,
ordered in early days from Viner and then from the firm that
was known first as Blanchard, later as Blanchard and Child,
and, finally, as Child and Partner. Another favourite present
was a portrait. But, on the whole, the family and higher
officials pre-eminently and the friends to some extent tended
to receive money gifts from the Earl far more frequently
than they received anything else. Even the Countess was no
exception to this rule. Such money was invariably distributed
by the receiver-general, who constantly entered in his accounts
that he had handed fifty, twenty or ten guineas to my lady,
or to one of the sons or daughters of the house, or to an
official, or even had sent it away to some other nobleman,
'on the order of his lordship as a gift.'

The receiver-general also ordered and paid for other
presents. When the Earl did not give his Countess money
he usually gave her jewels. These were not always bought
from a goldsmith. A great deal of buying and selling of
this kind went on between friends. In 1669 the Dowager
Countess of Northumberland sold the Earl of Bedford a pair
of ornaments made in the shape of roses set with fourteen
large diamonds, for which the Earl paid her three hundred
pounds in all. There was perhaps some special occasion
which the Earl wished to commemorate this year in his gifts
to his wife since in the same month he bought for her from

the goldsmith Gomeldon, a necklace of thirty-three Oriental pearls, for which he gave the big price of £1,820.

As for the children of the house, whether the Earl's own sons and daughters in the fifties or his grandchildren during the later years, they had many a present from the father or grandfather.

Gifts of money in reply to public appeals were of frequent occurrence. The havoc wrought by the Great Fire of London necessitated during many years afterwards appeals for building funds for the replacement of certain public buildings. The Earl contributed towards the rebuilding of both the College of Arms and St. Paul's.

> *December* 1672.—Received then of Mr. George Collop, by the appointment of the Right Honourable William, Earl of Bedford, the sum of ten pounds, being his benevolence money according to his subscription made towards rebuilding of the College of Arms in London, consumed by the late fire there, in compliance to His Majesty's commission issued in that behalf. I say received by me, FRANCIS SANDFORD; Rouge Dragon; *Collector*. £10 o o

> *January* 1678.—Received 16th January 1678, of Mr. George Collop, by the hands of Mr. Dawson, twenty pounds given by the Right Honourable the Earl of Bedford towards the rebuilding of St. Paul's church, London, I say received, per WILLIAM PHILLIPS. £20 o o

St. Paul's church was not the only building by Sir Christopher Wren in whose construction the Earl assisted. He had always had particularly close relations with Trinity College, Cambridge. Both his elder sons, Francis and William, had been undergraduates there and he was for long the lessee of certain of the College lands in Hitchin. Consequently, when an appeal was made by the College for the building of their proposed library, he sent them the handsome sum of a hundred pounds.

November 1676.—To Mr. Thomas Boughey, Receiver for Trinity College in Cambridge, given by his lordship towards building of a library in the said College. £100 0 0

No doubt this was partly at the instance of Mr. Thornton. The latter was intimately acquainted with Dr. Isaac Barrow of Trinity College, the mathematician, who was helping to collect the subscriptions.

Dr. Isaac Barrow to Mr. John Thornton at Woburn Abbey.

TRINITY COLLEGE
July 19*th,* 1676.

DEAR SIR,
Premising my hearty thanks to yourself for promoting our affair with so good success. I request you to present my humblest thanks to my lord of Bedford for his lordship's noble bounty to our College, the which I shall soon presume to do myself again in a more solemn manner, in company with my brethren. It is very acceptable to us and cometh seasonable, for that lately we have had not much encouragement and have been at great expense, having driven on our work very briskly. I have sent you some schemes of our library, designed by Sir Christopher Wren, according to which we build, whereof you may please to present one to his lordship, another to Mr. Russell, and the rest to dispose of as you think convenient. I could wish your leisure could suffer and your curiosity dispose to come and see our work and let us have the happiness to see you, which would be a great satisfaction to
Your very affectionate friend and faithful servant,
ISAAC BARROW

Our Receiver at London is Mr. Boughey, dwelling in Token Yard, in Lothbury.

Besides such subscriptions as these and the presents, the gratuity list was for the most part a matter of constant small payments. The casual gratuities, which had cost the Earl much in 1641, continued to be matters of daily occurrence, whether to other people's servants or the ubiquitous door and gate keepers.

But neither the gentleman of the privy purse, in his detailed accounts, nor the receiver-general ever made any attempt to distinguish between presents in money of the kind that to-day would be called tips and money given in actual charity. Everything was put under the head of gratuities.

The legal obligations of the Earl for the relief of the poor were met by the bailiffs of the respective estates and were entered in their accounts. When, as was sometimes the case, the Earl gave in charity a small additional sum over and above what he was bound to give, this was also accounted for by the bailiff.

Another legal charge for the relief of the poor, happily not of annual occurrence, was also paid by the bailiffs. This was the rate or tax imposed on all landowners in 1665 for the relief of those infected by the plague. The payments for Woburn and the district were made late in the year— October and November—and were paid to the constables. The Earl's share for Woburn, with the adjoining lands, came to about twenty-two shillings. Perhaps the rate covered all that was necessary to be done in Woburn in the way of relief. For the sufferers in London in this year of trouble the Earl made, through the receiver-general, a handsome voluntary contribution.

1665.—To Mr. Bennett, treasurer, his lordship's voluntary gift towards the erecting of a

pesthouse—£10; to Monsieur Cardonnel by his
lordship's order towards the relief of the poor
visited in Westminster—£10; and to Mr.
Patrick by like order towards relief of the poor
visited in St. Paul's, Covent Garden—£10. In
all   £30 0 0

The Great Fire, disastrous as it was in certain respects,
was at least salutary in that it burnt up certain plague-
infested areas. But it was another stroke of ill fortune for
the poor. The plight of those left homeless was far from
being remedied within one year or even two and for several
years in succession the Earl of Bedford contributed sums of
either ten pounds or five pounds towards their relief.

The gentleman of the privy purse always handed his
master a sum of five shillings whenever he went to take the
Sacrament and lesser sums for other purposes in church.
Often an especial appeal would be made either for a work of
mercy, such as a contribution for the help of those languish-
ing in prison, or for one of missionary intent.

Appeals for mercy to be shown in practical form for all
prisoners and captives still had an especial significance in
the seventeenth century. Every few months the Earl of
Bedford instructed his gentleman of the privy purse to give
money for those prisoners who lay in His Majesty's prisons
both in London and in Bedford. A certain amount for this
purpose was also given through the churches, particularly
through St. Paul's, Covent Garden, while at other times
special collectors would appear. Without such assistance
the prisoners could hardly have hoped to spin out their
miserable lives.

The word 'captive' had a wider connotation. The Turk
was still a menace to Europe. He was still making captives
in the Mediterranean and selling them into slavery. Appeals
for funds that should redeem these wretched men were yet

being made, if no longer so frequently as in the two previous centuries. The Earl of Bedford gave five pounds in 1670 to the collectors of Covent Garden for the redemption of slaves out of Turkey. In 1683 he received a more direct appeal.

The humble petition of Elizabeth Newman, widow, Showeth

That your petitioner's son served His Majesty on board the 'Royal James' till ordered out of the same by Sir Richard Beech at Portsmouth into the ship 'Posthorse,' the which was carrying soldiers for His Majesty's service: That from thence the said ship, being bound for Calais, was in her voyage thither taken by the Turks on the 3rd of January 1680, and carried to Algiers, where your petitioner's son doth still remain in most miserable slavery, having one hundred pounds laid on him for his redemption.

The appeal did not go unanswered, but the Earl of Bedford did not feel able to send more than one pound to Mrs. Newman.

A more hopeful sign was a single appeal that was made to the Earl in 1661 to help 'support a converted Turk.' He supported him to the extent of two pounds.

Other missionary work concerned the conversion of the Jews, which was an ever-present question, and in 1686 the Earl subscribed ten shillings for the support of a converted Jew.

The plight of the poor generally is amply illustrated by the ever-recurring entries in every account book, not that of any one official only, of a penny, sixpence or a shilling given to 'a poor man' or 'a poor woman,' who appeared at some door or more often was encountered on the road. But among those were to be found representatives of three classes of persons each of which constituted a special problem.

The 'poor'—the adjective is always affixed—mad woman, or sometimes the 'distracted woman,' was a person constantly encountered begging on the roads. For some reason, as far as the Earl of Bedford's accounts are concerned, the trouble here seems to have been confined to the female sex. It was always a mad woman who begged and never a mad man. Possibly this points to more drastic means being taken to deal with the one who was likely to be more dangerous. That there must have been a very large number of these miserable women on the highways is not left in doubt. Nor, equally, can it be doubted that if every one gave on the same scale as the Earl of Bedford they must one way and another have received a good deal in charity.

The second significant figure who came a beggar to the door, or who was found on the highway, was the 'poor discharged soldier,' or the 'poor wounded soldier.' A little had already been attempted in the way of helping maimed and injured men. That little was, of course, quite inadequate. Oliver Cromwell had recognized the difficult problem of the future of the discharged soldier who was well and fit. But neither his proclamations nor those of Charles II, who in this matter followed in his footsteps, whereby it was sought to make things easier for such to get employment, were really effective. All account books, including those of the constables and the overseers of the highways, testify to the number of soldier beggars who, in the seventeenth century, were still passing up and down the roads, although the claim that has been made for these, that they were more respectable and peaceful than their Elizabethan predecessors is probably justified.

The third figure on the roads was a very different class of person from either mad woman or discharged soldier. The gentleman of the horse frequently found at the door of the stables a Frenchman, or sometimes a Frenchwoman, who either begged outright, or who asked for and was often given a small job of work. The books of the gentleman of the privy purse tell exactly the same tale, except that he had to hand out much more money and at more frequent intervals than had his colleagues. Such persons, the French refugees who were to all intents and purposes beggars, constituted one aspect of the problem presented by the arrival of the Huguenots in England and perhaps the most difficult one to solve. The account books show that even as late as 1700 many of these men and women were still asking and receiving alms, although a good proportion of them had been brought under the various schemes which had been created to help with their relief. To these schemes also the Earl gave freely. A monthly contribution of two pounds at least to 'the Charity House for the poor French' appears to have been a regular payment for some years. He also subscribed generously, usually twenty pounds at a time, to the fund administered by the ministers and overseers of the French Church for the relief of their poor countryfolk.

The amount of money given either by subscription or as casual charity to those refugees a great number of whom were unable to help themselves was considerable. But all were not helpless. An earlier flood of *émigrés*, also fleeing from religious persecution, had brought to England a family from whom had sprung the first Governor of the Bank in Threadneedle Street. Every *émigré* could not be a Houblon, but among the new-comers were many, perhaps a majority, who needed a very little help in order to be able to stand upon their own feet and make contribution to the country which had welcomed them. Such help was freely given by the Earl of Bedford. He took an especial interest, perhaps at the suggestion of Mr. Thornton, in the outburst of Huguenot literature so many examples of which found a place on his shelves. He did more than buy the authors' books ; he helped the authors themselves. So also he constantly gave a present of anything from three to five pounds to some Frenchman, often a French minister, who had employment but who was in need of a little additional assistance.

CHAPTER XIX

GETTING AND SPENDING

(i) HOW THE MONEY CAME IN

W HEN Mr. Collop took up the office of receiver-general to the Earl of Bedford sometime between 1658 and 1660, the system upon which the finance was worked was still that which had obtained in 1641. The only noticeable change was that some time during the fifties the bailiff at Thorney had begun to make use of a bill of exchange for the purpose of transmitting his rents, thus following the example long since set by his brother bailiff in Devon. Monies from the other properties continued to be delivered in coin by their respective bailiffs. The bill of exchange only operated to advantage over a long distance. Otherwise it was more troublesome for the receiver-general to have to go to Lombard Street to fetch the money than it was for the bailiffs to bring the bags to him direct.

What the amount thus received at Lady Day and Michaelmas each year by the receiver-general on behalf of his master really represented is no easier to calculate for the years after the Restoration than for 1641, the year of the Earl's first account book.

For the purpose of the general accounts the receiver-general was only required to note the figure of the amount sent or handed to him half-yearly by the bailiff of each estate after the latter had balanced his own accounts. How much of this represented rents, how much fines, or even whether perhaps the sale of a small piece of land was included, was never clearly defined.

All that can be asked, therefore, is what, after all, was the only thing that was of immediate interest to the receiver-general, namely, how much was there to spend?

The answer is that whereas in 1641 the yield from the estates, including wood and other sales, had been round about £8,500, later on the figures fluctuated between ten and fourteen thousand pounds. The higher figures belong to the years in which many fines for renewals of leases were collected from one or other of the estates.

The rise in the total sum received depended upon many factors: in the first place, the greatly increased rent roll with the fines from Covent Garden; in the second, the profits from the development of the Thorney estate with reference to the draining of the fens; and, finally, a small but universal improvement in all the other estates. Woburn, for example, which had formerly shown a steady loss each year, was now paying its way and even showing a profit.

The years after 1658 were indeed years of prosperity for the Earl of Bedford. But it was a case of prosperity spread somewhat irregularly over a long period rather than one of a steadily increasing rental. Years in which big receipts came from the estates occurred at intervals throughout the entire period, counterbalancing other years in which the profits were lower.

The Earl of Bedford would have been a rich man had he had only his rents upon which to depend. But he had a good deal more than this. In 1641 he had been forced to save on anything and everything that he possibly could in order to find the interest for and ultimately to pay off the bonds given by his father as well as his own debt. By 1660 and probably earlier, as a result of economies exercised during the years of the Commonwealth, he was in a position to lend money at interest instead of borrowing it. At first perhaps two or three thousand pounds were employed in this way. Later this amount was considerably augmented by the savings of those years—there were not a few of them—at the end of which there was a balance over and above what was wanted for immediate purposes.

These transactions were of three kinds. Money was invested in the Company of Adventurers for Draining the Fens; loans were made to private individuals; and money was lent to tradesmen.

There was every reason why the Earl of Bedford should invest money in the fen enterprise. This he did at frequent intervals in sums varying from one hundred to as much as a thousand pounds. The money was always being put in and then taken back again, for the practice of the company was to borrow, pay back and then borrow again.

The long list of private individuals who borrowed from the Earl included such well-known names as those of the Duke of Albemarle, the Earls of Portland and Bristol—the latter a brother-in-law—Lord Holles, Sir Richard Temple and Sir Walter St. John.

Such loans to private persons were made for even shorter periods than those to the Company of Adventurers, often for less than a year, sometimes only for weeks or months. Those who borrowed did so as a rule because they had temporary need of gold, the supplies in their own money chests having sunk low. But presently their rents would come in.

The interest normally paid by all of these alike, including the Adventurers, was the six per cent. which had been made statutory in 1651, replacing the former eight per cent. But in a few cases the Earl took only five per cent. Sir Walter St. John was certainly only paying five per cent. on a loan in 1686.

The security offered might be a mortgage, the most usual and obviously the best, or a bond.

The tradesmen to whom loans were made also paid six per cent. interest and offered the same kinds of security. But in their case the sum involved was rarely more than one hundred pounds and was usually a good deal less. Also such a loan, in contradistinction to the others, often continued over a number of years. This may have been and probably was because in many instances it came to be considered as a more or less permanent investment. On the other hand, some tradesmen were never able to raise the money for repayment. The Earl lent Henry Kirk, the Indian gown seller, several sums of money, but poor Henry Kirk, whose business went to pieces when the fashion for négligé gowns waned, was never able to pay all the interest, much less repay the capital. Ultimately, the debt was forgiven him, or rather his son and successor, by a special clause in his noble patron's will.

The business of repaying and re-lending does not make the transactions any easier to disentangle, particularly in the absence of the distinction recognized by later generations between capital and income. Everything that came into the Earl of Bedford's chest was treated as income, whether it was the repayment of a loan, or interest on it, or, what was most often the case, a mixture of the two. The best that can be made of the figures as they stand is to say that the Earl was lending over a period of thirty-five years sums varying between three thousand and twelve thousand pounds, for which he received the six or five per cent. interest. How much money was out on loan at any one time depended entirely upon the surplus that could be spared from the requirements of the receiver-general, who had to dovetail one year in with another. A sum of as much as six thousand pounds might be and was not infrequently repaid during a year, but perhaps only three thousand of it would be lent out again because more was wanted for the household. On the other hand, a year of big profits from the estates and moderate expenditure at home meant that a good deal was available for lending.

The loans were returned in coin. With the fluctuations

in the value of gold, the receiver-general had sometimes to go to the trouble of analysing the kind of coins in which he was repaid, whether gold or silver and, if of the former, whether of what he called 'old gold' or of the new Guinea gold.

Great care also had to be exercised in fixing the time for repayment. If the dates were badly calculated, or if any debtor failed to return the money at the expected moment, the receiver-general might himself be hampered for want of ready money. This did occur on various occasions. Then it was necessary for Mr. Collop or Mr. Fox to resort, as they put it in the accounts, to 'Monies borrowed for the present supply of his lordship's occasions.'

On such loans, generally borrowed only for a very short period and in small amounts, the Earl paid the regulation six per cent. At first the creditors were men of much the same status as himself and as those to whom he lent money, obviously his friends. Here, however, was one exception. During the time when the sons of the house were abroad, an occasional entry was made that money had been borrowed from Mr. Luce, the exchange agent. It is fairly obvious that what had happened was that it was not convenient to send up the ready money for the bill of exchange and that, therefore, Mr. Luce had lent it, receiving it back with the six per cent. interest.

In the meantime, amid all these transactions of lending and borrowing, certain changes were taking place in the administration of the Earl's finance, changes which concerned the money chest. Some time during the middle sixties, Mr. Collop began at intervals to take a proportion of money from the chest and lodge it with the goldsmith, Viner. The latter paid six per cent. upon the money, which could be withdrawn at fifteen days' notice. Here was a method by which money earned interest instead of lying idly in the chest and yet could easily be obtained when needed. The Earl and his receiver-general were a little old-fashioned here, for the practice had been fairly common for some time before they adopted it. But it was characteristic of the Earl that, eager as he was to follow up new ideas in agriculture for the benefit of his estates, he was somewhat cautious in doing so elsewhere.

This practice of depositing money with a goldsmith and the consequent lower balance of money in the chest was the first stage in the elimination of the chest itself, although that neither Mr. Collop nor his successor, Mr. Fox, lived to see.

The next stage followed upon the connection of the Earl of Bedford with another firm of goldsmiths, that of Robert Blanchard, who, in 1663, had succeeded William Wheeler at his house of business called the Marygold and had married Wheeler's widow. The Earls of Bedford had apparently had no transactions with Wheeler. But the fifth Earl often bought plate from Blanchard after the latter had taken over the business and in 1675 the goldsmith had accommodated him with a loan of a thousand pounds. Here was a significant departure from the practice of borrowing from a fellow peer or friend.

Two years after Blanchard had lent the Earl money, another transaction took place between the firm and the Earl. In 1677 Mr. Collop noted that he had sent Mr. Robert Blanchard and Mr. Francis Child, goldsmiths, on the 6th of July, a sum of four hundred pounds 'to be paid on demand.'

This, unlike the money that was only payable at fifteen days' notice, earned no interest.

1677.—To Mr. Robert Blanchard and Mr. Francis Child, goldsmiths, the 6th of July 1677, by his lordship's order, to be paid on demand. £400 0 0

1679.—Received of Mr. Robert Blanchard
and Partner the 3rd of April 1679, being due
on their note payable on demand, dated the
10th March last.   £220 0 0

Mr. Blanchard had indeed now taken a partner, whose
name was destined to obliterate that of his master in banking
circles. In 1656 a boy named Francis Child, the son of a
Wiltshire clothier, had been apprenticed to a London goldsmith called Hall. The youth had next been taken into
Mr. Blanchard's firm and, with a slight departure from
tradition, had, in 1672, married not that gentleman's
daughter, but the next best thing, his stepdaughter,
Elizabeth Wheeler. Thence, by a natural and proper step,
he had become a partner.

The money deposited with the goldsmiths, for which,
when it was wanted, it was not even necessary to wait fifteen
days, allowing for the practical difficulties of fetching the
money from Lombard Street, served yet a little further to
depreciate the importance of what was kept in the chest.

When, on the 21st of August 1682, Mr. Collop died
suddenly in the midst of his duties, the chest contained only
ninety-three pounds, an entirely inadequate sum according
to previous ideas. This ninety-three pounds was promptly
taken in charge by the Earl himself—'Now in the said Earl's
custody' said the account book—to be passed over, with the
key to the chest, to Mr. Fox, the new receiver-general.

Then, in the time of Mr. Fox, the chest suffered one more
blow at its supremacy as the Earl's banking centre. Hitherto
all money that came in had been placed first of all in the
chest, even when it would be taken out again to be put into
the custody of the firm which since 1681 had been Francis
Child and Rogers, for Child, succeeding to the business on
Blanchard's death, had himself taken a partner. In 1687,
for the first time, a certain important part of the rents—

those from Thorney—never reached the chest at all. Instead of negotiating a bill of exchange by which the money was delivered to Mr. Fox, the Thorney bailiff now sent it direct to Messrs. Child and Rogers 'for his lordship's service and use.' The receipt from the goldsmiths was then delivered to Mr. Fox that he might keep his accounts correctly.

Hereafter this practice was regularly followed for all the Thorney rents. Moreover, the bailiff there no longer kept them back, until all, or nearly all, were in, as he had hitherto done, in order that the bill of exchange might be negotiated for the full amount, but sent the money to the Marygold in instalments.

April 1688.—Received of John Carryer, by the hands of Robert Grantham, the sum of one hundred pounds by the order of Ralph Peirson, Esq. [bailiff of Thorney], and for the use of the Right Honourable the Earl of Bedford. I say, for my master Francis Child and Partner, JOHN LUND.   £100   0   0

Neither in the general accounts nor in the isolated bills and notes, which continue after 1694 until the Earl's death in 1700, is there evidence that the practice was ever extended in so far as the estates were concerned, not even for Devon. But it is noteworthy that the money due to the Earl from the Company of Adventurers was paid through Child and Rogers at least as early as 1687 and very probably some years earlier.

Mr. Fox, like Mr. Collop before him, only aimed at submitting to his master at the end of each March a statement of what had come in and what had gone out. Nor did he make any distinction between the money he himself had received and what had gone to Child and Rogers. The entries in the accounts of the money due from Thorney and that from the Company of Adventurers were both kept in their traditional places, which happened to be well in the middle of the list of items. The only distinction made was a note affixed to these particular entries that the money had been transmitted direct by the persons concerned to Child and Rogers. For Mr. Fox it was all money that he had in hand. He, like his predecessor, remained as much master of the balance with Messrs. Child as each was of the other balance in the chest. They alone deposited money and they alone withdrew it.

On the other hand, the Earl of Bedford kept an extremely close watch on everything that was done. Messrs. Collop and Fox carried out the transactions, but under the direct and close supervision of the Earl. It is rare indeed that any paper relating to the money brought in does not bear his signature, showing that it had passed through his hands and that he had authorized the transaction. Everything, too, had to be shown in the final audit.

This careful management of his business affairs gave the Earl a position of comparatively stable finance, which was by no means the case with all his fellow peers. Nevertheless, even for him, the difficulties surrounding the question of ready money involved at times a hand-to-mouth existence.

Once, for the space of two years, it seemed possible that prosperity might not continue. The years of 1665 and 1666 were a time of stress and even terror for every one in the country. The financial stringency consequent upon the Dutch Wars had begun to be felt when first the horror of the abnormal incidence of the plague, which caused 1665 to be characterized as the plague year, and next that of the Great Fire fell upon the kingdom. The material consequence of both was to accentuate the financial crisis. The Earl of Bedford, for one, found himself at the end of 1665 short of something over a thousand pounds in the rents he derived from Covent Garden. The bailiff there had died and—it is not surprising—it proved to be difficult, if not impossible to get in the arrears of rents he had not yet collected. Some of the arrears were made up in subsequent years, although the Earl had to wait for them. Others remained bad debts. The Great Fire wrought no such havoc on the London property, but, for some reason that is not clearly stated, in 1666 other rentals failed. In particular, nothing was received from Thornhaugh in the east, and the Woburn Abbey estate showed a bad loss. On top of this came the extra war taxation. The Earl of Bedford found that he could not re-lend much of the money which had come in and was himself obliged to raise some small loans. It was, however, entirely characteristic of him that in face of his difficulties he promptly took measures to cut down his expenses. Every department in the household, particularly that of the clerk of the kitchen, showed a diminution for these two years. It was the easier done because the conditions of the time made simple rather than extravagant living natural and desirable.

(ii) HOW THE MONEY WAS PAID OUT

The Earl of Bedford exercised an even closer supervision over the money that was paid out than he did over what was paid in. No single item of all that Messrs. Collop and Fox distributed from the chest ever escaped their master's notice.

The picture that stands out of first Mr. Collop and then Mr. Fox is of someone who sat constantly beside the great painted chest in Bedford House grasping its enormous key in his hands and handing out gold and silver. The picture is not far wrong. What is astounding is that either of the receivers-general should have found time to do all that they did seeing that both of them had the supervision of all the business affairs and that Mr. Fox exercised the office of legal adviser as well. They had, of course, assistants, and one of these was allowed to keep the key and to distribute money when his superior was away in the fens or elsewhere. But anything that he gave out had to be reported and a careful account of it kept.

For the master of the house himself the receiver-general was still banker. As in 1641, so to the end of his life, when the Earl or Duke wanted ready money for his personal and private use he informed his official of the fact, the requisite sum was handed over to him and he duly gave a receipt.

Most of these receipts were endorsed, as had been those in 1641, that the money had been given to the Earl for his private use. Sometimes, however, the receiver-general was told that it was wanted for a specific purpose and then it was so entered up.

February 1690/91.—Received this 18th day of February 1690/91, of my servant John Fox, ten pounds to give unto Mr. Martin, the lawyer, of Lincoln's Inn. I say received by me, BEDFORD

February 1690/91.—Received this 20th day of February 1690/91, of my servant John Fox more ten pounds to give unto Mr. John Conyers, the lawyer, of the Temple. I say received by me, BEDFORD

When the Earl was handling his own money he preferred to use the useful and convenient coin which was called the guinea. Very often the receiver-general could not supply these from the coins he had in the chest. It is noticeable that a very large number of the rents were paid in what the receiver called 'old gold' or silver. Hence the necessity that was upon him, when his master asked for money, to effect an exchange at a goldsmith's.

May 1690.—Received this thirteenth day of May, Anno Domini 1690, of my servant John Fox three hundred guineas, for which he is to be allowed upon his account three hundred twenty and five pounds, so much being

375

paid by him to Mr. Harrison, goldsmith, for the said guineas. I say received by me, BEDFORD

There is no evidence at all that the Earl and Duke of Bedford, even during the latter years of his life, ever departed from this custom of getting his private spending money from his receiver-general instead of making a personal application to Child and Rogers. Nor does it appear that on those occasions when he particularly wished to pay someone—perhaps a lawyer—personally he ever gave a note on his goldsmith bankers for payment to bearer, although this precursor of the modern cheque was being used to some extent by others during the eighties and freely during the nineties. The first note of such a kind that has been preserved at the Marygold is one given by his grandson.

The lord and master of the house not being given to roam from home and certainly never very far away from his receiver-general, it was a simple matter for coin to pass from hand to hand. Nor was there any difficulty in handing the Countess her money and receiving her receipt.

Of the two girls, Diana, who married so young, never had a regular allowance. But Margaret, when she was still living unmarried as a middle-aged woman in her father's house, was given two hundred pounds a year for her personal expenses. When she did marry she received, as her elder sister Diana had done, a dowry of six thousand pounds.

The payments to the sons of the house presented greater difficulties. The young men were frequently away. Consequently the receiver-general had to carry out a series of banking transactions for them.

All the sons, once they were grown men, had allowances of between three hundred and four hundred pounds a year. When William married a settlement was made which ensured him an annuity of two thousand pounds a year, payable out of the rents of Woburn and Thorney. Settlements were also made when the other sons married, but the annuities payable to them were only five hundred pounds a year.

Whether it were an annuity or an allowance, the money was always paid over by the receiver-general, usually twice yearly. But since the young men were often away and also, like others, sometimes wanted their allowances paid in advance or readjusted, first Mr. Collop and then more especially Mr. Fox had to carry out a series of more or less elaborate transactions on their behalf. One or another would frequently arrange with their father's official to pay their allowance, or part of it, by means of a bill of exchange. They also sometimes used him as a banker, asking him to make payments on their behalf and to deduct them from the amount of their allowance due.

William Russell to Mr. George Collop at Bedford House, London.

EDINBURGH
21 *June* 1666.

MR. COLLOP,

At ten days after sight of this, my first bill of exchange, (my second not being paid), pay unto Mr. Roger Jackson at Devonshire House for the use of Mr. Richard Ward the sum of one hundred pounds sterling for the value received here of the said Mr. Ward, and place the same to the account of

Your affectionate friend,

WILLIAM RUSSELL

The money affairs of William, the ever perfect, gave but little trouble. Nor, to do them justice, did those of his three brothers, Edward, Robert and James. With George, the youngest of the family, it was far otherwise.

This young gentleman's career, until his comparatively early death, was one of perpetual getting into debt, whether as a married man or no. About 1676 he was dispatched to that refuge for straying sheep, conveniently distant from home, a colony. The settlements in North America would, it was hoped, be sufficiently far off to solve the problem of his existence. This was an error of judgment. During the three years he was away there arrived at Bedford House in the Strand a number of bills of exchange which he had given either in New York or in Boston to be paid in London, these quite over and above the tolerably generous allowance which was being sent to him.

NEW YORK
April 11*th*, 1679.

Exchange £200.

Twenty days after sight of this, my first per exchange, my second and third not paid, pay unto Mr. John Robinson or order the sum of two hundred pounds sterling, value received, as per advice of GEORGE RUSSELL

To the Right Honourable the
Earl of Bedford at Bedford
House in the Strand.

When he returned matters were no better, for he embarked on a career of visiting his father's friends and borrowing money by means of similar bills of exchange, which were then transmitted to Bedford House.

During the later years one son at least, Edward Russell, had an account with Child and Rogers. So also had William Russell's widow, Rachel.

Edward Russell to Mr. Fox.

23*rd September* 1682.

MR. FOX,
I pray pay unto Mr. Francis Child the sum of forty-nine pounds on my account, this being the three and twentieth day of September 1682.   EDWARD RUSSELL

GETTING AND SPENDING

After the receiver-general had entered in his final account the payments which he had made to each member of the family during the year, he set out his wage list and, after the wage list, the money, called imprest money, which he had advanced to the heads of departments for their current expenses. All these payments were made in hard cash, in the case of the wages twice yearly, in that of the imprest money every month. Such of the recipients who were required to do so distributed the money again in cash to their subordinates. Sometimes difficulties would arise. The receiver-general was perhaps at Bedford House and had not left sufficient imprest money with the gentleman of the horse or the steward of the household at Woburn Abbey to meet all their requirements, or something unforeseen in one of those departments would have arisen. Then these officials, occasionally aggrieved, would dispatch the creditor, or a messenger on his behalf, to London, asking the receiver-general to pay him. The letter was treated as and called a bill of exchange, which was to be set down to the account of the official who made the request. When it was necessary for Mr. Collop or Mr. Fox to transmit money to a bailiff on one of the distant estates, Thorney or Devon, he likewise did so by means of a bill of exchange.

That every transaction of this kind should be duly entered to the account of the person involved was very important. Every head of a department had to prepare annually his own detailed balance sheet, which was submitted in turn to the receiver-general, to the Earl and sometimes an auditor as well. If one of the three were omitted, it was never the Earl. More than this, every single bill paid by any member of the household was preserved and ultimately came into the possession of the receiver-general, who docketed it. Before it reached his hands and, moreover, before it had been paid, it had been submitted elsewhere. Of the thousands of isolated bills that have survived there are few indeed which do not bear the authorization for payment in the hand of the lord and master. The only marked change that occurred in the procedure was that, as years went on, he grew definitely more economical of words. In the forties and the fifties a long statement, always in his own hand throughout, was the order of the day.

1650.—Good fellow pay unto Dingley for three weeks expenses beginning the 18th of June and ending the 9th of July 1650, the sum of £28. 17s. 10d., which, together with the twelve pounds he had in his hands the week before, makes up the whole sum for those three weeks and twelve pounds more to buy in provisions for this week that comes in, being now the 9th of July 1650. BEDFORD

From the beginning of the sixties onwards the statement was still in his own hand, but many fewer words were used.

1681/2.—Bingley pay in full of this bill the sum of nine pounds nine shillings, being March 22nd, 1681/2. BEDFORD

In certain cases he even contented himself with signing a sentence similar to the above which had been written by someone else. This he must always have felt as evidence of overwhelming pressure of business, for to the end of his life he preferred to make all entries and notes, as he wrote his letters, in his own hand, with little difference in his handwriting, which was as firm when he signed 'Bedford' in his eighties as it had been when he signed 'W. Bedforde' in his twenties.

The legal expenses incurred by Mr. Fox, whether before he was acting as receiver-general or after, followed on those of the other departments.

Lastly, the receiver-general entered in his statement of accounts a number of miscellaneous items, which included such taxes as he had paid, gifts and rewards and, finally, collected into two divisions, 'Necessary' and 'Extra-ordinary' expenses. The last might be anything from the purchase of a picture to one of a tub for the kitchen which had had to be bought in a hurry and the bill for which had not gone through the steward of the household.

With all these bills, by whomsoever paid and of whatsoever nature, there is no indication that any one of them was ever settled during the Earl and Duke's lifetime by means of an order to bearer drawn on Child and Rogers.

The final statement was drawn up to be ready on the 25th of March. It would not be far wrong to say that the total amount paid out for all expenses, excluding loans and taxes, was something like an average of nine thousand pounds in a normal year during the sixties and seventies and then rose to ten thousand pounds and more, during the later years. That is allowing for the necessity endured by the receiver-general of making one year fit in with another.

The balance sheet drawn up, it went to the auditor. If and when he passed it, it was submitted to the Earl, who, provided he was satisfied, marked it:

Examined and allowed by me, BEDFORD

The relief on obtaining the Earl's signature must have been considerable and the receiver-general and the auditor, with any select official whom they invited to join them, sat down to a dinner to celebrate the occasion with, it is to be hoped, good appetites.

(iii) TAXATION

The section which the receiver-general called 'Public Payments and Taxes' by no means included everything that a later generation would have called taxation. In the first place, the receiver, as always, was only concerned with what he himself actually had to pay out. In the second place, his view of what did or did not constitute a tax caused him to distribute his obligations under many and various headings at different times.

The confusion which, to the modern mind, is evident in the history of the taxation of the Earl of Bedford was merely the result of the general situation. The theory that the Crown should live of its own was still at the back of men's minds, although it was only too evident as the years went on that it was ceasing to be tenable. But since direct taxation was still regarded as something that should only be imposed on especial occasions and at irregular intervals, neither the authorities who put on the tax nor the people who paid it saw their way clearly. The result was thoroughly unsatisfactory. Special taxes were imposed under a variety of names. But an old method of assessment was always resorted to, partly on account of convenience, since the lists were there, and partly perhaps—important point—because it was thought less likely to arouse resentment than an entirely new arrangement. Hence the extreme difficulty, if not impossibility, to assess with anything like accuracy, even on general lines, the amount that anyone had to pay.

Certain regular payments had, of course, to be made. But in the case of the Earl of Bedford, since they were for the most part connected with land, they do not appear in the accounts of the receiver-general. In Devon the tenths payable on the Tavistock estate amounted to just over two hundred and seventy pounds a year. But this sum was paid by the steward of the west and never came into the receiver-general's accounts at all. He was merely interested in the balance from the rents which the steward sent him up. So also with the lesser payments due on the other estates.

Two regular payments due on land, as long as they were

exacted, the receiver-general did make. The first of these was an annual payment for the Woburn estate of £68 18s. 0½d., which he seems to have thought of as a kind of tax. It was really nothing of the kind, but was the rental which had been imposed when the estate was granted. It was ultimately, in 1671, bought up by the Earl.

The receiver called the second payment 'Fen taxes.' These were payable on that part of the Thorney estate which had been brought into the scheme for draining the fens and on certain other lands used for the same purpose in which the Earl of Bedford had an interest. The entire amount was just under two hundred and twenty pounds a year. How long before 1660 these payments had been made is doubtful. They certainly continued until the end of the Earl's lifetime and from 1676 onwards were always paid by Messrs. Child on behalf of the Earl by order from the receiver-general, the only instance of thus dealing with a tax. Thus all payments connected with Thorney were unique in the use made of the firm of goldsmiths as a medium for the transactions.

With certain other taxation, some of it regular and some incidental, the receiver-general had also to grapple.

After 1662 one tax had to be paid regularly until it was abandoned in the first year of William and Mary. This was the extremely unpopular hearth tax of two shillings on everything that was defined as a hearth. It was unpopular because the Act which imposed it in 1662 had made it a recurring annual payment to the King, his heirs and successors, and still more so because it implied inquisition into private dwellings.

The Earl of Bedford paid for Woburn Abbey, where, out of ninety odd rooms, eighty-two hearths were reckoned to be effective, £8 4s. 0d. a year. For Bedford House in the Strand, with sixty hearths, he paid six pounds and for his other houses sums varying in amount between five pounds and thirty shillings.

Besides the hearth tax there was the regular recurrence of what the receiver-general called 'Public Payments.' By these he meant small payments of every possible kind, omitting those which were paid by the bailiffs. The principal was the militia tax, when this was imposed, but he usually also reckoned in such things as the constable and highway rates, repayments of certain small taxes which had been paid by the Earl's tenants, with allowances for tithe and the grinding of wheat and so forth. The amount he so gave out fluctuated between thirty and forty pounds a year.

The shocks came when 'Extra-ordinary Payments,' as the receiver-general carefully called them in his account books, were demanded in the shape of sudden calls, taking a different form nearly every time. The first of these was the re-imposition in 1660 of poll money for one year. For this the Earl of Bedford paid a hundred and eleven pounds in all. In 1661, poll money having been temporarily abandoned, the Crown asked for a free and voluntary present from Peers and Commons. The amount in the case of a Peer was fixed at four hundred pounds. Mr. Collop succeeded in getting the money together and paying it over on 15th July. His neat and orderly mind, which comes out in every line of his statements—he was far more orderly than his successor, Mr. Fox—knew not how to classify this. He put it down not among his 'Public Payments' or taxes, not even separately, but gave it a place among his 'Necessary Payments,' cheek by jowl with the 'provision of a nurse for William Russell in the time of his illness.'

Neither the poll tax nor the free gift prevented a further call in 1663, when the old form of tax on land and property called the subsidy was revived. The Earl of Bedford paid five hundred and sixty pounds, which was followed up by five hundred pounds the next year. This the receiver-general quite definitely recognized as a true tax and entered it as such, adding to his accounts under what Act it was authorized.

All these payments were but preliminary to the crisis of 1665 and 1666. With the burden of the Dutch War on their shoulders, Crown and Government were as badly put to it for ready money as many of their subjects. Precisely at a time when they themselves were finding it most difficult to get in ready money, men in the position of the Earl of Bedford were called upon to find money for a Royal Aid, or rather for two Royal Aids. It says something for the system of finance as worked by the Earl of Bedford and his servants that his receiver-general was able to pay over without much delay the two thousand pounds which were assessed upon the Earl. The entry in the account book was 'Monies lent by his lordship to the King.'

Twice again, in 1666 and 1678, poll money was imposed. But what the Earl paid in this respect had now sunk to thirty-three pounds in each case. This tax gave Mr. Collop no trouble at all. He knew all about it and put it under its proper heading.

When, after the coming of William and Mary to the throne, a form of land tax was devised, that did not worry Mr. Fox, for it was the business of the bailiffs, not his, to deal with it.

CHAPTER XX

FIFTY AND SIXTY YEARS ON

THE fiftieth year after the Earl of Bedford's succession to
the title found him at Woburn surrounded by children and
grandchildren. There were some sad gaps. His wife, Anne,
had gone. Francis had gone. William had died in Lincoln's
Inn Fields. George's unsatisfactory career had come to an
end with death. But the other sons and daughters were
prosperous and well married. The lively Robert had become
the staid Clerk of the Pipe and the electors of Tavistock
were to return him seven times as their burgess. His elder
brother, Edward, who had embarked on a military career and
had been one of the first to join the Prince of Orange on his
landing, was destined to sit as many times as Knight of the
Shire for the county of Bedford. All of them, sons and
daughters, when they were not at the abbey, were writing
long and affectionate letters to their father. And to someone
else than their father. Mr. Thornton still reigned supreme
at Woburn Abbey and in Bedford House, and, to do him
justice, in the hearts of his former pupils. The Earl bore
with his ever-increasing interference where health was concerned with resignation and no doubt was tolerably grateful
to him, even if he refused the treatment.

Thornton's life had been full of many rewards for the
labour he had expended on the family, some disappointments
and one tragedy. He could never have felt George to be a
satisfactory specimen. But then George had never been his
pupil after babyhood, having been taken away from his care
to be sent to school. The bitter and tragic memory centred

round William, the well-beloved, upon whom such high hopes had been fixed. By special permit from the King, the tutor had been allowed to see his former pupil after the trial and condemnation. What passed between them then remains their secret. Set free from hopes and fears, their minds fixed on the hope of the world to come, the belief which William had so fervently expressed in his last letters, that he had been wrongly condemned, may well have sustained them both at the end.

In the everyday life at Woburn Abbey and at Bedford House both the Earl and Mr. Thornton had found and continued to find their consolation in the younger generation. William had left a son, Wriothesley, less than three years old at the time of his father's execution, and two daughters, Rachel and Katherine, then nine and seven years old respectively. Their mother, the widowed Lady Russell, had shown courage and determination enough at the trial of her 'dear lord,' as she endorsed all his papers, to win the admiration of some even of her enemies. She was far too important a person to be ignored in the matter of her children's education, but she was content to leave a great deal to their grandfather and to their father's former tutor. In the matter of religious and moral training, she and Mr. Thornton were in perfect agreement. All her opinions were such as to incline her to think very highly of the kind of teaching Mr. Thornton was likely to give and she willingly entrusted her children to him. In his own old age, he was in his element training the grandchildren as he had trained the children before them. 'What several heinous sins,' asked he in writing to Rachel, afterwards the Duchess of Devonshire, 'can you reckon up in our first parents eating that forbidden fruit?' 'Desabedince and angreatfulness and prid and unbeleaf and murder and senshuelety, steling,' was the response of little Rachel, then ten years old, and, lest a sin should go amissing, she added two splendidly large etceteras.

Nevertheless, Rachel and Katherine, charming children as they are shown in their portraits, counted for very little in one respect compared with their brother Wriothesley. When the last decade of the seventeenth century opened the Earl of Bedford knew that, as far as human eyes could see, the great inheritance of title and lands would pass to this grandson. He had not always felt such certainty.

From the moment when the attainder of his son, William, had been pronounced, the Earl had asked himself whether or no the estates might not be forfeited, if not at once at least on his own death. Even if they were not held forfeit, might not William's son be excluded from the inheritance? In 1685 the accession of the Duke of York as James II had increased his uneasiness to a point where it had become acute and he had made up his mind to take legal opinion. Questions had been submitted to several learned justices, including Pollexfen, afterwards Chief Baron, Pemberton, afterwards Chief Justice, and Holt, afterwards Lord Chief Justice. Their replies, given in their own writing and carefully preserved at Woburn, had been eminently satisfactory. Either or both of the first two, Pemberton and Pollexfen, might have been suspected of a bias in favour of the inquirer, for Pemberton had sat at Lord Russell's trial and had afterwards been removed from Bench and Privy Council for want of zeal against the prisoner, while Pollexfen was known to be antagonistic to the Crown. But no such doubt could have been felt as to Sir John Holt, he who had pronounced the dispensing power legal and took the sternest view of treason. Yet Holt on this point had agreed absolutely with his learned colleagues that, in the first place, neither the estates nor the title could be forfeit since the attainted man, William, Lord Russell, had never possessed either. In the second place, all had held—and this must have been even more pleasing to the Earl—that William's son and no other was, after the death of his father, the natural heir of his grandfather. No impediment existed to this for the same reason as before, the father 'having never been seised of the Earldom' and having, in fact, had nothing that he could have forfeited. If—and it was Pemberton himself who had pointed this out—the father had been Earl and had held the lands, the answer must have been very different indeed.

The Earl's mind had been set at rest, or perhaps it would be safer to say partly at rest. A little lingering doubt remained. He was an old man; the heir was a child; and there were many forces at work which might easily deprive that child of what had been pronounced to be his. There was nothing like making assurance doubly sure, once that became possible, when England had changed her King. The first Parliament of William and Mary passed the Act which reversed the attainder of William, Lord Russell, and declared the condemnation null and void. The declaration of this by Letters Patent was handed to the Earl in April 1689.

The Earl knew now that, did the boy live, he and the Russell inheritance were safe. No questions had been asked concerning the Bloomsbury property. That estate was still Rachel, Lady Russell's especial charge and care. As she grew older she lost no whit of either courage or determination and, seated in Southampton House, hardened gradually into a resolute middle and old age. Her boy's grandfather was a co-trustee of the property with her. But the Earl was not particularly interested in Bloomsbury. No prevision told him that this would be an even more important piece of property than Covent Garden. As for the beautiful Southampton House, he hoped his grandson would never live there. Bedford House in the Strand had been good enough for him and he did not wish his descendants to part with it. This attitude of mind might have been attributed to lack of resiliency in an ageing man—by those who did not know the Earl. It is much more likely to have been the consequence of indifference to the Bloomsbury property and even perhaps to a faint dislike of it, for he showed neither lack of vigour nor of keenness in other directions.

For one thing, he now began to plan a gradual expansion of the Woburn estate, whereby adjacent lands might little by little be bought in. He was aware that this must be a long process extending far beyond his own lifetime. But the planning of the preliminaries must have given him much satisfaction. He would have been even more satisfied could he have foreseen that his great-grandson, John, the fourth Duke, would proceed with the scheme and carry it out on an undreamed-of scale.

But the Earl of Bedford was singularly blessed in his old age in finding a number of new interests in life and work. For the Dukedom that he was shortly to receive he cared but little. It was always said, indeed, that he accepted it only with reluctance. For other possibilities which opened out before him he cared much.

The creation, however, in 1694 of the Dukedom of Bedford and the Marquisate of Tavistock—conveyed by those Letters Patent with a highly ornate coloured and gilt border, for the carriage of which the messenger had been rewarded with sixpence—had a special significance. The preamble stated that the Earl had received this step in the peerage by reason 'that he was father to the Lord Russell, the ornament of his age, whose great merit it was not enough to transmit by history to posterity.' The new monarchy had set the seal upon Thornton's belief in his former pupil, and by reason of the execution of his father Wriothesley Russell would become not only sixth Earl, but second Duke of Bedford.

The boy's grandfather was more interested in the marriage project of the next year. His own sons had waited until thirty and even forty years before they had entered into matrimony. For his grandson, Wriothesley, he arranged a match when the lad was only fourteen and a half. The bride was a year younger, a girl of thirteen. Her name was

GRANDSON AND GREAT-GRANDSONS

On the wall : Portrait of Wriothesley, second Duke of Bedford.

At his mother's knee : Wriothesley, third Duke of Bedford.

Seated on the table : John, afterwards fourth Duke of Bedford.

Elizabeth Howland and she was the daughter of John Howland, who owned much property in Essex and Surrey. More
important, she was also the granddaughter of Sir Josiah
Child, the Chairman of the East India Company, who had
made his manor at Wanstead, both house and park, the
admiration of all beholders.

The history of these two families, that of Howland and of
Child, had been one of trading romance. John Howland,
a draper in Cheapside, in the reign of James 1, had left a
short will showing an extremely modest, not to say tiny,
fortune, hardly worthy to be called a fortune at all. But the
drapery business prospered. Within the next forty years
Howland's son had bought the ancient manor of Tooting
Bec, with Streatham, and had been pricked Sheriff of the
county of Surrey. After that the rise of the family and their
continued acquisition of property was, in the word of con-
vention, rapid. Since at all times it has been reckoned a good
and commendable thing for money to wed money, there was
every reason why in 1681 an alliance should be arranged for
the then John Howland, lord of the manor of Tooting Bec
and much else besides, with Elizabeth, the daughter of Sir
Josiah Child. The story of the bride's family was a good
parallel to that of his own.

Richard Child had been a clothier of London when the
Howlands were drapers in the same city. He had sprung
from a family in the Midlands, that of Child of Worcestershire, who, like their contemporaries bearing the same
surname in Wiltshire, had long been engaged in the trade
of wool and cloth which had created so much of England's
wealth. The Childs of Wiltshire gave London a great banker.
From the Childs of Worcestershire had sprung two East
India Company magnates, for the two sons of Richard Child
of London became respectively Governor of the East India
Company in Bombay and ruler in all but name of the same
company in London. Josiah, the younger son of Richard,

was in theory only one of the Committee of the East India Company in the City. In practice he was its head, whom none dared disobey, for it was he who, having bullied and browbeaten his fellow members into acquiescence, led them on to triumph. He did well for the Company and even better for himself and his family. Before his daughter Elizabeth left the great house at Wanstead to marry John Howland of Streatham, his elder daughter, Rebecca, had made an alliance with the Marquess of Worcester. The clothier's son ultimately numbered among his grandsons a Duke of Beaufort and among his great-grandsons two successive Dukes of Bedford.

The noble houses of Somerset and Russell had judged an alliance with that of Child well worth while. But whatever advantages his grandfather, the Duke of Bedford, thought might result from the marriage, Wriothesley, on his wedding day, had no such serious thoughts. In the early morning of Thursday, the twenty-third of May 1695, he left Bedford House for Streatham, seated in a coach beside his grandfather and attended, as Luttrell noted in his diary, by 'several other persons of quality.' Luttrell counted the coaches and there were twelve in all. That in which the Duke and the boy were seated was drawn by six horses. An echo of the stable arrangements at Woburn is found in a bill which shows that the horses, although perhaps not the coach, were hired for the occasion.

Mr. Brown's bill to Streatham.

May 1695. For six horses going out of town on Thursday, returning the next morning. £2 5 0

Gregory pay in full of this bill the sum of two pounds five shillings, now being the 31st of May 1695. BEDFORD

The wedding took place with all due pomp and ceremony in the private chapel of the Streatham manor house. Burnet, Bishop of Salisbury, who had stood at the side of the bridegroom's father that day in Lincoln's Inn Fields, performed the rite. Then, after the banquet, arose a hue and cry. The bride and bridegroom were missing. They had slipped away after dinner to play together and in their play the costly point lace trimming of the young lady's dress had been torn to pieces. She was found hiding in a barn, while her new lord and master was strolling back with seeming innocence to the wedding company.

After the wedding, the two only met at intervals for some years. The young bride remained with her mother and the groom was sent abroad with a tutor. But his grandfather and her mother saw a great deal of each other. If Mr. Thornton and Rachel, Lady Russell, were kindred souls, so were the Duke of Bedford and Mrs. Elizabeth Howland, the daughter of Josiah Child. The two constantly visited each other and Mrs. Howland came often to stay at Woburn, always paying for the board of herself and her servants with great exactitude. The lady was as rigidly Evangelical in her religious views as even Mr. Thornton could desire. She was, judging by her own account books, very nearly as good a woman of business as her father had been a man. It was only right and proper that the strong-minded daughter of Josiah and niece of John Child should, in particular, be interested in the East India Company and its vessels, in which she had a considerable amount of money invested. Her daughter's grandfather-in-law began likewise to participate in that interest.

That the Duke would take up shares in the ships of the East India Company went almost without saying. Apart from the dividends which he hoped to derive from the ventures, it was an excellent way of importing goods for himself. Fine pieces of Oriental china appeared in the withdrawing-rooms and parlours at Woburn and in Bedford House. But his interest in the East India Company went beyond these things. He threw himself heart and soul into a new project.

Part of the Howland property lay along the Thames-side. With the two women, the astute Mrs. Howland and the able Rachel, Lady Russell, who came into the business as mother of Wriothesley, the Duke planned and carried through first the building of a dry dock and then that of a wet dock at Rotherhithe.

Within the dry dock, which was leased to a shipbuilding firm called Wells, two vessels, both destined for use in the East India Company, were built in the Duke's lifetime. The one was named very properly the *Tavistock*. The other was completed only shortly before the Duke's death and one of his last acts was to cause his grandson to present the ship to the East India Company.

East India Company Court Minutes: India Office.

June 1700.—The Right Honourable the Marquess of Tavistock now presented to the Court a new ship of three or four hundred tons burden, building at Mr. Wells his yard, to serve the company in a voyage for India whensoever they have occasion, to be commanded by Captain Meyers.

Three hundred years and more before this entry was made, and long ere India had risen on the horizon of English seamen, Stephen Russell and Henry his son had sent their ships—barges and pinnaces—to Bordeaux and La Rochelle, lesser voyages than the Indiamen made but involving as many perils—perils from the sea and perils from foes, for trading-vessels were fighting-vessels in the fourteenth century as in the eighteenth. When the Duke of Bedford bade his grandson hand over to the East India Company the ship which he had ordered to be built for them, he was bridging the gulf of centuries between himself and that Stephen

Russell who, in a ruder, rougher and yet rich and vital England, must often have stood on the quay at Weymouth watching one of his gallant little vessels, laden with goods for the Gascon ports, making her way out into the Channel. The Russells had gone back to sea trading again.

The Duke might have thought of the past. Could he, with prophetic eye, have looked into the future and seen his East India Company vessel once more leaving port fifty-five years later, at a time when his great-grandson owned most of her shares, he might have observed on board her a somewhat dispirited man. The ship had been named the *Streatham* and her log from the moment when she sailed down the Thames on her first voyage in 1700 still lies at the India Office. It was on the 5th of April 1755 that her captain wrote:

Saluted Captain Clive and his lady at their coming on board.

The defender of Arcot, whose savings had all been swallowed up on his first visit home, was about to return to India.

But when the *Streatham* was put together in Wells yard the story of Clive and India lay far ahead. The Duke of Bedford did not live even to see the ship start on her first voyage. He was eighty-seven years old now, a remarkable age for a man of those days to attain to, and it was noticed that his extraordinary vigour of body was at last beginning to ebb. No sudden or grievous illness overtook him. 'His lamp of life was not blown out,' said Dr. Freeman, who preached the funeral sermon at Chenies, 'but the oil wasted by degrees and the flame went out.' It was an apt metaphor for the peaceful slipping away from life of William, Duke of Bedford. He died on Saturday, 27th September 1700, in Bedford House in the Strand, where his father had died before him. 'He wants us no more,' wrote his daughter

Margaret to Mr. Thornton, 'though all that knew him must always miss him.'

Thornton, of course, was still there. He survived his lord for nearly five years, dying in extreme old age early in 1705 in the household of Rachel, Lady Russell, whither he had retired. In his will he left the pictures of the boys he had taught back to the family, and to his old friend Thomas Gregory, sometime gentleman of the horse and afterwards gentleman of the privy purse at Woburn Abbey, he bequeathed his pair of globes which he had always kept in his own chamber.

The evening of Thornton's life was blessed by the affection of William Russell's children. It was well for Thornton that this was so, for he had had the unhappiness of seeing many younger than himself go before him, even to the dearly beloved Diana. She, her sister Margaret and her two brothers, Robert and James, died in quick succession after their father. Only Edward, of all those who had grown up at Woburn Abbey, survived the old tutor.

The house built on the site of the old abbey at Woburn went on for another fifty years. But already in the time of the second Duke flaws were beginning to appear in the building with alarming frequency. Whatever the young man might or might not have done in the way of rebuilding, everything was put an end to by his own death in his thirtieth year from smallpox.

Sarah, Duchess of Marlborough, in one of her outspoken letters to her grandson-in-law, the third Duke, Wriothesley's son and successor, another Wriothesley, told him roundly that in her opinion the house would shortly tumble down about his ears, to which the young man, whom Sarah always oppressed by her vigour, replied wearily that it would last his time. That was true enough. He was one of the weaker branches of a sturdy tree. It was left to his brother and successor, John, fourth Duke of Bedford, to see that tinkering with the structure would do no good and that he had better rebuild. But he informed his architect, Flitcroft, that the north front, with its grotto, and part of the west wing, must at all costs be preserved.

During the third week of July 1752, the furniture was gradually moved out of the old house so that the work of pulling down could be commenced. Most of it never went back again. The Duke had his own fancy for the grotto. But he had no fancy at all for the old-fashioned chairs, tables and beds. New furniture, the splendid new furniture of the mid-eighteenth century—from the English workshops, from France, from Holland and, last but not least, brought over by the East India Company, in which, like his great-grandfather, he took so much interest—for a new house.

Already, even before all the old furniture was out, the work of destruction which had to precede construction had been commenced and on the 29th of June men had begun to underpin the library, in which the fourth Earl had spent so many of his days. 'One of the most rottenest walls I ever saw,' wrote Flitcroft's surveyor angrily to his master, condemning in the most proper fashion his predecessor's work.

Within the next few months Flitcroft's building was rising on the site of the seventeenth century mansion. But some of the salient features of the latter were retained to remind new generations of what had gone before.

Bedford

INDEX

Acaterer, 117, 126, 163

Accounts: auditing, 115; books, 53, 126, 127, 129; estate, 52, 115; household, 52, 115, 117, 126-7, 129, 160, 211; personal, 116; petty cash, 126, 130; stable, 211; irregular method of accounting, 129

Acts of Parliament: Navigation Act, 186; private, 58

Ale and Beer: children's ale, 77; brewing, 179-80; purchase of beer, 179, 180

Alington, Diana, wife of Lord Alington of Wymondley, daughter of the 5th Earl of Bedford, widow of Sir Greville Verney, 76, 111, 148, 149, 216, 291, 293, 305, 323, 376, 396

Apothecaries, 63, 308, 312, 313-4, 320-1

Apparel: for ceremonial occasions, 25, 83, 86-8, 295-6, 328-30, 330-2, 335; wearing apparel, 336-41; children's, 53, 76-7, 94-5; cleaning and repairs, 342-3; Indian gowns, 294, 342, 368; mourning, 53; sewing done at home, 339-40; for staff, 120, 121, 122, 123, 204, 245; trimmings and accessories, 337-40; yearly expenditure, 329, 335, *see also* Liveries.

Arms, College of, 42, 358

Arms, Russell, 283; re-engraved on creation of dukedom, 335

Ashmole, Elias, Windsor Herald, 271-2

Baber, Sir John, royal physician, 303

Bacon, provision of, 135

Bailey, Captain, 57

Bailiff, 117, 161; accounts, 127, 129, 160, 360; at Thorney, *see under* Thorney

Baldock, hawking at, 231

Barber, 77; surgeon, 308, 309

Barge on Thames, 56, 202; liveries for bargemen, 203

Bath, Order of, 19, 25

Bath, visits to, 221, 224, 304

Baxter, Richard, 267

Bedford House, Exeter, 20, 47, 71

Bedford House, Strand, 33, 37-9; 41, 44, 143, 176, 215, 389, cleaning of, expenses, 213-5; description, 38-9; furniture, 70; garden, 239; gardener, 138; hearth tax, 383; money assembled in chest at, 41, 46-9; reconstruction, 37; staff, 125, 143, 213; tapestries, 38, 70-1, 299-300

Bibles, 269

Billiards, 237, 238

Blanchard, Robert, 370, 371

Blanchard & Child, goldsmiths, 357

Bleeding, 308-10, 311, 312

Bloomsbury property, 111, 389-90; Southampton House, 389

Boat, hire, 56; *see also* Barges

Books and Manuscripts, 262-79; bindings, 263, 268, 273; bought in sheets, 267; catalogues, 262-3; antiquarian, 272; of ceremony, 271-2; dictionary of the Ethiopian language, 273; educational, 75-6, 97, 270; general, 272; Huguenot, 276, 364; manuscripts, number, 263; missing, 263, 264; newsbooks and newsletters, 270, 278-9; poets, 266; political, 272; printed, 265;

INDEX

Dorchester, fire at, 282-3

Dorset, property in, rentals, 46

Dukedom, creation of, 330, 333-4, 334-5, 390

Duncombe, Sir Samuel, 61-2

Dunstable, 211, 231; dinner at, 231

East India Company, 391-5; ships, 394-5

Education, 72-8, 110-11; books, 75-6, 93; Continental tours, 93, 95-109; governess, 95; tutor, 72-6; travelling tutors, 92, 97-110; see also Schools.

Elizabeth, Queen, 21, 286

Embroidery and needlework, 120, 348

Essex rebellion, 17, 38

Eworth, Hans, portrait by, 285

Falconry, 226-34; head falconer, 230-1, 235

Fens: drainage of, 26-7, 43, 46, 50, 80-1, 155, 367, 372; taxes, 383

Field, John, gardener, 241-59 passim; wife of, 323

Fiennes, Celia, 244

Finance: audit, 115, 373, 379, 381; balance sheets, 379; bills of exchange, 47, 48, 97, 365, 377-8, 379; cash in chest, 41-2, 42-4, 51, 61, 49, 370-2; cash, payments in, 51, 368-9, 379; changes in administration, 365, 369-70; charges on estate and debts, 49-51, 66-7, 81, 366, and allowances, 51, 376-7; economy necessary, 43, 50-1, 53, 147, 373-4; imprest money, 117, 203, 379; income, amount, 365; income, sources and method of collection, 44-9, 67; increasing income, 79, 366; investments, 367; loans at interest, 366-9, 370; receipts and payments not clearly defined, 365,

368, 381-2; settlement of estate, 58-9; supervision by Earl, 373, 374, 380; transactions through goldsmiths, 47, 352, 370-2, 376, 378, 381, 383, 369-70; yearly expenditure, 53, 65-6; see also Receiver-general

Fire, the Great, 147, 358, 373, 374, 361

Fish, 132, 134; for ponds at Woburn, 159-61; supply for household, 128, 153, 156-7, 172; varieties, 140-1

Flitcroft, Henry, architect, 22, 396

Flowers, 239, 243, 244, 253; flowering shrubs, 253

Footmen, 118, 204, 231

France, refugees from, 224-5, 363; tour in, 93-102; wine trade with, 184, 186

Fruit, 132, 134, 145, 146; melons, 256-7

Fruit-trees, 151, 152, 240, 246-53; orange, 256, 258; potted trees, 256

Fuel: charcoal, 178; coal, 162, 173, 174-8; wood, 178-9

Funerals, 35, 42-3, 326-7

Furniture, 32, 38, 42, 397

Game: presents of, 19, 235; supply for household, 136, 153, 156-8, 159; transport, 158-9; venison, 128, 235

Games, 237-8

Gaming, 61, 65

Garden: alterations, 151, 244-5; exchange of plants, 255; glass frames, 256, 257; herbs, 239; labour, 245; lay-out, 243; lists of plants and seeds, 240-1, 254-5, 259-61; kitchen garden, 243, 244, 253-5; orange house, 258; statuary, 243, 246; stoves, 258; wilderness, 239; see also Flowers, Fruit-trees, and Orchards

2 C

401

INDEX

Gardeners: appointments and names, 138, 239-40, 241, 247, 248; of other estates, 247, 249, 250

Gardens, nursery, 241, 242, 247, 248, 249-50, 252-3

Garter, Order of: Book of Statutes, 271; Georges, 332; history of, 271; installation, 271, 330-3

Gheerhaedts, 286, 288

Gifts: christening, 64, 356-7; at Christmas, 354-6; church collection, 361; to friends, 64; gratuities, 43, 59, 60, 61, 91, 121, 136, 360, 362; at New Year, to and from sovereign, 64, 348-54; public, 358-60

Glass, from Venice, 192

Gloves, 340-1

Gold: guineas, 351; rise in price, 351; see also Plate

Goldsmiths, transactions through, 47, 352, 369-70, 371-2, 376, 378, 381, 383

Grain: corn, see that title; granary, 165; hempseed and coleseed, 153, 179

Guns, 227, 236

Hampshire, estate in, 111

Hampton Court, 232, 233; garden, 250

Henrietta Maria, Queen, 69, 71

Hockliffe, Hockley in the Hole, 211-2

Holbein, Hans, drawing, 283-4

Home Farm, none at Woburn, 128

Horse, gentleman of the: account books, 224-5; appointments and names, 83, 202; duties, 118; 203-4, 224, 235; salary and lodgings, 202

Horses, 54, 205-7, 222, 223, 392

Horse-racing, 227, 237

Houblon, James, 187, 188, 189, 197; John, 188; Peter, 188

Household: administration, 52; expenditure, 129, 143, 148-51; contribution by visitors, 149-50; linen, 62; materials, 214; plate, 62

Howard, Frances, Countess of Essex, Countess of Somerset, 15, 29

Howland, Elizabeth, wife of John, daughter of Sir Josiah Child, 391, 394; daughter of, 391-3

Hunting, 232-4, 235; coursing, 234; stag-hunting, 232; wolf-hunting, 226; head huntsman, 235, 236

Imprest money, 117, 203, 279

Italy, tour in, 105-10

Jewellery, 330, 348, 349; presents to Countess, 357-8; Georges, 332

Jones, Inigo, 22

Kennels, 54; see also Dogs

Kew, garden at, 247

Kitchen, clerk of: appointments and duties, 117, 121, 126, 139, 143, 154; accounts, 129, 149, 160; improved status, 162, 139

Kitchen: staff, 121; utensils, 126-7

Kneller, Sir Godfrey, portraits by, 295-7

Lace, 339

Laundry, 213-4

Leasure, Sir Stephen and Lady, 14, 16, 17, 18, 19

Lefèvre, Claud, portrait by, 292

Legal adviser, 115-6

Legal expenses, 58, 59, 380

Leighton Buzzard, 137, 156; market, 131, 135, 151

Lely, Sir Peter, portraits by, 290-1, 293-5

Librarian, 73

Library, 262-79; see also Books, and Pamphlets

Linkmen, 48

INDEX

Swords, 341
Swyre church, brasses in, 283
Sydenham, Dr. Thomas, 311, 318

Tapestries, 38, 70-1, 299-300
Tavistock estate, 20, 27; bailiff, 365; Bedford House, Exeter, 20, 47, 71; income from, 45-6, 47; sale of land, 66-7; steward, 47; tenths on, 45
Tavistock, marquisate, 390
Taxation and taxes, 43, 45, 65, 80; detailed, 381-5
Tea, 169-70
Tennis, 237, 238
Thorney estate: bailiff, 153; cattle breeding, 153-6: development, 128-9; drainage, 26-7, 46, see also Fens; granary, 165; payments from, 365, 372, 383; supplies from, 128, 136, 152-62; taxes, 383
Thornhaugh, 16, 20, 46, 374
Thornton, John: tutor at Woburn, 72-7, 110; books bought by, 274, 276-7, 328; letters to, 98, 102, 107, 109; friendship with Lady William Russell, 387, 393; death, 396; references, 82, 97, 116, 212, 265, 266, 292, 304, 305-6, 307-8, 317, 323, 325, 359, 364
Tithes, 384
Tobacco and pipes, 345-6
Toilet accessories, 344
Tortoiseshell boxes, 346
Touchwood, 346
Tradesmen, names of, 165, 169, 172, 179, 187, 197, 198-9, 200, 208-9, 259-61
Transport, 142, 158-9, 170-1, 173-4, 174-5, 202, 211; of cattle, 155; of goods to and from Bedford House, 210-13; by water, 160-1, 163, 175, 202, 247, 251-2
Travel: expenses, 54-5, 221-4, 303; by coach, 40, 55, 56, 57, 59, 211-3, 346-7; by hackney carriages, 215; on horseback, 55, 212; by sedan chair, 61-2, 210, 347; by water, 48, 56-8, 97, 203
Trunks, portmanteaux, 213
Tunbridge Wells, 197, 221-4, 304
Turks, war with, 108-10; prisoners of, 361-2

Umbrellas, 343-4

Van Dyck, Sir A., portraits by, 25, 31, 288-90
Verelst, S., portrait by, 291
Verney, Sir Greville, 111, 148
Viner, Thomas, goldsmith, 47, 48; Sir Robert, goldsmith, 357, 362-4

Wandon Heath, 236
Wars: with Dutch, 176, 186, 187, 373, 383: with Turks, 108-10
Watchmen, 123, 125
Water supply, 63
Westminster Hall, 90
Westminster School, 14, 94; portrait of schoolboy, 292
Whipsnade, 231
Whitnoe Grange, 202
Wigs, 341-2
Will of 4th Earl of Bedford, 35
Windmill, 163
Wines and Spirits, 183-201; bottles, 184, 189; brandy, 200-1; champagne, 183, 192-3; corks and stoppers, 184; customs, 185, 187, 191, 193, 201; expenditure on, 197; at funerals, 327; import laws, 185, 189; licences, 185, 189-90; methods of purchase, 184-5, 193-4, 198, 199; pirated, 186; port, 183, 197, 200; smuggling, 186
Wisbech: market, 155

INDEX

Woburn Abbey: description, 23-4; grotto, 23-4, 397; hearth tax, 383; neglected condition, 17, 19-21; principal residence, 19; rebuilding, 22-4, 397; royal visits, 21, 29, 71, 71-2

Woburn estate: attempt to sell, 17; expansion, 390; history of acquisition, 19-20; losses, 374; rental, 383; survey, 22

Woburn: market, 131, 135